GUIDE

M<small>USEO</small> <small>DEL</small> P<small>RADO</small>

J<small>OSÉ</small> L<small>UIS</small> S<small>ANCHO</small>

© ALDEASA, 2000
Legal Deposit: M-1110-20001
I.S.B.N.: 84-8003-982-5

Design: ALDEASA
Published and Produced by: ALDEASA
Layout: Myriam López Consalvi
Translation from Spanish into English: Philip Knight
Photographs: Museo del Prado Archives
Photomechanical Production: Lucam
Printed by: Estudios Gráficos Europeos, S. A.

Cover Illustration: Diego de Velázquez. *Philip III on Horseback* (detail).

Printed in Spain

INDEX

The Museum

The history of the collections and
the institution 6
The building 8

The Collections in the Villanueva building

GROUND FLOOR 17
Spanish painting in the XVIII
and XIV centuries 18
Spanish painting in the XV and
XVI centuries 18
Flemish painting in the XV and
XVI centuries 20
Albrecht Dürer and German Renaissance
painting 28
Italian painting in the XIV, XV
and XVI centuries 30
Venetian painting in the XVI
century 36
El Greco 46
Spanish Court painting in the second half
of the XVI century 50
Leoni sculpture 52
Classic sculpture 54
Greek art, from Archaism to Classicism ... 56

THE BASEMENT 63
The Dauphin's Treasure 64

FIRST FLOOR 69
French painting in the XVII century 70
Italian painting in the XVII century 72
Dutch painting in the XVII century 76
Flemish painting in the XVII century 78
Spanish painting in the XVII century 102
Velasquez 110
Spanish painting in the XVII century
(continuation) 130
XVIII century Spanish painting 140
Goya 144

SECOND FLOOR 157
Goya (continuation) 158
European painting in the XVIII century ... 170

The Casón del Buen Retiro

THE CASÓN DEL BUEN RETIRO 183
The Casón del Buen Retiro:
XIX century Art 184

INDEX OF ILLUSTRATIONS 192

THE MUSEUM

The layout recently established in the Museum enables the visitor to follow a route which traces the historical development of the Art of Painting from the Early Middle Ages until Francisco de Goya. Apart from this succession of painting, ancient Graeco-Roman sculpture is exhibited. Appropriately, this type of sculpture is described here between Renaissance and Baroque works, taking into account that the association with these creative styles not only indicates the extent to which the statues on display resulted from the fashion for collecting prevalent in that period but it also shows the link between the princely liking for "galleries of antiquities" and other objects representing Court Art during the modern age. These objects are located in nearby rooms and include the sculptures created for Philip II, especially those by Pompeo and Leone Leoni, as well as the Dauphin's Treasure.

THE HISTORY OF THE COLLECTIONS AND THE INSTITUTION

Inaugurated on November 19th 1819 as the Royal Museum belonging to the monarch, the institution takes up a tradition of collections which goes back to the sixteenth century, specifically to the period of Charles V, although it is true that royal patronage was exercised in previous reigns as can be seen from the works owned by Isabel the Catholic that are now housed in the Royal Chapel of Granada. Factors such as the absence of a fixed location for the court prevented steady accumulation until the sixteenth century. Therefore, the collection stems from the first urge to collect on the part of Charles V and, above all, on the part of his son Philip II, always from the standpoint of two important artistic styles: on the one hand, the northern European or Flemish style with its devotional spirit and, on the other, Italian classicist art. Both monarchs were clients of Titian, whose status in the general context of the Venetian School establishes one of the fundamental aspects of the royal collections and even their role with regard to the Spanish masters as a true academy or school of learning. This was the role of the Alcázar and subsequently the Royal Palace until the Museum was founded. The beginnings of the sculpture collection, both classical and Renaissance, also go back to that time.

The golden age of royal collections was the reign of Philip IV. He stepped up purchases of Venetian paintings and became the patron of Rubens, thus re-establishing links with Flemish painting already under baroque influence. Through fortunate purchases, like the one made at an auction held by Charles I of England, gifts from the Spanish viceroys in Italy and from Queen Cristina of Sweden, Philip IV built up the most important art collection of his time.

This passion for collection was maintained throughout the reign of Charles II who brought Luca Giordano to Spain. Under the first Bourbon, Philip V, the fashion for collections received new impetus, this time with a wider taste even taking in schools of painting which had until then been less appreciated by the

Spanish monarchs such as the Dutch School. Throughout the eighteenth century, the arrival of French and Italian painters or other international art influences gave a cosmopolitan perspective to the Bourbon royal collections. This outlook was maintained intact until the breakdown caused by the Napoleonic Wars which resulted in appreciable losses for the collection. Shortly before the conflict, the first efforts to create a Royal Museum had been made, encouraged by the neoclassicist Antonio Rafael Mengs. But it was Joseph Bonaparte who in 1809 created a Museum of Painting. This was however based on works originating from extinct religious communities. There has been much debate about the reasons why Ferdinand VII founded the Royal Museum. Apart from expressing a change in personal taste as regards the decoration of palaces, the Museum also reflects the general themes of official culture derived from the French Revolution whose benchmark was the creation of the Louvre Museum. Following the king's death in 1833, the Museum went through a very serious crisis. As it was considered to be the private property of the monarch, the Museum was on the point of being divided in two between his two sons. A decision having been reached in favour of keeping the collection together, it became a part of the Royal Treasures in 1865. This remained so until the 1868 Revolution brought definitive nationalization of the collection.

Until that time, the Museum was somewhat limited by its historical origins. As a result, there existed a collection of great quantitative and qualitative importance but one which was still a long way from expressing the ideals and content appropriate to an overall view of the history of painting. Practical circumstances of an ideological and ultimately historical nature meant that many Spanish and foreign schools of art were inadequately represented. An important change took place in 1872 when the Museum merged with the so-called *Museo de la Trinidad* (Trinity Museum) which had been inaugurated in 1838 with collections made up of objects originally belonging to monasteries in Madrid and the surrounding area. Due to its origins, the Museo de la Trinidad provides very significant examples of

Tiziano Vecelio di Gregorio. *Charles V at the Battle of Mühlberg.*
Oil on canvas, 332 χ 279 cm. Ref. n° 410.

seventeenth-century religious painting from Madrid. Unfortunately, the limited capacity of the building and the absence of a consistent long-term policy frustrated this project to a large extent, giving rise to a policy of mere depositing. At this time, the Museum was a lively institution, without chronological limits. In this sense, contemporary nineteenth-century pictures acquired by the state were added to the Museum collection in line with the typical National Exhibitions of the time, a situation which did not change until the creation of the *Museo de Arte Moderno* (Museum of Modern Art). On account of its national status, this period saw the Prado become the object of important bequests and donations. This, together with a successful purchasing policy, enabled gaps to be filled or even the completion of historical collections. Among the contributions made by private individuals, some of the most prominent were those by Emile D'Erlanger in 1881 – *Pinturas Negras de Goya* (Black Paintings by Goya) –, the widowed Duchess of Pastrana in 1889, Pablo Bosch in 1915, the count of Cartagena and Fernández Durán in 1930, F. de A. Cambó in 1940-41, and Manuel Villaescusa in the present day.

During the seventeenth and eighteenth centuries, the royal collections constituted a school of learning providing essential instruction for Spanish and foreign painters. Likewise, in the second half of the nineteenth century at the height of the Velasquez revival, the Museum was a vital source of inspiration for preimpressionists and impressionists alike.

Following the critical situation faced by the Museum during the Civil War culminating in 1939 in the great exhibition of Geneva which displayed some of the Museum's most notable treasures, the Prado embarked on a new phase characterized by an equally new phenomenon – mass tourism.

In 1971, paintings from the nineteenth century, which had until then been kept in the Casón del Buen Retiro building, were returned to the Museum itself.

Similarly, in recent times, a general restructuring of the collection has been undertaken. To this effect, appropriate parliamentary approval

was obtained in 1995. Also in that year, the architectural complex or building area was enlarged, a project which had been the subject of several controversial proposals.

THE BUILDING

The history of the building acquires great importance in terms of the image of the institution. The *Museo del Prado* (Prado Museum) building is regarded as the masterpiece of Juan de Villanueva, the best exponent of Spanish Neoclassicist architecture. The building is situated in the most historic avenue of Madrid and was also largely designed to provide a parallel route to the tree-lined Prado boulevard. In fact, the building warrants a visit as a monument in itself, not just as the building housing the art collection.

In the history of Madrid, the area of the city known as the Prado has been very important. The original core of Madrid – medieval, Arab and Christian – was located next to the Royal Palace. From this nucleus, the city grew eastwards, towards the roads leaving Madrid for Alcalá, Aragón and Valencia, through land descending in a gentle slope to reach the Channel of a stream. A pleasant place, full of trees, which was by nature a foremost location for the inhabitants of Madrid to settle – the Prado. Along these paths and tree-lined walks, local devotion gave rise to hermitages which, throughout the centuries, became important places of worship in Madrid such as *Nuestra Señora de Atocha* (Our Lady of Atocha). The devoutness of monarchs founded *El Monasterio de San Jerónimo el Real* (The Royal Hieronymite Monastery), established by Henry IV and transferred here by Isabel the Catholic. Since then, the monastery has been one of the main venues for royal events – the investiture of princes, royal weddings and funerals. In 1561, Philip II set up the Royal Court in Madrid. Consequently, the city grew and took in the Prado, whose tree-lined avenues were becoming even more pleasant with fountains. These avenues thus became the place for a daily stroll by the inhabitants of the city and all those who came to the court of the Catholic Monarch or

Brambila. Prado Museum. West and South Façade, 1830.

Comoroni. Lithography of the Northern and West Façade, c. 1824.

with pretensions on business. The literature of the Golden Age, especially plays, is full of scenes of gallantry set in the Prado, Madrid.

Therefore, it is not surprising that *El Prado de San Jerónimo* (The Meadow of Saint Jerome) should be the location chosen by the Count-Duke of Olivares to create a new Royal Site – the Buen Retiro – to the delight of the monarch whose will he dominated. Both the park, dotted with recreational buildings, and the palace, decorated with a magnificent collection of contemporary Italian, Flemish and Spanish painting, gave the Prado all the makings of its literary, artistic and historical brilliance.

However, the image of the Avenue within the city stems from the Age of Enlightenment, specifically from the reign of Charles III, an illustrious monarch who made the Prado into a true reflection of "public happiness".

Although the palace of the Buen Retiro was the official residence of the Court in Madrid during a large part of the reign of Philip V and the whole reign of Ferdinand VI, the *Paseo del Prado* (Prado Avenue) did not undergo any improvement in the first half of the eighteenth century. Nevertheless, Charles III and his minister, the count of Aranda, commissioned the architect José de Hermosilla to carry out a complete redesign from 1767 onwards. The streams were channelled underground and the space standardized, flattened and widened.

Lines of trees were planted and fountains added extra beauty. The old *Prado de San*

Jerónimo (Saint Jerome's Meadow) was transformed into the *Salón del Prado* (Prado Salon), a lovely avenue in the shape of a Roman amphitheatre, bordered to the north by the fountain of Cibeles and to the South by the fountain of Neptune with the centre situated at the fountain of Apollo alternatively know as the *Cuatro estaciones* (Four Seasons). Also at that time, other avenues were standardized, namely the Prado de Recoletos to the North and the Prado de Atocha to the South. These avenues were adorned with beautiful fountains such as the Alcachofa in Atocha or the *Cuatro fuentes* (Four Fountains) at the junction of Huertas Street with the Prado.

In this way, the Prado became the mirror image of the capital city of the Age of Enlightenment, thus fulfilling the wishes of Bourbon reformism. As a result, the surroundings of the Prado were adorned with especially significant monuments. Outstanding among these is the *Puerta de Alcalá* (the Alcala Gate), the work of Francisco Sabatini and designed as a triumphant arch in honour of Charles III himself. This programme of monument construction began in the 1760s and in spite of the disappearance of some of its main elements such as the railings along the Buen Retiro towards the *Paseo del Prado* (Prado Avenue), the magnificence of absolute power adopts a classicist architectural language inspired by the Romans.

A series of outstanding buildings lent a special atmosphere to the Paseo del Prado in the reign of Charles III. Not only the appearance of

9

the buildings but also their contents made this corner of the city into a showcase of the Age of Enlightenment, giving it meaning as the avenue of science. The new general hospital together with the Gate of Atocha and the Royal Botanical Gardens were the first steps in this programme. At the end of Charles III's reign, during the administration of the Count of Floridablanca, the programme was enriched by two more foundations to be housed in two equally magnificent buildings designed by Juan de *Villanueva – El Real Gabinete de Ciencias Naturales* (the Royal Museum of Natural Science) and the Astronomical Observatory.

The Royal Museum of Natural Science had been established some years before by Charles III on the second floor of the *Real Academia de Bellas Artes de San Fernando* (the Saint Ferdinand Royal Academy of Fine Arts). This institution still occupies the same site in Alcalá street today. At the beginning of the 1780s, the humble nature of the headquarters was coupled with the need to build a pavilion as a "chemical laboratory" with classrooms next to the Botanical Gardens. In 1784, a proposal was made to combine all these functions in a single building next to the Botanical Gardens and the Prado.

The minister, the Count of Floridablanca, awarded the project to his favourite architect, Juan de Villanueva. Born in Madrid in 1739, Villanueva was the son of a sculptor and the step brother of another architect, Diego, who gained importance by introducing theoretical French texts. Villanueva had excelled as a student in the recently created *Academia de San Fernando* (San Fernando Academy). He had obtained a scholarship to study in Rome, a city in which he stayed from 1759 to 1763. On his return, Villanueva gained distinction as the architect for the Hieronymite monks at The Escorial, for the heir to the throne – the Prince of Asturias and future Charles IV – and for the heir's brother, Prince Gabriel. Villanueva acquired prestige by designing country houses for these two princes and the house intended for their retinues. In addition, he designed the house to be occupied by the Minister of State – Floridablanca himself. All of these houses were situated in San Lorenzo de El Escorial. Villanueva also carried out other work

for the two princes. These projects won him the support of the minister. In 1797, following the death of Sabatini, Villanueva was rewarded with the post of chief architect, the most prestigious and best-paid job that a professional architect in Spain could attain at that time. Villanueva carried out this role until his death in 1811. Without wishing to diminish the importance of Villanueva's other work such as the Astronomical Observatory (1790), close to the Prado Museum and well worth a visit, or the Church of the *Caballero de Gracia* (The Knight of Grace) (1789), the year 1785 saw the start of the project which should be considered as Villanueva's masterpiece in Madrid – *El Gabinete de Ciencias* (the Museum of Science). From here onwards, we will call this building by the term 'the Museum' as the architect himself did in his writings.

Largely on account of what he had learnt in Rome, Villanueva constitutes a sharp caesura with regard to the late Baroque architecture at the Madrid Court where he had started his professional development. The museum represents Villanueva's architecture in synthesis. It is a serious and impressive piece of work meticulously following the classicist style but one in which the proportions and the subtlety of detail please the eye and prevent monotony. The design is basically composed of the geometrical figures of the circle and the square, both in terms of the large structures and also the spaces and recesses. The effect is one of great serenity. The quality of the design is ensured with the utmost care and is evident in the craftsmanship and the construction of the building itself. The monumental mass and the solidity of the domed structure are complemented by the objective beauty of the excellently crafted high-quality materials. The fine brick masses in the end pavilions form the basis of a contrast in colours and the stone (grey granite and white stone from Colmenar de Oreja) is sculpted with the utmost refinement not only in decorative terms but also in matching the different structural elements. This is strongly evident in, for example, the lintels of the Doric porch, those of the lower gallery facing the Avenue and those of the Ionic rotunda. No less magnificent than the masonry is the brickwork on the vaults which remain just as the architect designed

Recoletos Avenue.

them, especially those on the ground floor and most notably those in the hall leading to the Avenue and the vault in the Ariadne room. In general the quality of the whole fabric of the building combines with the grandeur of the proportions to lend an imposing style to the most undecorated spaces such as the patio of the southern pavilion. Unfortunately, Villanueva did not get to see his masterpiece completely finished and subsequent changes disfigured a large part of the interior.

The main structure of the building as well as the architectural detail on the façade clearly express the three original functions of its interior. The large longitudinal volume of the gallery, parallel to the tree-lined walk, in itself expresses the sense of linear trajectory which the Museum of Science was to follow. On the other hand, the central hall and its porch facing the Avenue, making a strong transversal axis with the gallery, suggest by their very form as a basilica that they could stage a public event for an audience or congregation, anticipating their future role as a con-

ference hall. Lastly, the southern pavilion, intended as a botanical school, has a quadrangular mass which resembles a palace or civil building and expresses an official role restricted to certain users. The northern pavilion was partly designed as a replica of the southern one so that its main columns solidly and symmetrically complete the longitudinal stretch of the façade extending towards the Avenue. Both pavilions thus express the beginning and the end of the gallery.

This type of construction consisting of five parts – a central structure, linked by two other intermediate sections to two end pavilions – had been a common approach in European architecture since the sixteenth century and had been particularly prominent in Baroque and French neoclassicist styles. Villanueva had already tried it out just one year earlier with the country house or recreational pavilion which he had built for the Prince of Asturias at El Pardo, near Madrid. But in the Museum, the architect develops his taste for accentuating large masses so that the façades are characterized by dramatic

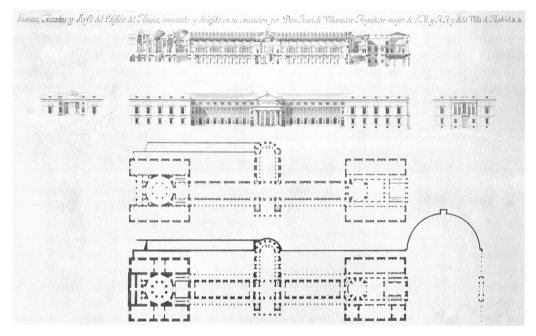

Plan of the building at the time of Villanueva.

projections and recesses with a powerful chiaroscuro effect. He manages to please the eye not only with the view from the front but also with foreshortening which, in spite of its exaggerated effect, is controlled by clear creative rationality. The recesses which in the end pavilions are situated in the centre of the short walls facing the Avenue, oriented towards the north and the south, are at the axis or the lateral intercolumn of the Doric porch. In this way, the pleasant scenic outlook provided by all these elements during a stroll down the tree-lined Prado Avenue is not a matter of chance. Villanueva had a liking for the effects of views other than from the front as regards classical elements of architecture. His preference has even been termed "romantic picturesque".

This magnificent architectural construction constitutes a fine example of the Museum-Library, a concept put forward by other contemporary European architects, especially Peyre. The two ground floors were linked by an outside ramp which bridged the difference in height between the Avenue and the top floor in a way which blended perfectly with the surrounding

natural features and created a very harmonious general aesthetic effect. Unfortunately, this ramp was removed in the nineteenth century when the level of the ground was lowered, It is to be hoped that the ground will one day be restored to its initial height as proposed by some of the most prestigious architects who have participated in the Museum project over the years – above all, Muguruza, Chueca and Partearroyo. However, this original concept explains why Villanueva did not make plans for a covered monumental staircase while devoting consummate subtle skill and attention to work on the whole interior space, in particular the large apsidal hall, the lecture room or meeting room, which he pictured as a magnificent basilica with Corinthian columns.

Villanueva's grand building was subjected to changing fortunes during its construction and suffered from the upheavals of the Napoleonic Wars before being completed.

Work began in the summer of 1785 and continued apace during the following years, driven on by Floridablanca and given generous financial support out of funds derived from the income or temporalities of the Jesuits who had

Francesco Bataglioni. *Ferdinand VI and Bárbara of Braganza in the Aranjuez Gardens.* Oil on canvas, 68 χ 112 cm. Ref. nº 4181.

been expelled in 1767. These funds were also used to finance the Astronomical Observatory from 1790 onwards. In 1788, with the foundations and containing walls already built and the ground levelled, work started on erecting the main walls. However, the rate of work slowed down from 1792 onwards when the minister was dismissed by the new monarch, Charles IV. Nevertheless, it appears that by 1808 the whole of the exterior of the building had been finished except for the large apsidal hall and that the building had been covered with lead and slate in compliance with Villanueva's plans.

The Napoleonic Wars caused so much damage to the unfinished monument but the conflict had hardly ended when first the Regency and then Ferdinand VII ordered the consolidation and completion of the building. In 1814 the project was awarded to a pupil of Villanueva's, Antonio López Aguado. At this time, it had still not been decided whether the building would serve its original purpose or whether it would be put to an alternative use. From 1815 onwards, however, what gained the upper hand was a decision to set up a Royal Gallery of Painting and Sculpture in Madrid and to use the Museum to this effect. This option became the official line in 1818 and the following year, the Prado opened its doors.

From then on, modifications to Villanueva's building started to be made according to new requirements and criteria. Although the architecture of the building has always been highly valued, until recently it has not been sufficiently 'heeded' in order to derive from its governing principles the most appropriate guidelines for successive necessary alterations.

In the middle of the nineteenth century, Narciso Pascual y Colomer embarked on the construction of the central hall or basilica, following a very different design from Villanueva's plans. Among many other alterations, one of the most significant was the extension to the rear eastern façade carried out from 1913 to 1968. An international competition was held with the aim of selecting proposals for an extension to the building. As a result, in 1998, a draft project by Rafael Moneo was chosen. This involved joining Villanueva's building to the Hieronymite cloister complex.

THE COLLECTIONS IN THE
VILLANUEVA BUILDING

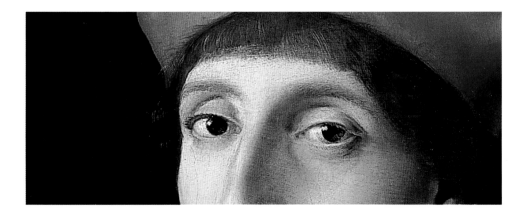

In order to follow this historical route, it is necessary to go through the lower Goya door and proceed through the rooms in the order shown here until you reach the other end of the building. Then, you must go back to Goya's door so as to cross the first floor in the same direction from north to south. The top floors of the end pavilions house European art from the eighteenth century and a part of Goya's works. Therefore, to obtain an integral appreciation of their contents, they should be viewed before entering the rooms in the southern pavilion on the first floor as indicated in situ.Lastly, in the nearby building called the Casón del Buen Retiro, Spanish art from the nineteenth century can be seen.

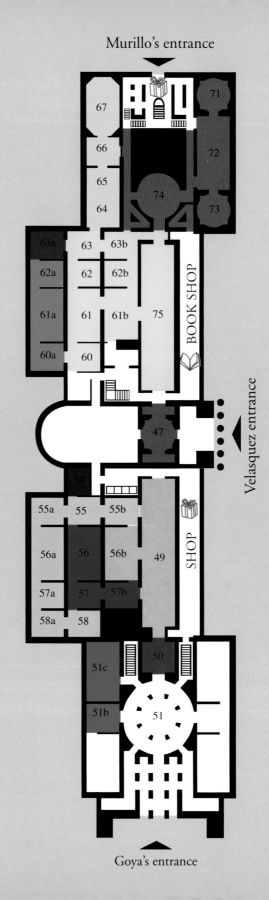

Murillo's entrance

67

66

65

64

71

72

74

73

63a

63 63b

62a

62 62b

61a

61 61b

BOOK SHOP

75

60a

60

47

Velasquez entrance

54

55a 55 55b

56a 56 56b

49

57a 57 57b

SHOP

58a 58

51c

50

51b

51

Goya's entrance

GROUND FLOOR

	ROOMS	PAGES
Spanish painting in the XIII and XIV centuries	(51b, 51c)	18
Spanish painting in the XV and XVI centuries	(50, 57b, 57 y 56)	18
Flemish painting in the XV and XVI centuries	(58a, 58, 57a, 56a, 55a, 55 y 55b)	20
Alberto Durero and German Renaissance painting	(54)	28
Italian painting in the XIV, XV and XVI century	(49 y 56b)	30
Venetian painting in the XVI century	(75, 61b, 61, 62, 63, 63b, 62b y 60)	36
El Greco	(60a, 61a y 62a)	46
Spanish Court painting in the second half of the XVI century	(63a)	50
Leoni sculpture	(64, 65, 66 y 67)	52
Classic sculpture and Greek art, from Archaism to Classicism	(74, 73, 72, 71 y 47)	54

SPANISH PAINTING IN THE THIRTEENTH AND FOURTEENTH CENTURIES
Rooms 51b and 51c

As an illustration of Romanesque mural painting, the Museum holds two noteworthy series of exhibits. There are six fragments of decoration from the church of *San Baudelio de Berlanga* (Soria) on indefinite loan from the Metropolitan Museum of New York. Among these fragments, the most prominent characteristics are the introduction of secular subject material and Mozarabic iconographic influence which, in turn, incorporates forms and themes of more remote Byzantine origin. A typical example of the Castilian Romanesque Style in the thirteenth century is the decoration, more over complete, in the hermitage of **Santa Cruz de Maderuelo** (Segovia) with Pantocrator in an almond-shaped halo on the vault and scenes from Genesis on the walls. The side walls and the base of the vault are filled with apostles and saints and above all archangels. The painting is schematic, very lively and expressive.

SPANISH PAINTING IN DE FIFTEENTH AND SIXTEENTH CENTURIES
Rooms 50, 57b, 57 and 56

Some of the largest pictures are assembled in room 50. The others are located beyond the first room of Italian painting dating from the fifteenth century.

Two important Castilian Gothic retables illustrate this style from the first half of the fifteenth century. The first reredos takes its name from archbishop **Don Sancho de Rojas** (Sancho of Rojas). It was created by Rodríguez de Toledo who, according to the records was producing work around 1400. This reredos preceded the extremely well-known one by Alonso de Berruguete in the church of San Benito in Valladolid. In the central panel showing the Virgin and Child, the said archbishop and the king of Aragón, *Fernando de Antequera* (Ferdinand of Antequera), both appear at prayer. The reredos of *La vida de la Virgen y San Francisco* (the Life of the Virgin and Saint Francis), the work of Nicolás Francés (died 1468), already displays international Gothiscism and bears out the master's origins.

Bartolomé de Cárdenas Bermejo was born in Cordoba and worked in the last quarter of the fifteenth century. He pursued almost the whole of his artistic career in the region of Aragón where he stood out strongly as one of the most significant exponents of the Flemish realist influence. His **Santo Domingo de Silos** (Saint Dominic of Silos) enthroned as an abbot, recorded as already having been painted in 1477, shows the figure sitting in a lavish chair adorned with personifications of virtues and dressed in sumptuous vestments. His face reveals distinctive individuality as can be seen in sketches originating from Van Eyck. More significant within the Flemish trend was Fernando Gallego, an active exponent between 1446 and 1507. *La Piedad* (Devotion) or *Quinta Angustia* (The Fifth Anguish), a highly dramatic panel, is a youthful work which, on a much lower scale shows in the figures of the patrons touches of international Gothicism. His son or brother, of whom hardly any record survives and who was possibly called Francisco Gallego, was according to some the painter of *El martirio de Santa Catalina* (The Martyrdom of Saint Catherine) which, from the point of view of iconographic interest, includes a nude protagonist.

The Franco-Gothic or Linear Gothic movement is illustrated by *El retablo de San Cristóbal* (Saint Christopher's Reredos) from the fourteenth century. The frame is painted with castles and lions, suggesting a possible royal donation. In the centre, Saint Christopher holds the Child while legends of saints are depicted at the sides.

The important panel of *La Virgen de los Reyes Católicos* (The Virgin of the Catholic Monarchs) dates from the fifteenth century. Two groups are positioned in front of the Virgin's throne. On the one hand, there are *Fernando el Católico* (Ferdinand the Catholic), Prince Juan, Friar Tomás of Torquemada, the inquisitor general or perhaps *San Pedro de Arbués* (Saint Peter of Arbués). On the opposite side, there are his daughter and apparently the chronicler *Pedro Mártir de Angleria* (Peter the Martyr of Angleria). The panel comes from the royal room at the Monastery of *Santo Tomás de Ávila* (Saint Thomas of Avila). Recently, it has been attributed to the Master of Miraflores.

Although a contemporary of Gallego, **Pedro Berruguete**, born around 1450, who was working actively in Urbino in 1477 and who died about 1504, represented a link between the Flemish tradition and

The church of Santa Cruz de Maderuelo. *The Creation.*
Mural painting. 498 χ 450 cm. Ref. nº 7284.

Bartolomé Bermejo. *Saint Dominic of Silos
enthroned as an Abbot.*
Panel. 242 χ 130 cm. Ref. nº 1323(p.19)

Reredos of Archbishop Sancho de Rojas (detail).
Ref. nº 1321(p.19)

the split brought about by the Italian Reinassance. Among his Dominican works, the most outstanding is the Auto-da-fé spread out into two different levels. The higher one shows *Santo Domingo de Guzmán* (Saint Dominic of Guzmán) and a group of inquisitors presiding on a platform under a throne whereas the lower level depicts the leading away and burning of several of those condemned. The great realism of this scene is of obvious iconographic interest as a portrayal of the practices of the Inquisition Court. A work of exceptional quality is *La Virgen con el Niño* (The Virgin and Child), inspired by works from northern Italy and essentially equidistant between the Flemish tradition and the knowledge that the artist had acquired during his stay in Italy.

A highly debatable work, currently attributed to **Paolo de San Leocadio**, is *La Virgen del caballero de Montesa* (The Virgin of the Knight of Montesa). It was painted in Valencia at the beginning of the sixteenth century and, although it has new Renaissance features, it retains a connection with the Gothic style. The painting was mistakenly overvalued and acquired by the state.

The portrait of Francisco Fernández de Córdoba y Mendoza was painted by the enigmatic **Fernando del Rincón** who worked actively from the end of the fifteenth century to the fifteen twenties. This small panel of around 1520 includes an inscription making clear both the name of the artist and the subject of the portrait whose coat of arms as a bishop are reproduced on the frame. Exceptionally, the frame is original. Shaped as an extended bust in ecclesiastical garb and biretta, the figure makes a strong impact with a vivid realistic image. This shows the benefit of skilful modelling, the studied use of chiaroscuro being a contributory factor.

The Renaissance burst fully onto the scene in the style of Leonardo Da Vinci with the work of Fernando Yáñez de la Almedina from Valencia who worked actively from 1505 to 1536.

He trained in Florence and was apparently a direct pupil of Leonardo Da Vinci. Exemplary in this respect is the tremendous *Santa Catalina* (Saint Catherine), regarded as the most beautiful Spanish painting from the sixteenth century. The clarity of the outline, with shades reminiscent of Leonardo, the grace of the figure and the classicist architectural background reflect a total assimilation of contemporary Italian Renaissance painting.

Vicente Juan Maçip, known as **Juan de Juanes**, enjoyed great historiographic favour until the nineteenth century as *"Rafael español"* (Spanish Raphael). Although he was in Italy and he knew Romanesque painting subsequent to Raphael, his work nevertheless connects with contemporary Flemish masters. In this context, Charles IV acquired a reredos originating from the church of *San Esteban de Valencia* (Saint Stephen of Valencia). Outstanding scenes from the reredos are *El martirio de San Esteban* (The Martyrdom of Saint Stephen) and ***La última cena*** (The Last Supper). The Martyrdom reveals Raphaelite touches with a clearly northern European sense of detail. The Last Supper achieved enormous popular success. It is a balanced composition with new features such as the still life. The picture takes on its own personality but shows a characteristic monotony and repetition of standard types.

Pedro Machuca was born in Toledo at the end of the fifteenth century and died in Granada in 1550. An architect and as such the creator of an edifice so significant in the advent of the Italian Renaissance as the Palace of Charles V in Granada, he was also responsible for *El descendimiento de la cruz* (The Descent from the Cross). The latter is a strange piece of work, designed as a nocturne in which the artist reveals his Italian training through a combination of Leonardo, Michaelangelo and the Mannerists. He was one of the first to introduce the mannerist movement into Spain. In the foreground, two children give a realistic, anecdotal and even humorous touch to the work. Another prominent feature is the strange anachronistic figure in armour. According to some, this piece stems from the artist's Italian period. For others, it dates from around 1517 to 1520, on his return to Spain.

FLEMISH PAINTING FROM THE FIFTEENTH AND SIXTEENTH CENTURIES
Rooms 58a, 58, 57a, 56a, 55a, 55 and 55b

The historical reasons of commercial contact and dynastic intermarriages but also the identification with the same style of devotion explain the abundance and wealth of Flemish work from the fifteenth and sixteenth centuries in the Prado Museum. In representation of the **Van Eycks**, the collection is

Jan van Eyck. *The Fountain of Grace and The Triumph of the Church over the Synagogue.*
Panel. 181 χ 116 cm. Ref. 1511.

Juan de Juanes or Vicente Juan Maçip. *The Last Supper.*
Oil on canvas. 116 χ 191 cm. Ref. nº 846.

initiated by a work connected with **Jan** who was in the Iberian peninsula in 1428 and 1429 – *La fuente de la gracia* (The Fountain of Grace). The origin of this panel is highly debatable as it was attributed to Jan's school, just as it had been thought that perhaps it had come from the Ghent School immediately before, or it has been suggested that it is an imitation of a reredos entitled *La adoración del Cordero Místico* (The Adoration of the Mystic Lamb) by Saint Bavón of Ghent, painted by a subsequent pupil. Structured in three planes, like the mystery plays in religious theatre of the period, it can be seen mounted on late Gothic architecture which is indeed reminiscent of the platforms staging these dramatic performances. At the higher level, God appears between the Virgin and Saint John. In the centre there are groups of angels on both sides of a small meadow (the only Van Eyckian trace of the countryside on this panel). The triumphant Church group is situated on one side and of the inner section and on the other side of 'the fountain' from which the picture gets its name and from which eucharistic shapes fall. This group consists of figures representing the corresponding dignitaries – the Pope, the Emperor, the Bishop, the King, etc. – and the Synagogue whose figure is blindfolded. The figure presides over a group of rabbis who are retreating in shock. Having come from the monastery of Parral in Segovia, it is probably a copy of a lost original work of which other lower-quality versions are known. The anonymous and mysterious Master of Flemalle is thought to be **Robert Campin**. The Master of Flemalle was born about 1375 in Tournai and he represents the link between his contemporaries the Van Eycks and the dramatism of Van der Weyden who, according to the records, he trained. The panel *Los desposorios de la Virgen con Santiago y Santa Clara* (The Betrothal of the Virgin with James and Saint Clare) in chiaroscuro on its external side constitutes a complex scene –two groups of people, one inside and the other outside a church that could be similar to Notre Dame du Sablon in Brussels. Two panels designed as little triptych doors are exceptionally interesting. One is entitled *San Juan Bautista con el maestro franciscano Enrique de Werl* (Saint John the Baptist with the Franciscan master Henry of Werl). According to the inscription, it was made in 1438. The panel shows a kneeling figure and, behind him, the protective saint. They are in front of a window through which a landscape can be seen. At the back of the room, a concave mirror reflects the scene with brilliant virtuosity. The accompanying panel, even more than the first, takes us into a contemporary Flemish interior, here acquiring the full characteristics of this artistic genre. This second panel is dedicated to Saint Barbara. The lady is sitting down reading with her back to the fireplace in a setting which meticulously reproduces every element making up a pleasant middle-class interior of the period. If it were not for the tower rising from the landscape in the background, it could be believed that the iconography corresponded to a Virgin of the Annunciation.

Roger van Der Weyden (c. 1399-1464) was the most dramatic and intense of the Flemish masters and therefore closer to Spanish sensitivity. Preserved here is his undoubted masterpiece *El descendimiento de la Cruz* (The Descent from the Cross), apparently the central panel of a triptych whose sides have been lost. Painted in approximately 1435 for the chapel of the Ballesteros family of Louvain, it interested Philip II to such an extent that he ordered Michel Coxcie to make a copy. Later, he acquired it through the bequest of his aunt, Mary of Hungary, despatching it to the Escorial where it remained until the Civil War. In 1939, the Head of State decided that it should be transferred to the Prado Museum together with some of the most significant pieces which had until then been kept at the Monastery. Here, Van Der Weyden displays his exceptional creative qualities, no less impressive for all the simplicity.

The picture is painted on a neutral golden background which does not indicate archaism. Rather, the aim is to highlight the figures as sculptural elements of a reredos, although with a bold set of intense colours that reveal an absolutely artistic expressiveness. It is structured along large-scale compositional outlines which impose order on what would otherwise be a confused mass. The two figures at both ends suggest respective closed curves while the corpse of Jesus, and the parallel lifeless pale figure of his mother, bring power to the central area with brilliant draping folds. Recently, it has been suggested that the hand of Robert Campin was instrumental in producing this panel.

Various copies testify to the complexity of another two important panels by Van Der Weyden – *La Virgen con el Niño* (The Virgin and Child) and *La Piedad* (The Piety). In the latter, the patron is not

Roger van der Weyden. *The Descent from the Cross.*
Panel. 220 χ 262 cm. Ref. nº 2825.

Roger van der Weyden. *The Piety.*
Panel. 47 χ 35 cm. Ref. nº 2540.

only on the same level as the divine figures but is also included in the scene as one more element in the composition. *La Virgen con el Niño* (The Virgin and Child), also called Madonna Durán after the name of the legatee, is one of the most exquisite pieces with rich draping folds meticulously perfected.

Dirk Bouts (+1475) is represented with a curious triptych whose central panel shows two stories, the Adoration of the Kings and the Visitation. His subsequent interest in realism of a domestic nature is already displayed in this work from his youth, dated around 1445.

Previously attributed to Van der Weyden, *El tríptico de la redención* (The Triptych of the Redemption) is actually an extremely important work by his pupil Vranke van der Stockt (c. 1420-1495).

Hans Memling (+1444) replaces the dramatism of his master Van der Weyden with a no less intense lyricism which emanates from his fragile pensive figures. One of his greatest works is this large triptych called *La Epifanía* (The Epiphany). Painted sometime between 1470 and 1480, it is very similar to another smaller one that he made for the Bruges hospital in 1479. It was inspired by one from his master. As a result of its grandeur and large-scale composition and the delicate skill with which each and every figure is created, the picture constitutes a first-class work of art whose artistic value is reinforced by its iconographic interest.

The monarchs in the central panel are in fact portraits of the Dukes of Burgundy. They are *Carlos el Temerario* (Charles the Brave) and *Felipe el Bueno* (Philip the Good). Acquired by Charles V, it was used as a reredos in the Chapel of the Palace of Aceca until 1849.

The Bruges school was characterized by devotional figures painted with a high degree of delicate skill. The leading exponent of this school was **Gerard David** (c.1450-1523). In *El descanso en la huida a Egipto* (A Rest During the Escape to Egypt), he gives equal importance to the landscape and the figures. Curiously, the Holy Family appear in the wooded background, signifying a return to wider perspectives in artistic representation.

Joachim Patinir (c.1480-1524) was the creator of the northern European landscape painting school. Although he portrayed reality in a relatively accurate descriptive style, he was capable of transformation in his own personal disconcerting and re-creative style. In this work, his distinctive blue and green shades stand out. He produced *Las tentaciones de San Antonio* (The Temptations of Saint Anthony) in collaboration with Quentin Masys, the creator of the figures. The picture shows knowledge of Italian Renaissance painting. A high wide-angle view of the landscape is a representation of the banks of the river Meuse and eloquently expresses the concept of nature from the human standpoint.

The above –mentioned **Quentin Massys** (1465-1530) combines the Flemish tradition with the teachings of the Italian Renaissance of Raphael and above all Leonardo Da Vinci. Massys was influenced by Leonardo's shading techniques (sfumatura) as well as being inspired by a certain sense of caricature undoubtedly originating from Leonardo's drawings. A work from approximately 1515 indicative of the artist's full maturity is *Cristo presentado al pueblo* (Christ Presented to the People) on a balcony of the praetorium against a background of strange Renaissance architecture. In this picture, the unusual low-angle view accentuates the exaggerated gestures of some of the figures.

El Bosco

Hieronymus van Aecken Bosch (c.1450-1516, Bois-le-Duc) known in Spain as El Bosco, produced an unequalled collection which was distributed between the Escorial and the Prado. It bears witness to Philip II's appreciation of this curious master whose complex type of representation, between burlesque and enigmatic, was then interpreted in moral allegorical terms. The signed triptych *La adoración de los Magos* (The Adoration of the Magi), painted around 1495 is for some his masterpiece. Closed off on the outside, the picture shows *La misa de San Gregorio* (Saint Gregory's Mass), almost all in chiaroscuro. At the side doors, the benefactors, a man and a woman are escorted by their patron saints. In the central area, the subject that gives its name to the piece includes the curious detail of a figure behind a curtain which could be the painter himself. The figure is pointing to his son. The panel entitled *Las tentaciones de San Antonio* (The Temptations of Saint Anthony) is a mature work, perhaps from around 1490. Strange monsters surround the subject of the picture. The theme lent itself to the artist's imagina-

Joachim Patinir. *A Rest During the Escape to Egypt.*
Panel. 121 χ 177 cm. Ref. nº 1611.

Hieronymus Bosch. *The Adoration of the Magi.*
Triptych on a panel. 138 cm. high. Each lateral flap is 33 cm wide. The central panel is 72 cm wide. Ref. nº 2048.

tion and he took it up again in various other versions. On account of its extremely high quality, the triptych of *El carro del heno* (The Hay Wagon) is evidently not a copy of the one preserved in the Escorial but instead an original work. Closed, it represents the theme of the traveller on the path of life. Open, it displays earthly paradise on the left and Hell on the right. The central scene, inspired by psalm 102 from the *Book of David* evokes the vanity of the world's pleasures. The high dignitaries of the time can be seen behind the wagon, arranged in the typical grouping of the Pope, the Emperor, etc., surrounded by people of all ranks who are vying to obtain hay from the wagon. In *La extracción de la piedra de la locura* (The Removal of the Stone of Madness), the scene from this artistic genre is transformed by means of the strange portrayal of the characters –the surgeon is touched by a funnel and the woman by a book.

Signed by *El Bosco* (Bosch) although some have maintained that he was not the artist, **La mesa de los siete pecados capitales** (The Table of the Seven Cardinal Sins) represents the sins in a circle around the figure of Christ, the Man of Pain. Four circular scenes at the corners of the square panel represent the final stages of the human condition according to Christianity – Death, Judgement, Hell and Glory.

Bosch's masterpiece and also his best-known and most highly-debated work, the object of successive contradictory interpretations, is the triptych called **El jardín de las delicias** (The Garden of Delights). Closed, it depicts the theme of the creation of the world in grisaille with surprising modernity. Open, the distribution is reminiscent of the triptych of the hay wagon. On the little left-hand door, there appears paradise with the scenes of the creation of Eve and the expulsion. On the left there is the delirious chaos of Hell while in the centre, you can see an allegory of sensuality and the sins of the flesh. For this, Bosch resorts to the scant life and usefulness of fruit trees such as the arbute or strawberry tree. This interpretation, as an expression of the banality of these earthly pleasures, was the view adopted by P. Sigüenza and all those who saw the work at the Escorial in the reign of Philip II. This picture, like the previous work, was brought from the Escorial. Attempts to go deeper into its symbolism or to search for its iconographic roots have come up with the theory that it was inspired by Saint Augustine's commentaries on the psalms or those of Saint Gregory on the Book of Job.

Bolder still is the theory that sees here a reference to the Adamites or brothers of the free spirit who promoted sexual promiscuity, conceiving of paradise in the Adamic terms which the panel evokes. However, it has not been proven that Bosch belonged to this sect. On the other hand, it is clear that even the mockingly anti-clerical depictions on the panel of Hell, with the Simoniac monastery of diabolical monks, contain a Christian moral warning. It is certainly true that whereas some of the themes in the triptych can be interpreted easily and directly, others are open to the most varied interpretations, from the iconographic – linking up with the classical and medieval tradition of monsters – to the psychoanalytical. In the context of its presentation to the Spanish court of the sixteenth century, it was taken as a game of ingenuity or allegorical craft perfectly suited to catholic orthodoxy. A similarity with Dante's Hell has been pointed out in the sense that although the panel corresponding to fire shows how fire devastates cities, it does not constitute a punishment for the damned. Instead, punishment comes from the icy cold, an expression of the absence of love.

The Prado conserves an extremely important panel by Pieter Brueghel the Elder (c.1525-1569), the head of a famous dynasty of artists and the main exponent, together with Muro, of the sixteenth century Flemish School. Although the theme of the panel is medieval, it links up with the concerns of Bosch as a painter of the nobility and the educated bourgeoisie in relation with the new northern European Christian Humanism. *El triunfo de la muerte* (The Triumph of Death), completed around 1560 or perhaps slightly later judging by its connections with another work of similar subject matter, in effect reproduces the old medieval theme of the dance of death from a traditional Flemish standpoint. There is a sense of fantasy clearly connected with Bosch. In addition, a tight, extremely delicate drawing in warm colours and refined expressiveness projects an image of total desolation which vividly transmits the situation of the Low Countries at that critical time. The work is designed as an accumulation of scenes on the road to the kingdom of death – an army of skeletons attacks and corners the humans and leads them to the coffin. Under the medieval concept of equality in death, the lifeless emperor can be seen in the top left-hand corner while in the opposite corner, two lovers, only concerned with themselves, are lost in thought.

Hieronymus Bosch. *The Garden of Delights or the Painting of The Strawberry Tree.*
Triptych on a panel. 220 χ 195 cm. Ref. nº 2823.

Hieronymus Bosch. *The Table of Cardinal Sins.*
Panel. 120 χ 150 cm. Ref. nº 2822.

Anton van der Haats Mor, known in Spain as **Antonio Moro** (c. 1519-1576, Utrecht) was a portrait painter. Although he was obviously influenced by the Italian Renaissance, he successfully attempted to reflect the psychological aspects of his subjects, thus initiating a highly significant trend in Spanish art. It is ño coincidence that he was a painter for Charles V and Philip II.

In 1554, Moro painted the portrait of Philip II's first wife, Mary I of England, who was called Bloody Mary by her protestant subjects. Painted on occasion of their wedding, Mary is holding the red Tudor rose in her right hand.

The great Flemish Romanesque artist **Michiel Coxcie** (1499-1592) painted the canvas *Santa Cecilia* (Saint Cecily). It provides a very high view of the saint playing the clavichord in the company of three singing angels. A characteristic example of the painter's synthesis art, so dear to his patron Philip II, it is recorded that the king paid the artist for the picture in 1569.

Recently acquired with funds from the Villaescusa bequest, the panel *Retrato de familia* (Portrait of a Family) was signed by the Flemish artist Adriaenz Thomasz Key (c. 1544-1590). It is an important example of this type of collective artistic representation. Against a dark background and dressed in black except for their collars, cuffs and white headdresses, the figures throng compositively around the seated figure of the father whose hand rests on a vanitas or a morally dead manifestation of nature made up of an hourglass, a skull and a book. According to now old conventions, males and females can be seen in tight distinct groups, separated here by the head of the family.

ALBRECHT DÜRER AND GERMAN RENAISSANCE PAINTING
Room 54

In spite of the close historical links between Spain and Germany, the collection of paintings from the latter country is relatively small in number. However, it includes works of great importance, particularly those by Albrecht Dürer (c. 1471-1528), known in Spain as *Alberto Durero*.

The leading exponent of Renaissance painting in Germany and the whole of northern Europe, he reproduces the knowledge he acquired during his stays in Italy in his own distinctively personal style. His *Autorretrato* (Self-Portrait) dates from 1498 when the artist was 26 years old. He is shown in luxurious apparel, wearing a cloak and gloves, looking more like a noble than a wealthy member of the middle class. His clear purpose in showing this attire is to present the freshly-won status of the artist, as it had been defined by the Italian Renaissance. The painting comes from the collection of Charles I of England. The window gives a view of a subtle, tightly-packed landscape, like a picture within a picture. Among the artist's portraits of male subjects, one of the most prominent is that of an unknown character. The picture was painted in about 1524. Attempts to identify the subject of the portrait have given rise to long and so far fruitless debate. It is more likely that he is middle-class rather than a noble. The intense concentration on his face shows how the artist has done his utmost to capture individual personality, a feature of Renaissance painting.

The panels of *Adán y Eva* (Adam and Eve) were painted in 1507, two years after the artist's return from Italy. As the first German portrayal of classic nudes, they caused a huge reaction among his contemporaries. The monumental nude figures are set against neutral backgrounds with no other boundary than the natural ground itself and, in the case of the Eve panel, the Tree of Knowledge with the Serpent. The date and the name of the artist also appear on the Eve panel while the Adam panel only displays the painter's monogram. Both panels were a gift from Queen Cristina of Sweden to king Philip IV.

Hans Baldung Grien (c. 1484-1545) incorporates Italian Renaissance teachings from a perspective of Germanic expressionist symbolisation which is not lacking in a certain brutality. Two noteworthy panels, *La armonía o Las tres gracias* (The Harmony or The Three Graces) and *Las tres edades y la muerte* (The Three Ages and Death), the latter still with truly medieval contents, stand out on account of their uninhibited Renaissance feminine nudes.

Lucas Cranach the Elder (1472-1553), a famous portrait painter and friend of Luther is represented with two scenes of hunts organized by the Elector of Saxony for Charles V at the Castle of Torgau. The paintings are signed and dated in 1544 and 1545 respectively. They are of great historical

Peter Brueghel, the Elder. *The Triumph of Death.*
Panel. 117x 162 cm. Ref. nº 1393.

Albrecht Dürer. *Self-portrait.*
Panel. 52 χ 41. Ref. nº 2179.

and iconographic interest and are attributed by some to his son.

ITALIAN PAINTING IN THE FOURTEENTH, FIFTEENTH AND SISTEENTH CENTURIES
Rooms 49 and 56b

The paintings in the museum from the Italian Trecento and Quattrocento periods are few in number but important. This is explained by the Spanish attraction to the Flemish world and by the late reassessment of these masters in the nineteenth century when the Spanish State could not compete with others in the new fashion for collections. The Cambó bequest served to alleviate these shortcomings with positively interesting works not only from a referential standpoint but also from an inherent one.

The two panels about the life of Saint Eloy – *San Eloy en el taller de orfebrería* (Saint Eloy at the Goldsmith's Workshop) and *San Eloy ante el rey Clotario* (Saint Eloy in the Presence of King Clotario) – are now attributed to the **Master of the Madonna of Mercy** from Florence, having previously been ascribed to Tadeo Gaddi. They are works from the Trecento period and apparently come from the predella of a reredos. The panels are claimed to be by Giotto and from Florence on account of the monumental figures, the folds, the mass, the perspective and the psychological advances reminiscent of Siena. Anecdotal detail and the stylishness of the figures also allude to Siena.

An outstanding work from the beginning of the Renaissance in the first half of the fifteenth century is *La Anunciación* (The Annunciation) painted around 1430 by Fra Giovanni da Fiesole, **Fra Angelico** (c. 1400-1455) with the help of the miniaturist Zanobio Strozzi, his oldest associate. The picture was painted for the Dominican monastery of Santo Domingo in the above-mentioned locality of Fiesole. With a still Gothic sensitivity but in a fully Renaissance mode, the large upper scene depicts the Annunciation in a porch in the Brunelleschi style. Next to the porch, Adam and Eve, who are dressed, are expelled from the Garden of Eden. The whole scene is marked by intricate preciosity. The five small panels on the predella portray *El nacimiento de la Virgen y los desposorios* (The Birth of the Virgin

and the Betrothal), *La visitación* (The Visitation), *La Epifanía* (The Epiphany), *La presentación del Niño en el templo* (The presentation of the Child in the Temple) and *La muerte de María* (The Death of Mary). The latter episode reveals an antiquated grouping and curiously from an iconographic point of view, includes Christ gathering up the soul of the deceased. This panel was acquired from the Madrid convent of the Descalzas Reales in 1861.

Antonello de Messina (c. 1430-1479) belongs to the full Renaissance of the second half of the fifteenth century. One of his leading works is exhibited – *Cristo muerto sostenido por un ángel* (The Dead Christ Supported by an Angel). This panel was painted in Venice approximately between 1476 and 1479 or perhaps on the artist's return to his native city. In any case, it was painted in the last few years of his life. The artist's technical development is brought out in the picture through the great intensity and pathos as well as the incredible brilliance of the sky. The painting combines what the artist learnt in Sicily and Naples with the knowledge he acquired in Flanders about oil painting techniques and realist meticulousness. Flemish influence is detected both in the detailed approach to Christ's hair and also in the sharp folds of the clothes. Behind an ascetic desert of bones and skulls, the landscape goes beyond a pleasant verdant area to show us the celestial Jerusalem, with a certain resemblance to Messina itself.

The Prado exhibits three famous panels by Alessandro or **Sandro Boticelli** (born c. 1444-45, died 1510) from the great Florentine Renaissance period. The panels deal with the **Historia de Nastaglio degli Onesti** according to the story told by Boccaccio in the Decameron. The concept evidently comes from the master, whose aristocratic distinguished design presides as much over the general composition as over the human and animal figures without being affected by the partial intervention of the artist's studio. The landscape, with the trees as columns, is more intellectual than realistic or descriptive. These episodes are put into focus by the story of the rejected lover who witnesses the wonder, repeated on certain dates, of the apparition of another who, after committing suicide for the same reason, chases the elusive damsel, tears out her heart and throws it to the dogs. Having seen all this, the first lover prepares a picnic so that his beloved will

Fra Angelico. *The Annunciation.* Panel. 194 χ 194. Ref. nº 15.

Boticelli. *The Story of Nastagio degli Onesti.* (Picture I).
Panel. 83 χ 138. Ref. nº 2838.

see this punishment and succumb to his desires. The fourth scene, which is still preserved although not at the Museum, shows the resultant wedding. The series of episodes was apparently made for a marriage between two members of the Florentine families of Bini and Pucci, whose coats of arms appear on one of the panels. The marriage took place in 1483, the date the series was made. These works originate from the Cambó donation of 1941.

The Padua School is represented by its chief exponent, **Andrea Mantegna** (1431-1506) with one of his masterpieces, the small panel entitled *La dormición de la Virgen* (The Dormition of the Virgin) which many consider to be one of the supreme treasures of the museum. Painted according to some around 1462 and according to others in 1492, it apparently forms part of a larger work. This belief stems from the fact that a panel is kept in Ferrara which shows Christ gathering up the soul of the Virgin. This panel could match the top of the panel exhibited in Madrid because, among other reasons, its half-pointed arched structure fits the lateral pilasters that finish off the scene on the Madrid panel. In spite of the limited surface area, Mantegna orchestrates the scene on a grand scale with great clarity and tremendous precision. The figures have a sculpturesque image and correspond to an architectural framework emphasized by the predominance of perspective, with an impression of depth is created both by the chequered surface and the open landscape behind the large window which offers an unmistakable view of Mantua with its lakes. This work reached the royal collection following the auction of the collection belonging to Charles I of England.

There are no works by Leonardo da Vinci in the Prado. However, there are paintings by his pupils such as **Bernardino Luini** (born between 1480 and 1490, died in 1532) whose *Sagrada Familia con San Juan* (The Holy Family with Saint John) is perhaps based on a sketch by the master. Leonardo's influence is apparent in the depiction of the figures, the smile of the Virgin and the characteristic shadows and transparency. Philip II received this work as a gift.

Rafael Sanzio de Urbino (1483-1520) was a leading figure in art historiography and fashion until well into the nineteenth century. He is extraordinarily well-represented in the museum on account of

having previously featured prominently in royal collections. The Prado holds extremely noteworthy works from the various stages making up his brief but dramatic artistic development. *La Sagrada Familia del Cordero* (The Holy Family of the Lamb) is a small panel signed and dated in 1507 illustrating his youthful Florentine phase with borrowings from Leonardo as regards the triangular design, the landscape and the characteristic *'Sfumato'* (gradual shading). The theme of the child with the lamb is reminiscent of specific drawings by Leonardo. But it is a very personal piece entirely from the artist's own hand. There exists a previous version with variations which experts cannot precisely date.

The solemn *Virgen del Pez* (Virgin of the Fish) dates from the beginning of his Roman period in about 1513. This was the artist's best phase as a colourist. The painting on the panel was transferred to canvas after its removal from Spain by the Bonaparte administration. Not only does the exact drawing show Florentine patterns but also the group of the Virgin and Child is reminiscent of classical statuary and that of Michelangelo. In the composition, the diagonal arrangement is superimposed on the triangular one. The former links the child with Tobias who carries the fish that gives the picture its name. Perhaps the colouring reveals elements of Sebastiano del Piombo. In producing the work, Raphael had the benefit of some measure of collaboration from Giulio Romano.

The most important work by Raphael in the museum and also the most highly-valued in royal collections since it was acquired by Philip IV is the **Caída en el camino del calvario** (Fall on the Way to Calvary). This painting was known historically as the *Pasmo de Sicilia* (The Wonder of Sicily), a corruption of the name of the Sicilian monastery where it came from, Santa María dello Spasimo. It was painted and engraved around 1516 and, as a logical consequence, became universally known with numerous copies being made, both complete and fragmented. It is a work of classical perfection illustrating Raphael's total maturity in his Roman period. The picture is extremely large and constitutes one of his last great altar pieces. Although it was personally created by the artist, perhaps he required the collaboration of Giulio Romano. The artist's signature appears on a stone in the middle of the composition. There is a dense structural complexity with a wide

Raphael. *A Fall on the Road to Calvary.*
Panel transferred to canvas. 318 χ 229. Ref. nº 298.

variety of attitudes and gestures, characteristic of Raphael's later works which reflect his interest in states of extreme tension, both physical and psychological. The tremendous structural balance is made more dynamic by the intersection of diagonal lines. According to some, the iconographic inspiration came from Dürer. Others see the imprint of Schongauer. The painting was transferred from a panel to canvas following the Napoleonic invasion. This was the last turn of events in an incredible series of hazards that make the survival of the painting all the more miraculous. Its recent restoration has revealed its superb quality in spite of the inevitable effects of the said transfer.

A masterpiece of Renaissance portrait painting is **El Cardenal** (The Cardinal), whose identity is highly debatable but who is perhaps Bandinello Suari. It is a mature work from about 1517. The panel represents an archetypal characterization of the Roman Cardinal of the day – refined, enigmatic and astute. The picture was undoubtedly painted by Raphael alone, as was usually the case with his portraits. Raphael uses only one colour scheme in an exceptional economy of resources that surprises the observer.

La Sagrada Familia del Roble (The Holy Family of the Oak) dates from round 1518 and is a characteristic example of this type of painting by the master. He was undoubtedly the artist but a substantial contribution was also made by Giulio Romano. This panel is very similar to that of La Sagrada Familia (The Holy Family), also called La Perla (The Pearl), given its contrasts of light and the special attention paid to the symbols of classical antiquity, whose exact significance is unknown, but which goes beyond the usual references to the defeat of the pagan world.

Philip IV added it to his collections after acquiring it in an auction held by Charles I of England. Also painted in about 1518, it shows not only the collaboration of Giulio Romano but also to a lesser extent that of Penni.

Some attribute La Sagrada Familia de la Rosa (The Holy Family of the Rose) to the said Giulio Romano. It was painted at the same time but the distinctive flower as well as other features could be later additions.

Transferred from wood to canvas in the previously-mentioned circumstances, La Visitación (The Visitation) is signed and is recorded as having been commissioned around 1519. On the left of the main theme is a depiction of the baptism of Christ under an outburst of glory, set out in large-scale but balanced terms. Although the genius of Raphael shines through in this tremendous composition, the participation of his pupils cannot be refuted. They include Perino del Vaga or the frequently-mentioned Giulio Romano. Some analysts believe that the work was produced entirely by Raphael's assistants.

The Prado holds some of the most important works by Fra Sebastiano Luciani, known as **Sebastiano del Piombo** (c. 1485-1547). These include the canvas Jesús con la cruz a cuestas (Jesus with the Cross on his Back), painted in about 1520 in the style of Michelangelo but, in pleasing synthesis, using fully Venetian techniques and colouring.

A leading work in devotional and funereal painting from the Italian Renaissance is La Piedad (The Piety). Signed, it was produced over a long period between 1533 and 1539. The picture was stored by the Casa Ducal de Medinaceli Foundation. It was painted in oil on slate for Francisco de los Cobos, the secretary of Charles V. The painting was intended for his Chapel of the Saviour in Úbeda. Its recent restoration has disclosed the magnificent sombre colour which is determined by the special platform. The iconography is along Venetian lines but apparently Michelangelo provided drawings for the composition.

Andrea del Sarto (1486-1531) paints La Virgen con el Niño, un santo y un ángel (The Virgin and Child, a Saint and an Angel), the latter being identified as Tobias and Saint Raphael. Saint Matthew has also been cited instead of Tobias.

The artist uses the magnificent technical resources which gave him the epithet of 'Andrea Senza errori' (Faultless Andrea). To these, he adds the 'sfumato' (gradual shading) of Leonardo, the Roman outlines of Raphael and Michelangelo's large-scale approach in order to achieve an extremely personal and unmistakable style. The picture probably symbolizes the defence of the authenticity of the Book of Tobias by Jesus Christ himself.

An outstandingly characteristic work by Antonio Allegri, **Corregio** (c. 1493-1534) is the wood painting transferred to canvas entitled **Noli Me Tangere**, dated about 1525. Already in the sixteenth century, it received eloquent praise from Vasari. With a morbid sensitivity closer to future

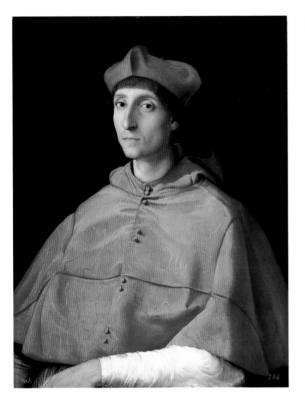

Raphael. *The Cardinal.*
Panel. 79 χ 61. Ref. nº 299.

Raphael. *The Holy Family.*
Panel. 144 χ 115. Ref. nº 301.

rococo than to the Renaissance, it portrays an ambiguous dialogue between Christ and Mary Magdalene against a very dense landscape in the background. The expressive intensity goes beyond naturalism. It belonged to the collection of Charles I of England, reaching Philip IV following the auction of this collection.

Francesco Maria Mazzola, **Parmigianino** (1503-1540) was a characteristic exponent of mannerism, the culmination of the full Renaissance. We can highlight two panels that provide an extraordinary insight into this new aesthetic outlook – the portraits of *Pedro María Rossi or Roscio, count of San Segundo* and of his wife *Camilla Gonzaga, with Three children*. The pictures were painted in about 1533 to 1535.

Agnolo Bronzino (1503-1572) was the leading exponent of early Florentine mannerism in portrait painting. He approaches his figures coldly from a considerable psychological distance. His technique is impeccable while the light is far from flattering. One of his most prominent portraits is that of Don García de Medicis, the son of the great duke Cosme I. It is 1549 and the subject is still very much a boy. With his left hand, he is grasping the cord which he is holding up to his collar. A small jewel with a horn-like amulet hangs down from his collar.

VENETIAN PAINTING FROM THE SIXTEENTH CENTURY
Rooms 75, 61b, 61, 62, 63, 63b, 62b and 60

The Venetian School from the sixteenth century was exceptionally well-represented in the royal collections, not only in that very same century but also increasingly during the next. It had a decisive influence on the development of painting in Madrid and the whole of Spain in general. From the Venetian Quattrocento period, the Prado holds the extraordinary panel entitled *La Virgen y El Niño entre dos santos* (The Virgin and Child Between Two Saints) signed by **Giovanni Bellini** (c. 1429-1516). It is a mature work that shows how the artist assimilated the new techniques from Antonello de Mesina and how he created the standard devotional painting which we call *'sacra conversación'* (sacred conversation). The piece stands out on account of its extraordinary colouring technique. As far as the iconogra-

phy is concerned, one of the characters could be Saint Catherine or Mary Magdalene whereas the other, judging from the arrow, seems to correspond to Saint Ursula.

The Canvas *Virgen con el Niño, entre San Antonio de Padua y San Roque* (the Virgin and Child, Between Saint Anthony of Padua and Saint Rock) has been attributed, not without a great deal of controversy, to the otherwise elusive or evanescent Giorgio da Castelfranco, Giorgione (c. 1478-1510). It was painted around 1510 and has an imprecise structure accentuated by the lack of a conclusion, a typical feature of this master. In more than one aspect, his work ties in with that of Titian. The figure of Saint Anthony is reminiscent of Titian. Recent critics have again taken up the theory that the picture was in fact painted by the young Titian.

Tiziano Vecellio (Titian) (1477-1576) was the leading figure of the Venetian school. All the styles and periods relating to him are present in the Prado museum in great qualitative and quantitative wealth, having previously formed a part of royal collections. Charles V and Philip II were his patrons and the collectors of his works. These collections grew substantially in the seventeenth century. His impact on Spanish painting is absolutely crucial.

The panel entitled *Virgen con el Niño, Santo y Santa* (Virgin and Child, Male and Female Saints) also named *Los desposorios místicos de Santa Catalina* (The Mystic Betrothal of Saint Catherine) perhaps portrays Saint Catherine and Saint George. The painting is in Titian's early style, still following in the footsteps of Giorgione, namely prolonging his sense of colour gradual together with soft shading and open sensuality. Apparently inspired by a composition from the said Giorgione, the picture may have been painted in 1505 or 1515. A splendorous work from this initial stage of Titian's great career, he already displays the distinctive golden colour scheme that became a characteristic feature of his work.

La Bacanal de Andros (The Bacchanal) and *La ofrenda a la diosa de los amores* (The Offering to the Goddess of Love) were painted in 1518 and were both signed. They were a product of Titian's early maturity and refer to a story by the Hellenistic Filostrato and also to poems by Catulo. The pictures were commissioned for an exhibition room at the palace of Ferrara where they were accompanied by a

Correggio. « *Noli me tangere* ».
Wood panel transferred to canvas. 130 χ 103. Ref. n° 111.

Bellini painting. The Bacchanal depicts the arrival of Dionysius on the island of Naxos. It is an enjoyable pagan reproduction. The bacchante, dressed in red, takes her lover Vilonate as the subject for the central figure in the foreground. Titian's departure from Rome in the seventeenth century caused a great stir in artistic circles who saw in this picture a vital benchmark in neo-venetian Baroque which was then in vogue. The offering to the goddess of Love surprises the observer with the infinite variety of attitudes present in the numerous flirtations.

As a portrait painter, Titian combines his technical talent with profound psychological perception. Great quality is evident in the signed portrait of *Federico Gonzaga, primer duque de Mantua* (Federico Gonzaga, first duke of Mantua). For some, it is a work from the artist's youth and for others, it dates from 1531, the year in which the subject of the portrait married.

La alocución del marqués del Vasto (The Exhortation of the Marquis of Vasto) was commissioned in 1539 and represents Alonso de Avalos addressing his troops. It expresses what some have termed Titian's 'mannerist crisis', partly brought on by the arrival of several Tuscan artists in Venice.

The magnificent portrait of Charles V was painted in Bologna in 1532-33. The King is standing with a dog and is dressed in the attire that he wore to receive the Crown of Lombardy. Not only does the picture initiate Titian's series of portraits of Spanish monarchs but it also begins a new type of Italian painting. In doing so, Titian incorporates the full-figure portrait into the artistic medium, a technique already common in northern Europe.

At Augsburg in 1548, the master painted the posthumous portrait of **Isabel de Portugal** (Isabel of Portugal), the wife of Charles V. He used previous portrayals as a basis. Although some critics blame the indirectness of the source for a lack of conviction in the portrait, others see an accurate reflection of the personality of the sovereign who is sitting in front of an open window which affords a view of a pleasant landscape.

The portrait entitled *Carlos V en la batalla de Mühlberg* (Charles V at the Battle of Mühlberg) was also painted in Augsburg in 1548 although the battle itself had taken place one year before. It is a portrait of the utmost importance, not only for its equestrian content.

The emperor is portrayed as a hero in this battle, greatly echoing the classical style. He appears against a wooded background landscape in which the river Elbe can be seen. The twilight setting matches the melancholic gesture of the figure. In spite of his victory, the ideal of 'Universitas Christiana' is seen as a difficult objective. This is undoubtedly the most important portrait with an equestrian theme in Renaissance painting.

The portrait of Philip II which was painted in Augsburg in 1550-51 shows the king on foot, partly covered in armour, with his right hand resting on his helmet. The painting was to be sent to Queen Mary Tudor of England in the context of the negotiated marriage arrangement between the nephew and the aunt. However, the picture did not please the subject. Technically outstanding is the treatment of the fabrics and the armour in which Titian displays extreme virtuosity.

La Gloria (The Glory) is a canvas painting of enormous dimensions. It was commissioned by Charles V in 1551 and completed three years later. It is a religious-allegorical-dynastic composition also serving as a collective portrait of the imperial royal family. Presided over by the Trinity, accompanied by the Virgin Mary, the picture sets out a congregation of figures in a grand circle with tremendous foreshortening. The patriarchs appear in the foreground. Among them are Charles V, Isabel of Portugal, the future Philip II and other royal dignitaries, shown kneeling and with a shroud. Titian had no hesitation in appearing in person with his own portrait at this zenith not only of the dynasty but also of its principal cause, the defence of Catholicism. Charles V took the canvas to his Yuste retreat where he asked to see it before his death. From there, it was transferred by Philip II to his favourite establishment and the new sacred site for the monarchy – The Escorial.

The canvas *La religión socorrida por España* (Religion Saved by Spain) was begun by Titian in 1566. It is of a similar symbolic nature but is painted in a different setting. The picture is a seascape with Neptune. Following the victory at Lepanto in 1571, Titian opportunely transformed a mythological picture into this political-devotional allegory. For this purpose, he disguised the classical god as a Turk. Titian sent the result to Philip II in 1575.

The Spanish court was not well-disposed to this type of symbolic expression, so remote from their

Titian.
Bacchanal of the Andrios.
Canvas. 175 χ 193. Ref. nº 418.

Titian.
Isabel of Portugal.
Canvas. 117 χ 98. Ref. nº 415.

own sense of realism, but Titian still produced a third work along similar ideological lines – *Felipe II ofreciendo al cielo al príncipe Fernando* (Philip II offering Prince Ferdinand to Heaven). The work was commissioned to accompany the portrait of Charles V at the Battle of Mühlberg. It was sent to Spain in 1575. Signed on a cartouche on one of the columns, it constitutes an allegorical portrait of Philip II. The evidence is the promise held out by the date 1571, the year not only of Lepanto but also of the birth of the said prince who nevertheless soon died. The accordance with the emphatic style characteristic of the genre and with the backdrop of a collonnade at one side, an angel bearing a palm descends on the royal dignitaries while in the foreground a chained Turk tells of the defeat of the infidel.

Returning to our review of Titian portraiture, we can highlight *El caballero del reloj* (The Gentleman with the Watch). The date of 1550 is generally accepted for this painting. With a magnificent use of light and shade, the piece addresses the iconographic problem of whether the watch is a symbolic element, as is usually the case in Spanish portraits, or whether it is merely an indication of the owner's trade and therefore without any underlying significance. Believing the second possibility to be true, some have attempted to identify the subject of the painting as a certain jeweller. Others believe that he is an effigy of the famous inventor Juanelo Turriano.

Titian's self-portrait dates from around 1565 to 1570. It shows the artist already very old. An exceptional work, it belonged to Rubens and, on his death, was purchased by Philip IV. It is an outstanding work as a result of its impressionist technique, achieved through bold brush-strokes away from the main outlines. Thus, it illustrates the master's final phase of stylistic development, splitting up painting and heralding the break-up of realism centuries in advance. A strong impact is also created by the psychological depth or introspection with which Titian approaches his own personality.

Mythology acquires dimensions in the leader of the Venetian School. The Prado holds some of the masterpieces produced by Titian in this genre. These works are sometimes subject to controversy due to their dubious classification or meaning, fluctuating between allegory and straightforward eroticism. This is what happens in the different variations on

the theme of Venus with an organist. The so-called *Venus y la música* (Venus and the Music) was painted between 1540 and 1550. Apart from its supreme qualities, a distinguishing feature is the miniature dog that accompanies the goddess. It is an exceptional canvas entirely in the artist's own hand. The way in which Titian reflects the corpulence of Venus is particularly noteworthy. The melancholic background landscape, with an arboreal perspective and a Renaissance fountain, ambiguously goes beyond the conventional concept of a garden. The bold nudity is augmented by the no less immodest uninhibited way in which the organist, dressed in contemporary apparel, directs his looks at the feminine figure.

The painting known as *Venus y el amor* (Venus and Love) is similar but of lower quality, perhaps owing to the participation of other artists. This picture is said to have been presented to Charles V in 1548 although there is considerable doubt about this. Cupid replaces the dog from the previous version.

Among the mythological nudes painted by Titian, the 'poems' intended for the future Philip II, then a prince, have been the object of particular interest from the point of view of the reaction to this genre in such an unauspicious setting as the Spanish court. It has not even been possible to establish for certain what guidelines were followed for installing these works as a part of palace decoration programmes. Consequently, we cannot be sure whether or not relatively good access was provided to these paintings away from the intimate circle of royal dignitaries.

Inspired mainly by Ovidio's *Metamorfosis* (Metamorphoses), Titian completed a series of 'poems' for Philip II. Three of these are today scattered among different places. At least from 1553 onwards, Titian worked on the two 'poems' now kept at the Prado –*Dánae recibiendo la lluvia de oro* (Dánae receiving the Golden Rain) and *Venus y Adonis* (Venus and Adonis). Given their date, these works reflect total maturity. The former is a golden composition in which everything shakes under the vibration of the painting. The previous version of Dánae Receiving the Golden Rain is today in the Museum of Naples. It received deserved criticism from Michelangelo for its lack of drawing. In fact, both versions are a radical expression of Venetian

Titian. *Self-portrait.*
Canvas. 86 χ 65. Ref. nº 407.

Titian.
Danäe Receiving the Golden Rain.
Canvas. 129 χ 180. Ref. nº 425.

colouring technique. The one in the Prado displays bold brush-strokes which fill the picture with a sensuality that even reaches the luxurious tapestries.

The accompanying painting of **Venus and Adonis** is a very personal work of art and was painted by Titian himself. There exist several versions of the picture including one in London which is sometimes considered to be an original and a replica of the painting in the Prado, produced soon afterwards. The second picture is regarded as providing a matching contrast to the first in the context of a mythological collection. In the second picture, Titian presents a back view of the feminine nude whereas in the first picture she is seen from the front. The famous description by the contemporary Ludovico Dolce explains and extols the difficult posture of Venus, presenting it as a real challenge.

Within the mythological theme, but in a different setting, Titian was the creator of the two surviving canvases in the series *Las Furias* (The Furies), also called *Los Condenados* (The Damned). The series portrays the punishment of four notorious legendary criminals. It was commissioned by Mary of Hungary in 1547-48. Two works of magnificent conceptual thinking are *Sísifo* (Sisyphus) and **Ticio** (Tityus), the latter having been confused with Prometheus. Unfortunately, these pictures were damaged in the fire at the Alcázar of Madrid in 1734. Despite this, they still display the extremely high original quality.

As far as biblical themes are concerned, Titian is represented by his superb *Adán y Eva* (Adam and Eve), signed on the stone in the lower left-hand corner. Painted in about 1560, it was perhaps inspired by Dürer. The painting was also damaged in the fire at the Alcázar. The magnificence with which Titian set out the theme attracted Rubens. When the Flemish artist visited Madrid in 1628, he produced a copy which is preserved in the Prado as well. Moreover, Eve's face was remade after the fire, naturally by an artist other than Titian. Apparently, the face is based on the completely separate design followed by Rubens in his reconstruction.

Salomé con la Cabeza del Bautista (Salome with the Head of the Baptist) is a canvas dating from about 1550. There exists a lower quality version in Berlin. Perhaps the picture presents the artist's own daughter, Lavinia, a technique very often used in Renaissance painting. Sometimes, a portrait was

clearly intended to create a divine atmosphere. In this case, however, the identity of the subject prevents this.

Despite his total mastery of secular themes, Titian took on the additional role of a religious painter with the ability to bring out the most intense pathos. *El Salvador, de hortelano* (The Saviour, as a Gardener), in which Jesus is presented in the form of an extended bust, would be a strange creation if it were not recorded as constituting a fragment from Christ's appearance to Mary Magdalene. Commissioned by Mary of Hungary, Titian worked on the piece in 1553.

In that same year of 1553, *La Dolorosa* (Our Lady of Sorrow) had already been completed. It is a work performed on marble and signed by the artist. Half of a figure with raised hands can be seen. This specific iconographic theme allowed Titian to intensify devotional dramatism in a way which suited the devotional style of his Spanish clientele. In 1554, Titian painted *La Dolorosa* panel for Charles V. The painting also shows half of the figure, this time with her hands crossed. The figure is characterized by a melancholy expression.

La Oración del Huerto (The Prayer in the Garden), painted from 1559 to 1562, is extraordinary both on account of its bold creative structure and also in its nocturnal setting. There is another version of this canvas painting in the Escorial. Its defective state of preservation does not prevent us from appreciating Titian's brave inventiveness. Large secondary figures are in darkness in the foreground. Behind, we can see a small-scale portrayal of the title scene, taking place in strong light.

El Entierro de Cristo (The Burial of Christ) projects the same dramatic style. Two very similar signed versions are exhibited in the Prado. By far the higher quality version is the picture commissioned by Philip II in 1559. Undoubtedly the work of the artist himself, some believe it was painted later. Like the other version, it depicts the burial of Christ, a scene made more solemn by the use of chromatic vibration. The second version contains many variations and was produced in about 1572. Most experts detect a certain degree of participation from members of the artist's studio.

Two beautiful versions of the same theme are *Cristo y el Cireneo* (Christ and the Cyrenean), probably dated around 1560, and *Jesús y el Cireneo*

Titian. *Tityus.*
Canvas. 253 χ 217. Ref. nº 427.

Pablo Veronese. *Venus and Adonis.*
Canvas. 162 χ 191 cm. Ref. nº 482.

(Jesus and the Cyrenean). According to some, the latter was begun by Giovanni Bellini although this theory has generally been discounted. It was presented to the Escorial in 1574 as the work of Titian and illustrates his capacity to tune into Spanish religious sensitivity, a traditional Flemish focal point of interest.

The canvas *Santa Margarita* (Saint Margaret) is a signed work of religious art in the category of legend. It portrays a scene from the Golden Legend in which the protagonist makes a dragon disappear with the sign of the cross. Painted in 1565, it contains a turbulent background of dramatic intensity with a village and the sea in the distance. For the painting, Titian obviously took into account the picture of the same name by Raphael, whose design he reworked with such chromatic fusion that the end product is unrecognisable from the first.

The Prado preserves a great deal of evidence of the artistic output of the Bassanos from the Venetian school. **Jacopo da Ponte Bassano** (born in 1510-15, died 1592) specialized in Biblical themes viewed from an everyday perspective. His pictures are full of figures related to the scenes from the genre, according to the preferences of his mostly middle-class clientele. *La entrada de los animales en el arca de Noé* (The Animals Entering Noah's Ark) gives maximum expression to these characteristic features. The virtuosity in his portrayal of the beasts can be considered totally naturalistic but the landscape and the human figures undoubtedly bear resemblance to the work of Titian who acquired this painting for Charles V.

Paolo Caliari, **Veronés** (1528-1588) was a leading exponent of the Venetian school. His work is characterized by lavish scenes, luxurious anachronistic garments, splendid architectural backgrounds and a clever perception of space. *La Disputa con los doctores en el Templo* (The Argument with the Doctors in the Temple) is dated 1548 according to the inscription on a corner of a book in the foreground. However the maturity of the work makes it unlikely that it was painted at such an early stage in the artist's career. The magnificent structure convincingly achieves the effect of creating space. Another contributory factor in attaining this effect is the superb architecture in the Palladian Style. The large dimensions and complexity of the picture are surprising. This is emphasized by the lavish figures among

whom there appears a gentleman of the Holy Sepulchre, perhaps the person who had the commissioned the painting.

Small in size but grand in concept, the canvas ***Moisés salvado de las aguas del Nilo*** (Moses Saved from the Waters of the Nile) is a fully mature work. It is difficult to be precise about its date which can be flexibly put at between 1560 and 1575. The picture has been considered a true artistic jewel. This description has never been better applied, given the stage scenery of the royal court, an extremely refined ambience in which Veronés evokes the landscape and the characters. The work is not without brilliantly exotic touches, manifestly justified here on account of the setting.

The same wealth of materials and lush vegetation fill the canvas painting entitled *Venus y Adonis* (Venus and Adonis) from around 1580. The artist creates a vibrant picture and is extremely skilful in producing lighting effects whose most delicate shades are focussed on the body of the goddess. Technically, Veronés achieves an effect which is close to nineteenth-century 'plenairism' and which makes this work an essential testimony of his personal contribution to the school.

Together with Titian and Veronés, Jacopo Robusti, **Tintoretto** (c. 1518-1594) makes up the great trio of Venetian painters. With a tendency to be capricious and close to mannerist contortion, he took the colouring techniques of his predecessors to their ultimate consequences before the Baroque style would do so. The grand ***Lavatorio*** (The Washing of the Feet) is a canvas painting from the artist's youth. It was produced in 1547 for San Marcuola of Venice. The painting presents numerous figures distributed in a complex pattern of space. The background is extended in an unmistakably Venetian architectural perspective ending in a triumphal arch. Through the use of position and looks, emphasized by the effects of light and shadow, the relations between the groups and figures who are positioned at regular intervals along the dynamic paving contribute to the credibility of the setting. This establishes the basis for the Baroque aerial perspective. The painting was acquired by Philip IV from an auction by Charles I of England.

Also works from his youth and dated around 1555 are the six *Historias bíblicas* (Biblical Stories) and *La Purificación de las vírgenes madianitas* (The

Pablo Veronese.
Moses Saved from the Waters.
Canvas. 57 χ 43 cm. Ref. nº 502.

Tintoretto. *The Washing of the Feet.*
Canvas. 210 χ 533 cm. Ref. nº 2824.

Purification of the Madianite Virgins), the latter in an oval shape. Together, they make up a typical Venetian ceiling. Velasquez apparently bought the works for Philip IV and, indeed, when the paintings were transferred to Madrid, they suited a bedroom ceiling at the Alcázar. With their rich colouring, splendorous vestments and magnificent architectural elements, they clearly belong to Tintoretto's Veronesian period.

Probably painted in the second half of the 1560s, *El Caballero con cadena de oro* (The Gentleman with a Golden Chain) is one of the artist's best and most widely distributed portraits. However, it has not proved possible to identify the subject of the portrait, two-thirds of whom is seen from a side angle and whose head is turned towards the observer. The composition is most unconventional although the colouring is very frugal in a characteristic show of restraint from an artist who, although Venetian, tended to use cold shades of light as opposed to Titian's golden hues.

Judith y Holofernes (Judith and Holofernes) is a great canvas painting produced between 1570 and 1580. It displays a fully mature style. Perhaps because of its bad state of preservation, historians have suspected a substantial contribution by the artist's studio. Nevertheless, the weaknesses evident in its completion give rise to increased interest in Tintoretto's contacts with Roman mannerism. The figures are clearly reminiscent of Michelangelo's style. In spite of these borrowings, the picture expresses a totally Venetian sensitivity with a free technique and characteristic contrasts of light. Incidentally, there are three Tintorettian versions of the episode preserved at the Prado, including this one.

A very well-known painting but one which is generally rejected by the critics is **La Dama que descubre el seno** (The Lady Revealing her Breast). This canvas painting is included among the boldest and most modern of Tintoretto's pictures, emphasizing his clear range and preimpressionist images. Some have considered the subject to be the courtesan Verónica Franco whereas others have identified her as the artist's own daughter, Marietta.

Luis de Morales, nicknamed *El Divino* (The Divine), was born in Badajoz about 1500 and died in 1586. He expresses a very personal spiritual combination of beliefs in which he links Italian Renaissance sensitivity with a technique of detailed preciosity in the Flemish style that he probably learnt in Seville where he must have got to know Pedro de Campaña. *La Virgen con el Niño* (The Virgin and Child) is an elegantly refined work that is conceptually related to the Mannerism of the time. The painting enjoyed great popularity and is a characteristic testimony from a time of traditional devotion, both Spanish and northern European. Several versions of the painting are preserved, three in the Museum itself.

EL GRECO
Rooms 60a, 61a and 62a

El Greco was an unusual artist in that he stayed outside court circles. Therefore, historically, just a few of his paintings were housed in Royal Palaces. Only latterly has the Prado been accumulating a significant collection of his works.

Domenikos Thetokópulos, El Greco, was born in *Candia* (Crete) in 1541 and died in Toledo in 1614. His basic Byzantine Style, Venetian training and subsequent stay in Rome do not prevent him from being considered a stalwart of the Spanish school, albeit unique and out of context. He did not obtain full historical recognition until the twentieth century. El Greco arrived in Spain, apparently attracted by the grand enterprise of the Escorial. However, his aspirations were frustrated by the failure of his *San Mauricio* (Saint Maurice). In 1577, he settled permanently in Toledo, a decision which has been the subject of frequent debate, given the relative decadence of the city at that time. El Greco's previous period prior to his arrival in Spain is represented in the Prado by a small Annunciation in a clearly Venetian style.

The Trinity is part of the first great commissioned work carried out by El Greco in Toledo in 1577 on behalf of the Dean of the Cathedral, Diego of Castile, for the monastery church of *Santo Domingo el Antiguo* (Saint Dominic the Elder). The choice of perspective is explained by the fact that it occupied the top section of the main reredos. The numerous traces of the influence of Italian painting reveal a type of expression that still relies on the teachings of that school although its future Mannerism is already evident. Thus, the cold range of colours is reminis-

Tintoretto. *The Lady Revealing her Breast.*
Canvas. 61 χ 55 cm. Ref. nº 382.

El Greco. *The Gentleman with his Hand on his Chest.*
Canvas. 81 χ 66 cm. Ref. nº 809.

cent of Venice, the angels hark back to Rome, and the large-scale bodies reflect the knowledge conveyed by Michelangelo. The proportions of the subjects in this work are in the realist mode. A wood engraving by Dürer from 1511 inspired the iconography which shows the Eternal Father with an oriental tiara holding up the dead Christ. The dove of the Holy spirit flies over them. The painting was acquired by Ferdinand VII.

El Greco arrived in Spain as a portrait painter, having assimilated the teachings of the Venetian School, particularly Tintoretto, but without letting himself be influenced by the type of court portrait painting then in fashion. He completely rejected this kind of refined concept in the Flemish Style. The extremely well-known *Caballero de la mano en el pecho* (A Gentleman with his Hand on his Chest) is signed but not dated although it is supposed to have been painted around 1580. It evokes the archetypal Spanish nobleman from the time of Cervantes. Some have called the work A Gentleman Taking the Oath. According to others, the protagonist had a disability in his left arm.

In any case, ... the lace collar... a medallion or scallop-shell... the scabbard for his sword... his possible identity, the subject of sarcasm from Borges, has given rise to a great deal of debate. Perhaps he is Juan de Silva, a Knight of the order of Saint James, marquis of Montemayor and the chief notary in Toledo. He undoubtedly influenced Velasquez who was able to see him in his studio. The recent restoration of the picture has removed the dark nineteenth-century background, a typical feature in a museum picture.

Un retrato de caballero (A Portrait of a Gentleman) was painted between 1584 and 1590. The identity of the nobleman is unknown but the portrait is considered to be one of the most captivating images created by El Greco and as such one of the most characteristic images from the Spain of Don Quixote. The protagonist's melancholic expression provides the main attraction in the picture.

San Andrés y San Francisco (Saint Andrew and Saint Francis) was painted in approximately 1590-1595 and signed by the artist. Its best-known projection is in the small reredos of the basilica of the Escorial. However, this does not mean that it no longer had any connection with the Venetian style of the holy conversations. Against a background formed by the Toledo landscape, Saint Andrew and Saint Francis appear with their respective attributes – the diagonal cross and the stigmata. It is the cross which provides the link and the basis of the composition. A vibrant work of great chromatic harmony, its iconography is subject to doubt. It probably derives from the circumstances of the person who commissioned the painting and would therefore make the picture a characteristic work of private devotion. The picture came from the Madrid monastery of *La Encarnación* (The Incarnation).

One of the main series of pictures for a reredos painted by El Greco belongs to the Prado. It was painted between 1596 and 1606 for another church in Madrid, the church at the school of *Doña María de Aragón* (Mary of Aragon). Incidentally, this institution was located very near to the Monastery of La Encarnación. Although the records show that only *La Anunciación* (The Annunciation) and *El Bautismo* (The Baptism) belonged to this series, it is assumed that several more pictures preserved here formed a part of the group of paintings. The Annunciation, signed on the step under the basket, is without doubt one of El Greco's masterpieces. The artist presents the typical distinction between the earthly and celestial spheres with a sharpness undiminished by the flamelike appearance of the image, highlighted by so many. On the other hand, the clarity is not quite so pure as in other pictures from the series. The painting merges into intense divine radiance that minimizes the effect of the realism of the surroundings. The outburst of glory is represented as an angelic concert. In the lower part of the painting, an unusual detail is the burning bush, taken from the story of Moses. Here it appears on the sewing basket. This disconcerting canvas is characterized by stylized figures among cotton-wool clouds. The dove of the Holy Spirit is the turning point between the two spheres. Like the previous picture, *El Bautismo de Cristo* (The Baptism of Christ) is also signed. In spite of the grouping together of elements in the picture, still in the style of Michaelangelo, the now glaring colours used by El Greco reveal the depth of his involvement with Mannerism.

La Crucifixión (The Crucifixion) probably belongs to the same series and is likely to have come from the top section of the reredos. It is also understood that *La Pentecostés* (The Pentecost) comes from

El Greco. *Saint Andrew and Saint Francis.*
Canvas. 167 χ 113 cm. Ref. nº 2819.

El Greco. *The Annunciation.*
Canvas. 315 χ 176 cm. Ref. nº 3888.

the same section. This work was remotely inspired by a work of Titian's and is likewise signed. The figures are presented as roaring flames amid strongly vertical spiritual tension. The foreground is occupied by two large-scale figures with their backs turned. In the background, many other figures make up a tightly-packed scene with the Virgin in the centre. The third apostle on the right of Mary seems to be the subject in a portrait and his face is a constant reminder of the face of Covarrubias. *La Resurrección* (The Resurrection of Christ) is also considered to be a part of this series. The painting eloquently expresses Mannerism, for example in the difficult postures taken up by the sepulchre guards. *Cristo abrazado a la cruz* (Christ Embracing the Cross) is a signed painting, dating arguably from between 1591 and 1605. More than half the body of Christ is shown. Many other versions are known to exist. The head of Christ is similar to the head of the figure in *El expolio* (The Despoliation) in Toledo cathedral.

The interesting picture *Julián Romero y su santo patrono* (Julián Romero and his Patron Saint) is from the end of the sixteenth century and the beginning of the seventeenth century. Saint Julian is standing and wearing a fleur-de-lis robe. It was believed for many years that he represented Saint Louis, the king of France. Romero was 'the one who had performed heroic exploits' and this famous portrait of him at prayer duly and graphically illustrates the chivalric ideals present in private devotion.

A recently acquired work, *La Fábula* (The Fable) corresponds to a basic theme that has given itself to the existence of several different versions. These versions have now been definitively attributed to El Greco after a controversy in which opinion tended to come down on the side of the Venetian Jacopo Bassano. Without attempting to detract from the importance of the clear Venetian influence, the painting constitutes a curious representation of a masterpiece from the ancient world, specifically the picture by Antifilo of Alexandria. However, unlike other versions that follow the Classical style in presenting only the central and front figures, here, as in some other works, a figure is visible on each side: a monkey and a figure in profile. The central figure is blowing a burning brand with which he is trying to light a candle held in his other hand. According to some, the scene comes from a Spanish fable with the character recast as a female figure. However, this theory can be totally rejected. The piece was painted in about 1600 although another version, also considered to be the work of the artist himself, dates from approximately 1570-1575.

The painting of *San Sebastián* (Saint Sebastian) must be from about 1600-1605. It shows rather more than half the figure and was created in the latter part of the artist's career. This work is similar to another from the Bucharest royal collection. In 1962, a fragment showing a part of the lower section of a painting was made known. This could belong to a picture of this type although not necessarily to this work even though the painting and the fragment are exhibited together. The differences between the image projected in this picture and the Saint Sebastian that El Greco had painted for Palencia Cathedral in 1577-1578 in a monumental Italianesque style exemplify his qualitative leap towards Mannerism.

A different level of light illuminates *La adoración de los pastores* (The Adoration of the Shepherds) which was painted about 1612 as a funeral altar for the burial of the painter himself in the church of *Santo Domingo el Antiguo* (Saint Dominic the Elder) in Toledo. A wonderfully preserved work, it provides an appropriate conclusion to the El Greco Collection housed in the Museum. Nevertheless, some mention should be made of a part from one of his paintings in the series on the Apostles. This part originates from Almadrones (Guadalajara) and is preserved in the museum although quality is much lower than that evident in a single picture of *San Juan Bautista* (Saint John the Baptist) which perhaps belongs to some other incomplete apostolate.

SPANISH COURT PAINTING IN THE SECOND HALF OF THE SIXTEENTH CENTURY
Room 63a

The influence of Antonio Moro on the one hand, and Titian, on the other, contributed to the establishment of a Spanish school of portrait painters at the court of Philip II. This continued into the early seventeenth century.

Alonso Sánchez Coello was born in about 1531-1532 and died in Madrid in 1588. He was a pupil of the Dutchman Antonis Mor who was called Antonio Moro in Spain. Coello perpetuated his mas-

El Greco. *The Resurrection.*
Canvas. 275 χ 127 cm. Ref. nº 825.

ter's work with the type of court portrait that would become general in the Madrid of Philip II. In these paintings, the subject is usually on foot and three-quarters visible. The pictures are characterized by a clinical objectivity that does not prevent the artist from portraying a deep perception of the personality of the subject. These portraits were painted against a neutral background, hardly decorated by any pieces of furniture that might indicate a palatial environment. Outstanding among these portraits is the one of *The Infantas Isabel Clara Eugenia and Catalina Micaela* together. In the portrait, the first princess is giving a garland of flowers to the younger princess. The artist painted another magnificent portrait of Princess Isabel Clara Eugenia in 1579. The signed picture shows the princess resting her right arm on a crimson armchair.

The portrait of *Prince Carlos* dates from approximately 1557. It was originally a full-figure painting but, following a reduction, the subject can now only be seen from the knees upwards. He was twelve years old at the time the picture was painted. Although this was one of Sánchez Coello's first works, it already shows a fully-developed personal style. However, it includes sharp contrasts in colour which are a departure from his usual methods and are more typical of other court painters. His free Venetian brush-strokes had at this time still not reached the heights that they would attain in subsequent phases. The enormous ermine coat is undoubtedly a tactical ploy in order to hide the Prince's deformity. The tragic fate of the prince could not yet be glimpsed. By contrast, the open window affords a view of a landscape showing Jupiter, the personification of Philip II. Next to him, there appears an eagle with one of the columns of Hercules, a reference to his successor.

The double portrait of *The Infantas Isabel Clara Eugenia and Catalina Micaela* dates from about 1575 and was the last time that they were pictured together. They turn slightly towards one another so as to avoid an excessively direct perspective. The painting is set inside a palace but the atmosphere is dark and unenhanced. Only the shadow of one of the princesses can be seen. This is a canvas painting with a colour scheme in discreet tones to reflect the sense of distance essential for a court portrait. There exists another version of the painting with variations.

The portrait of *Isabel Clara Eugenia* was signed in 1579 and presents the subject from the knees upwards. The artist depicts the thirteen-year-old princess with a majestic precision more in keeping with an adult member of a royal family. Following court conventions, the princess rests her right hand on the back of an armchair and displays a handkerchief in her left hand. Once again, the court background lacks any specific content such as architectural features and only includes a window frame. Sánchez Coello paints the jewels with free rather than exact brush-strokes. In doing so, he does not display the preference shown by northern European artists for minute detail.

The portrait of **Catalina Micaela, the duchess of Savoy,** was painted in about 1584. It has sometimes been attributed to Sofonisba Anguisciola. This is a mature piece of work by Sánchez Coello and reveals the influence of Titian, already latent in his earlier work. A previous emphasis on detail now gives way to a more complex style which in certain aspects involves the merging of colour and drawing.

Within court circles, the portraits by **Juan Pantoja de la Cruz (1553-1608)** are some of the most outstanding. He painted the portraits of Philip III and his wife, Margarita of Austria. The latter was signed in 1606. The paintings make up a pair although the backgrounds in each picture are different. In her portrait, the queen follows conventional practice for high-ranking dignitaries by resting her right arm on the back of an armchair and carrying a handkerchief in her left hand. However, the background of the picture shows the inside of a room characterized by the symbolic thick curtain whereas the king's portrait is set in front of a tent with landscape in the background, this in spite of the protagonist's marked pacifism.

LEONI SCULPTURE
Rooms 64, 65, 66 and 67

The Prado museum exhibits a remarkable collection of sculptures in bronze and marble by Leone Leoni (c. 1509-1590) and his son Pompeo (c. 1530-1608). They were Milanese sculptors in the service of the Spanish crown. Their importance in Italian Renaissance statuary combines with the historical value of a series of portrayals of the Habsburgs.

Alonso Sánchez Coello.
Catalina Micaela, the duchess of Savoy.
Canvas. 111 χ 91 cm. Ref. nº 1139.

Leoni. *Isabel of Portugal.*
Marble of Carrara. 183 cm. high. Ref. nº E-260

However, the Habsburg kings themselves did not look very favourably on this art form, to the extent that Philip II even refused to include such works in the decoration projects for his palaces.

The group depiction of *Carlos V y el furor* (Charles V and the Fury) was commissioned in 1549 by the emperor together with another seven pieces, three in bronze (like this work) and four in marble. The precise destination of the series is nevertheless unknown. The piece in question was signed by both sculptors on the base and dated 1564. Yet this date refers to the completion of the sculpture. The main work was carried out in 1551-53. The piece undoubtedly reveals the influence of the sculptures on the pantheon of Maximilian I in Innsbruck. It also contains echoes of Donatello and Michelangelo. The abstract personification of the Fury does not refer to a specific victory or a particular military exploit but instead to the succession of triumphs which made the king the epitome of a hero of olden times. This explains the boldness shown by Leone in displaying the armour as capable of being dismantled in the Roman style, thus allowing Charles V to appear nude. As far as the Spanish mentality was concerned, this iconographic solution seemed doubly unbecoming. In the Italian Renaissance, Cellini completed his *Perseus* with a similar composition, i.e. by adding a defeated figure.

The work commissioned in 1549 also included *Charles V* in marble. The king is on foot, wearing half a suit of armour, a cloak and a sash. Design and posture are very similar to those displayed in the abovementioned work. Striding forward with his right foot, the monarch raises his corresponding arm, holding not a lance but a sword. Sculpted around 1553-1554, the piece shows that Leone Leoni, so closely involved with the world of crafted metalwork, proved more skilful with metal than with stone.

The bronze statue of the *Empress Isabel* was also commissioned in 1549. It was signed by both sculptors in 1564, a date that once again refers to the completion of the piece, the main work having been carried out from 1550-1555. A rigid hieratic figure, this work was directly inspired by the statue in the mausoleum at Innsbruck of Charles V's aunt, Margarita of Austria. The face of the already deceased sovereign, *Empress Isabel,* was based on an equally posthumous portrait of her by Titian. Once more

from the same date and the same commissioned work, the Empress Isabel in marble is a replica of the previously mentioned work with a few variations. It was completed in Madrid in 1572.

Again signed by both sculptors in 1564 but essentially produced between 1551 and 1553, the statue of Philip II in bronze bears an inscription presenting the protagonist as the son of Charles V and the King of England. Compositively, it follows the guidelines laid down in the group of the Fury without being affected by the references to the pantheon of Innsbruck. Portrayed as a classical hero with refined grandeur, the king is resplendent in Roman-style armour whose virtues are taken by Leoni from the reverse sides of the king's own medals.

The style from the Innsbruck sculptures is also borne out in the bronze statue of *Mary of Hungary*, once again signed by both sculptors in 1564 but made around 1553. This piece was commissioned by the subject herself for her Flemish palace of Binche. She is presented on foot and dressed as a widow. The design is much more lively and dynamic than that for the statues of her august parents.

Probably commissioned in 1549, the two marble reliefs of *Charles V* and *Isabel of Portugal*, sculpted by father and son between 1550 and 1555, present the monarchs in profile within rich caryatid frameworks. Rather than sculptural technique, the piece demonstrates the art of the engraver of medals. It was not in vain that Leoni resorted to the designs that he had previously used to depict the emperors in medals. This time, he applies them to convey the emperor's cold and distant dignity.

CLASSIC SCULPTURE AND GREEK ART, FROM ARCHAISM TO CLASSICISM
Rooms 74, 73, 72, 71 and 47

There are two hundred Greco-Roman sculptures in the Prado. Ancient Greek art is represented by copies, some Hellenistic but for the most part Roman and dating from the first and second centuries AD. However, the importance of these copies is often very great due to the loss of the originals. In general, the versions in the collection reflect old Roman taste. This really appreciated Greek works from the fifth century but also expressed a preference for Renaissance and

Mary of Hungary.
Ref. nº E-262.

Relief of Charles V.
(Between 1550-1555). Ref. nº E-291.

Baroque pieces, especially when together, while likewise having a particularly favourable regard for the Neo-classicism or Neo-atticism of the second and first centuries B.C.

'Classical' sculptures were assembled by the Austrian royal family. These were mostly copies or contemporary versions, like the ones brought back by Velasquez from his second trip to Italy. Apart from this, the greatest period for the addition of important ancient sculptures to the Royal collection was the reign of Philip V. At this time, two collections built up in Rome during the seventeenth century were acquired for the Palace of San Ildefonso. These belonged to the marquis of Heliche –Gaspar Méndez de Haro y Guzmán–, and to Queen Cristina of Sweden.

La sala de las musas (The Hall of the Muses) constitutes a tribute to the exceptional sovereign Queen Cristina, who settled in Rome following her abdication and conversion to Catholicism. Her equestrian portrait painted by a French artist stands over the series of eight muses that decorated a room in her palace where she presided over informal discussions seated as the ninth muse, the one that had not found the others at the Villa Adriana theatre in Tivoli. They are Roman copies of original Hellenistic pieces from the second half of the second century BC and were made for the Emperor Hadrian around 130-140 BC. The only real head is that of *Clio*, generally the best preserved. The head of Caliope is old but from an Aphrodite added in the seventeenth century. Polimnia's head was also made at the time and so too was the image of Talia showing a likeness to Queen Cristina herself. Other figures of heads are attributed to the sculptor Valeriano Salvatierra, a pupil of Canova and Thorvaldsen. Salvatierra restored the items from the collection when they were brought from La Granja in 1839.

Clitia is a re-created work by a pupil of Bernini Giulio Cartari based on a Roman fragment which is the lower part of a bust of *Ninfa* (Nymph), a copy of an original late Hellenistic work showing the influence of classicist studios who were expressing the styles of Rhodes and Ionia about 100 BC.

The Ariadne rotunda shows that even in ancient times, classical designs could make a comeback. These included those of Praxiteles which inspired the so-called *Venus de la concha* (Venus of the Shell) and the **Venus del delfín** (Venus of the Dolphin),

Roman copies from the middle of the second century AD from original Hellenistic works dating from the middle of the second and third centuries BC respectively.

The figure of *Ariadne*, giving the room its name, is lying on the beach at Naxos after being abandoned by Theseus. This work is a Roman copy from the middle of the second century based on an original by Rhodes or Pergamo. It typifies the liking for synthesis, characteristic of the middle of the second century BC, with wet folds in the style of Fidias and a classicist face. This piece, together with the Vatican and Medicean Cleopatras, all derive from the same original. The Medicean Cleopatra is presented by Velasquez in one of his *Vistas de Villa Medicis* (Views of the Medici Villa).

The beautifully made *Young Man at Prayer* is a Roman copy from the beginning of the first century based on an original Neo-attic work from the start of the first century BC.

The two busts of the *Emperor Hadrian* and his favourite *Antinoo* can be dated around the year 135. Numerous depictions of this young man were produced in Rome and in the eastern provinces of the Empire as a result of his canonization, declared in the wake of his early death. However, it is rare to find a bust like this one. In fact, only eight of this type are preserved. The inclination of the head and the eyes in shadow lend a fresh air of melancholy to the Greek classicism.

Fully representative of the archaic period is the archaic Ephebus or Kouros, a work from the school of Naxos around 550 BC. This piece presents the direct front view, a regular feature of archaic art. However, a contrast is already provided by the movement that begins to express itself in the virile body. The work is a Roman copy of an original Greek creation from the middle of the fourth century BC, the prelude to all permanent classicism in the following centuries.

Art by Fidius is represented through the **Athena Promacos**, a Roman version or revision, with the introduction of new elements in the composition formed by a monumental bronze statue. It was paid for with loot from Marathon and it presides over the Acropolis in Athens. This copy seems to resemble the original in the way that the peplo falls in great parallel folds whereas those in the higher section, although in the Fidias style, reflect a subsequent style by the master. Thus, the copier from the second

Giulio Cartari.
Clitia. Ref. nº E-22.

The Dolphin Venus.
Marble. 200 cm. high. Ref. nº E-31

century AD was able to make subtle modifications to the original from the fifth century BC.

The liking for wet folds, created by Fidias, was perpetuated by several adherents. Among these pupils, the most notable was Calimaco, the legendary inventor of the Corinthian capital and the creator of the originals of the four reliefs showing Menades dancing. Roman copies were made in 140 AD.

The impressive *Atenea* is one of the best versions of the lost original by Miron which was situated next to one of the corners of the Parthenon, associated with that of the Satyr Marsias. The slim and fairly rectilinear shapes, the linear folds, the very flat surfaces and the dramatic shadows are characteristic of the severe style from the middle of the fifth century. The head is a modern copy of another version that exists in Frankfurt produced by the same workshop.

The grandest style shown by Fidias is visible in the small marble copy of the monumental ivory and gold sculpture that presided over the Parthenon, the *Atenea partenos*. This work was the object of numerous imitations in antiquity.

The *Diadumeno* is one of the best reproductions from antiquity of the original by Policleto. It dates from his period in Athens, in this case about 425 BC, and is later than *The Doríforo*, a work that he had created in his home town of Argos. His insistence on perfect anatomical harmony made this piece a model for all ancient classicism.

The copy of the *Leda,* attributed to Timothy and dated around 370 BC, not only presents a smoothly modelled nude female figure but also relates the figure to the space in a much more active way.

The palatine *Apollo,* a copy by Scopas, is particularly noteworthy because of the cloak with bold folds although it was very much restored in the Baroque periods. Copies of some of the most famous pieces by Praxiteles are preserved in the Museum. His art comes from the middle of the fourth century BC. These sculptures include *La cabeza de la Afrodita* (The Head of Aphrodite) by Cnido, whose graceful beauty fascinated the Hellenistic and Roman world, and *El sátiro en reposo* (The Satyr at Rest). The latter expresses a peaceful rather than an agressive concept of nature. The Baroque restorer exaggerated the praxitelic curve by crossing the right leg in front and not the left leg from behind.

The various schools from the Hellenistic period are quite well represented in the Prado. One of the most prominent works is the *Faun of the Kid,* a characteristic piece from the Pergamo School with its triangular structure dominating the space agilely covered by the figure. It is related to the groups commemorating victories against the galetians.

The magnificent and colossal bronze *Cabeza* (Head) dates from around 300 and was designed to form part of a statue almost three and a half metres high. It is supposedly the image of a certain Diadochos or of Hefestion, or perhaps it portrays Meleagro. The statue may be a genuine Greek work.

Hipno (Hypnus), the god of sleep, who travels the Earth with light footsteps, is a sculpture illustrating the synthesis characteristic of early Hellenism. The anatomy is praxatelic but the posture reminiscent of Leocares. Another piece drawing inspiration from Praxiteles is *Eros y el Apolo Citaredo* (Eros and the Apollo Zither Player) following on from the original attributed to Timarquides.

With regard to sculpture that had become totally Roman, the *Venus, llamada de Madrid* (Venus called from Madrid) was inspired by a Hellenistic design attributed to Lisipo. It presents the body covered by a tunic. The extremely well-known **Grupo de San Ildefonso** (The San Ildefonso Group) is one of the greatest examples of neoattical classicism from the time of Augustus. It is an original neoattical work from the beginning of the first century AD. It is generally thought to represent Castor and Pollux offering a sacrifice to the infernal goddess Persephone. Thus, her posture and expression reflect the pain of separation when Castor dies and Pollux ascends into heaven. However, Winckelmann believed them to be Orestes and Pilades in Tauride, offering a sacrifice to Artemis. The one with the burning torch presents a smoother version in the style of Policleto and the other imitates the posture of the Praxitelian Sauróctono while the goddess evokes an archaeological vision of the archaic style. The head of *Antinoo* shows the restoration work carried out by Ippolito Buzzi in the first third of the seventeenth century when the sculpture left the ownership of Ludovisi and came into the possesion of Cardinal Massimi. He then cherished the piece as one of the most precious works of art in Madrid. It was later acquired by Cristina of Sweden.

Athena Promacos.
Ref. nº E-24.

The Augustus or *Tiberius* reveals a characteristic heroic nude from the classical Greek tradition. Based on designs by Policleto, the head dates from the seventeenth century.

La apoteosis del emperador Claudio (The Apotheosis of the Emperor Claudius) is an important work from the first century although it underwent extensive restoration in the seventeenth century. This period saw the addition of the pedestal, a gift from Cardinal Ascanio Colonna to Philip IV. The bust of Claudius was lost in the fire at the Alcázar in Madrid.

As a result of their size, four colossal sculptures have been placed in the lower central hallway of the Museum. *Demeter* is the better-preserved copy. A Roman work from the third century, it is based on a grand original of V century A. D. The piece is attributed to Alcamene or Agoracrito and is reminiscent of the art of the Parthenon. The original destination of this work was the shrine to this goddess of cereals in Eleusis. The thunderous *Jupiter* is an original Roman work typifying the grandeur of imperial classicist eclecticism from the end of the first century. The anatomy was inspired by Policleto but the head is more expressive and was therefore influenced by later designs. It may be the one installed by Domitian in the Capitol when rebuilding the temple of Augustus.

The colossal *Poseidon* or *Neptune* comes from the school of Aphrodisias, active around 130 AD and based in Corinth. The same taste is evident with a physical structure inspired by Policleto, a posture reminiscent of Lisipo and Hellenistic influence visible in the dramatic expression.

The colossal *Apollo* is a Roman work remade in the Baroque period for Cristina of Sweden and destined for the guardroom of her palace in Rome.

The San Ildefonso Group.
Ref. n° E-28.

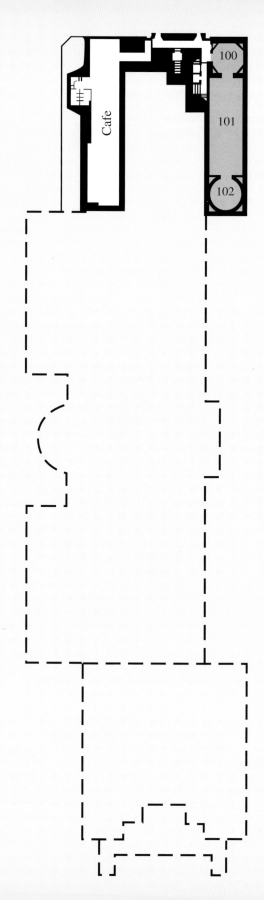

THE BASEMENT

	ROOMS	PAGES
The Dauphin's Treasure	(51b, 51c)	64

THE DAUPHIN'S TREASURE
Salas 51b y 51c

This collection consists of glasses and other tableware items made in hard and precious stones with crafted settings. It gives us a three-dimensional view of one of the most luxurious aspects of European courts during the Renaissance and Baroque periods, an atmosphere brought out by the majority of the paintings in the Museum. The name of this collection is that of the previous owner immediately prior to its incorporation into the Spanish Royal Collection. He was Louis de Bourbon, the Great Dauphin, son of Louis XIV. However, he did not live to inherit the French throne. He died in 1712, three years before his father, thus fulfilling the prophecy predicting that he would be "Son of a King, father of a king, but never king". Indeed, his son, Philip V, reigned in Spain from 1700 onwards. The Dauphin's free assets, i.e. those not tied to the crown of France, were distributed among his three children. Logically, the king of Spain was awarded those assets which were easiest to transport, their value also being taken into account. As a result, he received magnificent pieces of furniture and this collection of "jewels". Philip V initially intended to house them in the Alcázar in Madrid. Nevertheless, when he set up the Royal Country House of La Granja de San Ildefonso, he ordered that the gems be taken there. They remained there until Charles III considered it appropriate that they should be displayed. Even so, Charles III put a greater value on the rarity and beauty of the minerals making up the jewels than the craftsmanship involved. Consequently, he put them in *El Real Gabinete de Historia Natural* (The Royal Natural History Museum), the first national museum to be open to the public in Madrid. There they stayed until 1839 when they were transferred to the Museum.

Only museums which, like the Prado, have been built up around their particular royal collections, such as the Louvre in Paris or the Palazzo Pitti in Florence, can present a collection comparable to this treasure. It is exceptionally important in the context of Renaissance and Baroque industrial art as the very high quality combines with the large number of pieces. In fact, there are 120 items including 49 made from rock crystal. 23 more were lost in two raids, one carried out as a consequence of the Napoleonic invasion and the other occurring in 1918. The beautiful leather cases with a golden fleur-de-lis pattern are to be found in the Museum of Decorative Arts.

Although it could be thought from the origin of the treasure that there would be an abundance of pieces demonstrating the tastes of Versailles, only a few were made during the reign of Louis XIV and practically all date from the sixteenth century and the first third of the seventeenth. Some of the items are French but the majority are Italian, as during those centuries Milan was the main production centre for this type of luxurious tableware intended for European princes.

For the most part, the glass vessels could be used for liquid and solid dishes, mainly sweets or preserved fruits. Yet to a large extent, their purpose could only be decorative, obviously in the case of the large glass vessels with cameos. The most common type of tableware on display is the drinking glass, including a great variety of shapes and outlines. One that stands out is the bernegal, a drinking cup with a wide top and a wavy edge. The drinking glasses used to have covers or *'sobrecopas'* (overglasses) but many of these were lost in 1918 when 35 of the pieces were disfigured.

The most attractive jewels are without doubt the hard stone ones. They are mostly agates and jaspers but there are also jades and lapis lazulis. The turquoise appears on only one glass as a coating. The chalecedonic agate displays a varied series of hues within its different-coloured layers. On the other hand, the jasper is largely green with reddish patches, the so-called 'blood-red diaspore'. A contrasting gentle and oily green is provided by the jasper. The deep blue of the lapis lazuli also contrasts with the bright blue of the turquoise. Craftsmanship with coloured enamel has helped to combine the precious stones and to enrich the different pieces.

The **Onyx Salt Cellar** is an absolutely essential part of the collection. It is held up by a golden enamel mermaid, indicative of the marine origin of the container. Until 1815, there was a dolphin between her legs. This beautiful piece of work comes from the first half of the sixteenth century and is possibly French. The striped brown agate is outshone by the beauty of the crafted enamelwork, completed with amazing virtuosity.

The magnificence can also be seen on the enamel base of a lapis lazuli glass. The base is shaped like a

Onyx Salt Cellar with a golden Mermaid.
17.5 cm. high. Ref. nº 01.

dragon. It can be seen too in the embellishment on some of the agate drinking glasses. Among the blood-red diaspore pieces, scallop shell number 17 is outstanding. It was made in about 1600. Prominent among the chalcedonic exhibits is the small boat with a cupid riding an enamel dragon. From the Bernegal category, we can highlight the chalcedonic piece-number 22, or the green jasper and white enamel piece-number 21. The Diaspor Tray and Jug decorated with pearls Nº 86. Most of these cameos are from onyx although some are from oriental cornelian and from lapis lazuli. Almost all of them were made in Milan. At the end of the sixteenth century and at the beginning of the seventeenth specialists in this art form thrived in Milan. They included Miseroni and Masgano as well as sculptors and lapidaries like Giacomo da Trezzo and the Leonis. However, among these cameos, there is at least one medieval one and several classical ones, particularly that of a veiled woman made of lapis lazuli on chest number 32. Unlike the cameos, the engravings seem mostly old.

Among the jade pieces, one of the most striking is a glass with dolphins. These were made in France at the end of the seventeenth century whereas the jade was worked in China. As far as the pieces containing precious stones are concerned, three cups stand out. One has gold with purple rubies and turquoises. Another has agate with gold and rubies while the third is blood-red with turquoises. The latter exhib-

it is a product of islamic, possibly Indian, art and contains heliotrope jasper. Some enamelled items are distinctive due to the simplicity of the themes. Decoration is very important on six glasses adorned with hard stones and on two chests.

Among the numerous pieces made with rock crystal, the most impressive, on account of the beauty of their reliefs, are *The turtle* boat and the *Glass with a hunting scene.*

Related to the Dauphin's treasure by the characters portrayed are a number of small bronze sculptures exhibited in the same rooms.

The small *Grupo de la cabeza de Meleagro* (The Group of Meleagro's Head) was produced by Giovani Bandini for the duke of Urbino about 1583-1584 and also belonged to Philip II. It ties in with a series of small equestrian images made in bronze. The most noteworthy are the following: a young Philip IV, attributed to Pietro Tacca and made in approximately 1615-1620, previously regarded as Philip III by Giambologna; Charles III by Gian Battista Foggini from 1690, originally among the figures of four prisoners; *Fernando de Toscana* (Ferdinand of Tuscany) by Giuseppe Piamontini, a pupil of Foggini. This piece was created in 1695 along the lines of the previous work; Philip IV by Lorenzo Vaccaro and made in 1702. It is a smaller model of the statue erected in Naples in 1705; Louis XIV, a piece that can be attributed to Guillermo de Groff.

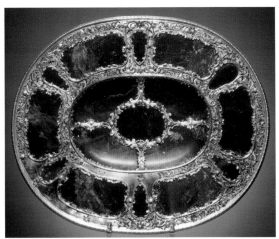

Diaspor Tray decorated with pearl.
44 cm diam. Ref. nº 86.

Diaspor Jug decorated with pearl.
17.5 cm. high. Ref. nº 86.

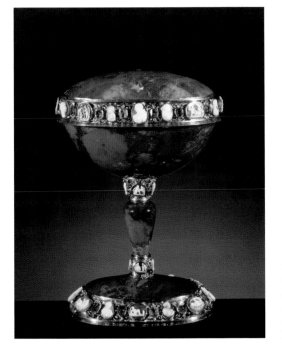

Goblet with a flower jasper decoration, adorned with
enamel and silver coated with gold. There are 23
emeralds and cameos of the chalcedonic and white
cornelian variety. The goblet is from the beginning of
the seventeenth century.
Ref. nº 40

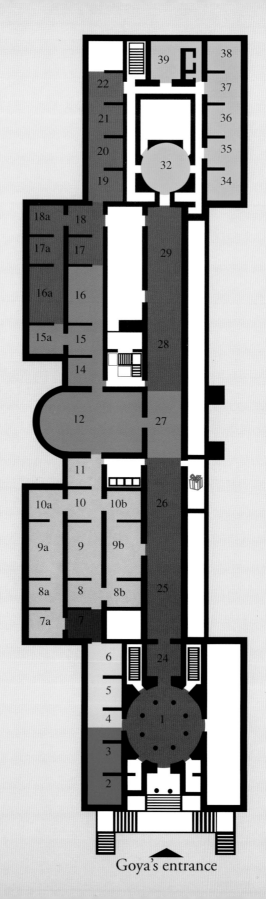

Goya's entrance

FIRST FLOOR

	ROOMS	PAGES
French painting in the XVII century	.................(2, 3 and 4)	70
Italian painting in the XVII century	.................(4, 5 and 6)	72
Dutch painting in the XVII century	..................(7)	76
Flemish painting in the XVII century	.................(7a, 8, 8a, 8b, 9, 9a, 9b, 10, 10a, 10b and 11)	..78
Spanish painting in the XVII century	................(18, 18a, 29, 28, 26, 25, 24 and 1)	102
Velasquez	...................(27, 12, 14, 15, 15a and 16)	110
Spanish painting in the XVII century (continuation)	......(16a, 17 and 17a)	130
Spanish painting in the XVIII century	...............(19, 20, 21 and 22)	140
Goya	.......................(32, 35, 34, 36, 37, 38 and 39)	144

FRENCH PAINTING IN THE SEVENTEENTH CENTURY
Rooms 2, 3 and 4

The continual confrontation between the Austrian royal family and the Bourbons throughout the seventeenth century did not prevent the acquisition for the Spanish royal collection of an important display of French painting from that time. **Simon Vouet** (1590-1646) painted *Virgen y Niño con Santa Isabel, San Juan y Santa Catalina* (The Virgin and Child with Saint Elizabeth, Saint John and Saint Catherine). The picture was created in Rome between 1624 and 1626. It is a very balanced work with twilight shades. Vouet developed as an artist in Rome before returning to Paris and veering towards classicist guidelines, a route that culminated in his decisive contribution to the creation of the Academy. Another work produced by him in Rome, this time in 1627, was the signed painting *El tiempo vencido por la esperanza, el amor y la belleza* (Time Beaten by Hope, Love and Beauty). A crucial work in his career, strongly featuring a landscape and light colours, it superimposes a distinctive compositive style on the Venetian flavour.

Nicolas Poussin (1594-1665) was one of the leading exponents of Baroque classicism. Some of his most notable canvas paintings are preserved at the Prado. A difficult artist, particularly concerned with matching form and content, he expresses a cold outlook out of step with contemporary sensitivities.

Parnaso (Parnassus), a youthful work from about 1631-1633, is equally reminiscent of Domenichino and of a fresco by Raphael. Venetian touches alternate with his geometric concept of nature, promptig him paint trees like columns. The theme is based on the coronation of a poet, perhaps Homer, by the god Apollo. In the centre, the beautiful nude female figure, characteristic of Poussin's intellectual taste, personifies the fountain of Castalia that rises on Mount Parnassus.

David vencedor (David the Victor) is also a youthful work and was painted in about 1630. It shows stronger traces of the Venetian style. Biblical and mythological themes once again merge in this picture as in so many canvas paintings from the seventeenth century. We can see how the figure crowning the king in the picture is an angel with the extended additional role of the personification of Victory.

Poussin designed *La caza de Meleagro* (The Hunt Meleagro) as a classical monumental frieze. It was created between 1637 and 1638 and was intended to be part of a matching pair together with *Un sacrificio a Priapo* (A sacrifice to Priapus) now in Sao Paulo. Trees, a column and a statue emphasize the effect of sculptural formality in the background landscape. This composition has a sideways focus. Both Nature and the figures are subjected to the dominance of reason, heralding French academic doctrine.

El paisaje con edificios (The Landscape with Buildings) is from about 1650-51 and displays beautiful Romanesque classicism. The picture is brightened up by the tinges of colour from some of the small figures. It is associated with *El tiempo tranquilo y sereno* (Calm and Serene Time), a picture forming a matching pair with the lost *Tempestad* (Storm). Passed over for a long time and even attributed to Dughet, it is now considered an important original work.

Jean de Boulogne, **Valentin** (1594-1632) was the painter of the great canvas *Martirio de San Lorenzo* (The Martyrdom of Saint Lawrence) which was part of a series along with another two. The active body of the saint is the focus and the catalyst of the composition as well as being the strongest element of chromatic intensity.

The Prado holds a remarkable collection of ten works of art by **Claude** Gellée, le Lorrain (c. 1600-1682), known in Spain as Claudio de Lorena. The canvas paintings *El vado de un río* (The Ford in the River) and *La salida del rebaño* (The Flock Leaving) were probably intended as decorative pictures for the Madrid palace of the Buen Retiro. They form a matching pair and date from 1636-37. In line with the expected style, small figures of humans and animals fill both pictures with life. The first, although an early work, already demonstrates Lorena's style but continues to reflect Carraci and the northern European world in the mysterious or sombre halo. The artist repeats this theme on many other occasions. The Ford in the River and the Flock Leaving were both painted solely by the artist and are extremely high quality pictures. Curiously, both canvases display landscapes rather than seascapes. Lorena's pairs of paintings usually include at least one picture with a coastal view.

El embarco de Santa Paula Romana en Ostia (The Embarkation of Saint Paula Romana on the

Nicolas Poussin. *The Parnassus.*
Canvas. 145 χ 197 cm. Ref. nº 2313.

Nicolas Poussin. *Landscape with Buildings.*
Canvas. 120 χ 187 cm. Ref. nº 2310.

Ostia) is one of the artist's absolute masterpieces. It was painted between 1639 and 1641 and forms a matching pair with *Paisaje con Tobías y el arcángel Rafael* (A Landscape with Tobias and the Archangel Raphael). The Embarkation of Saint Paula Romana on the Ostia was part of an important batch of commissioned works intended to decorate the palace of the Buen Retiro. As usual, the artist got an associate to add the small figures. Here, the painter is shown to be a leading exponent of 'classical' landscapes in the Romanesque style, with a single point of escape and a control of light in colour gradations that anticipates the achievements of impressionism. The picture confirms that his best scenes are those of ports and harbours. This, essentially, was one of the main stages in the development of Lorena's concept of the landscape, an outlook that would be of such fundamental importance in shaping a new humanized Nature based on the intellectual approach predominant in England in the eighteenth century. It would be impossible to explain the future landscape garden without these evanescent backgrounds.

In the accompanying canvas painting, A Landscape with Tobias and the Archangel Raphael, the architectural features of the previous picture give way to masses of trees. Claudio de Lorena completed this picture with a range of the richest and most varied shades. In both pictures, the light enhances the theme or the reason for the journey, parallel to the idea of transformation. However, the motive for the journey in the first picture is rejection of the world whereas in the second, the topic is love of the family.

Georges de la Tour (1593-1652) painted only a small number of pictures. His *Ciego tocando la zanfona* (A Blind Man Playing the Barrel Organ) was recently acquired by the Prado. An unknown work until recently, it was painted at some time between 1610 and 1630 although the precise date is not clear. It probably forms part of a larger full-figure canvas. The painting enables us to appreciate the way in which the artist contemplated scenes from the genre. This represented the antithesis of the intellectualist or sensualist classicism expressed by other contemporary French artists.

San Juan Bautista (Saint John the Baptist) was painted by **Pierre Mignard** (1612-1693). This very correct and delicately completed work of art was commissioned in 1688 by Philip of Orleans for his son-in-law Charles II.

ITALIAN PAINTING IN THE SEVENTEENTH CENTURY
Rooms 4, 5 and 6

Italian painting from the seventeenth century developed into two parallel trends, naturalism and classicism, later opening out into so-called decorative Baroque. Benefiting from the good traditional relations between Spain and Italy, the Museum holds notable and varied examples of the work of the most significant Italian masters. These pictures originate from royal collections.

The extremely important *Crucificado* (Crucified) is the work of **Federico Barocci** or Baroccio (c. 1535-1612). A great canvas painting, it has recently been the subject of continual reassessment as a paradigm of devotional pathos from the Counter-Reformation. Produced in 1604 for the duke of Urbino, who left it for Philip IV, the painting reveals a sensuous technique originating from Correggio. It is believed that the most beautiful Italian landscape of the time was precisely the one set out in the background of this picture, namely the city and palace of Urbino.

The work of Michelangelo Merisi, **Caravaggio** (1573-1610) is not represented in the Museum in spite of his specific importance not only in seventeenth-century Italian painting but also in Spanish art. This great tenebrist has consistently been credited with the canvas *painting David vencedor de Goliat* (David, the Victor over Goliath).

This is a compressed but well-completed work. As a youthful painting from around 1600, it reflects his progress in the control of the effects of light and shadow. A recent X-ray photograph has shown that another very different head lies under Goliath's head. The latter coincides with designs used by the artist at that time. This modification has prompted critics to declare this painting authentic.

Annibale Carraci (1560-1609) was a member of the Bologna School of classicism. In his Venus, *Adonis y Cupido* (Venus, Adonis and Cupid), he offers an eloquent example of the clarity, idealism and balance present in this artistic trend, so different from the style of Caravaggio. Painted in about 1590, it provides evidence of the eclecticism characteristic of his circle with a very elaborate concept of intellectual beauty and rotund corporeity as opposed to the previous whims of the Mannerists.

Claude de Lorena. *Landscape, Saint Paula Romana embarking on the Ostia.*
Canvas. 211 χ 145 cm. Ref. 2254.

Compositively, the figure of Venus stretches across the space in a great diagonal sweep against the serene background landscape.

Also from Bologna, Giovanni Francesco Barbieri, **Guercino** (1591-1666) was the painter of *Susana y los viejos* (Susana and the Old Men). A piece from his youth, it was painted in 1617 and shows that at this stage, he still had a long way to go before reaching his greatest mature classicism. The picture contains a union of diverse influences, the most prominent being Venetian luminosity. This painting was commissioned by Cardinal Ludovici together with *Lot y sus hijas* (Lot and her Daughters) which is not in the Escorial and is a typical female nude created on a Biblical pretext.

The art of Domenico Zampieri, **Domenichino** (1581-1641) is classicism at its peak. His work is represented by the *Arco de triunfo* (Triumphal Arch), painted between 1607 and 1615. As indicated by the inscription on the tablet, the work was dedicated by Giovanni Battista Aguchi to his patron saint. Aguchi was a political figure who indeed fulfilled the role of classicist theorist. The picture is an allegorical religious rerepresentation of a classic architectural theme in a very erudite style, full of emblems. The serene standard landscape bears the hallmarks of Carracci.

Daniele Crespi (born c. 1598-1600, died in 1630) from Lombardy was the painter of *Piedad* (Devotion), a work from his period of balance between Mannerism and a restrained Naturalism.

This canvas painting dates from 1626 and has a very limited range of colours. It shows the bent figure of Christ in the foreground in an awkward position being supported by the Virgin. A picture repeatedly copied in its time, Ribera undoubtedly knew the work as he made direct use of it.

Bernardo Strozzi (1581-1644) was a Genoese painter whose eventful life ended in Venice, where he made a decisive contribution to the renewal of the local school of art. *Veronica* is a work from a very advanced stage of his career and was created in about 1625-30. Without doubt, it is much better than the other three known versions of the picture. A full-figure Veronica is seated and dyagonally is holding out a cloth with a face of Christ in the Baroque style. The painting comes from the collection of Isabel of Farnesio, pointing to the possibility that it was acquired in Seville where Genoese work was plentiful.

El sacrificio a Baco o bacanal (The sacrifice to Bacchus or Bacchanal) was painted around 1634 by the Neapolitan artist **Máximo Stanzione** (1585-1658) for the Madrid palace of the Buen Retiro. This piece comes from his more classical side in the Bologna style. A very large high-quality signed canvas painting, it contains an extremely complex structure in which the central female figure is the focal point of the composition.

A characteristic piece from the art of Rome at this time is *El pintor Francesco Albani* (The Painter Francesco Albani) portrayed by his pupil **Andrea Sacchi** (1599-1661) in around 1635. With a magnificent very light technique and great powers of observation, Sacchi depicts his master without leaving distinctive professional traces, as opposed to the more general approach to making a portrait of a painter. Because of its colour, the body merges with the background in a relatively uniform plane. There is a copy or replica in Rome dated 1664.

Likewise, **Carlo Maratta** or Maratti (1625-1713) presents the portrait of his master *El Pintor Andrea Sacchi* (The Painter Andrea Sacchi). Once again, there is a lack of identifiable professional elements. Dated around 1650, it is therefore quite a youthful work among Maratta's pictures. It was previously thought to be a self-portrait by Sacchi. Instead, his favourite pupil here demonstrates deep psychological perception in an informal view of the master.

The versatile Gian Lorenzo **Bernini** (1598-1680) has been credited with *Un autorretrato* (A Self-portrait), although not with total certainty. The picture contains a great deal of sketchwork and is dated about 1640. There exist other versions of the painting.

Gaspar Dughet (1615-1675) was the son of French parents but to all intents and purposes he was an exponent of Italian art. He was a brother-in-law and pupil of Poussin although he was also influenced by Claudio de Lorena. His *Paisaje con Magdalena* (Landscape with Magdalen), painted at some time between 1660 and 1670, shows an extremely wide border, explained by the difficulties that his work posed for the critics. This picture stands out as a magnificent piece from the artist's most mature and distinctive phase. With complex lighting effects and tightly-packed detail, this canvas illustrates the essential contribution made by Dughet to the history of landscape painting.

1

Guercino. *Susana and the Elders.*
Canvas. 175 χ 207 cm. Ref. 201.

Dughet. *The Penitent Magdalene.*
Canvas. 175 χ 207 cm. Ref. 136.

The Calabrian **Mattia Preti** (1613-1699) was the painter of *La Gloria o Cristo glorioso y Santos* (The Glory or The Glorious Christ and Saints). This work dates from 1660 and was created by the artist when he was fully mature. It shows great originality in merging very different artistic influences to achieve a brilliant result worthy of decorative Baroque. Perhaps designed to adorn a ceiling, it is seen from a perspective of *'de sotto in sú'* (looking upwards). The Venetian influence is identified on two different counts; directly, through the range of colours and indirectly, from Ribera's figures which are closer to the most serene art. As far as the complex iconographic set-up is concerned, a number of saints can easily be recognised in the foreground. They include Saint Francis, Saint Jerome and Mary Magdalene.

Luca Giordano (1634-1705), known in Spain as Lucas Jordán, exemplifies the culmination of Italian decorative Baroque painting. He was already known at the Madrid court before Charles II called on him to paint vaults in the Escorial and the Casón del Buen Retiro. The ten years he spent in Spain explain why so many of his pictures are in royal collections and therefore in the Museum of the Prado. Nicknamed "Fra Presto" on account of the incredible speed with which he completed his work, he was a skilful imitator and very good at combining styles. *El sueño de Salomón* (Solomon's Dream) belongs to a series from 1693-1694 on the story of the said Biblical monarch and of David. It is a straightforward transfer to canvas of his frescoes in the basilica of the Escorial. Here, he depicts an episode from the Book of Kings, an unusual development in painting. His characteristic uninhibited but solid technique is not without splendidly refined colours. In a curious compromise between Biblical and pagan-classical themes, the goddess Minerva appears over the sleeping figure in her role as the symbol of wisdom.

DUTCH PAINTING IN THE SEVENTEENTH CENTURY
Room 7

In the seventeenth century, Holland was by now independent from Spain and gave rise to a splendid school of painting reflecting a middle-class or capitalist society ideologically distinguished by the Calvinism of the elite. For obvious historical reasons, the Prado lacks an adequate display of this art dedicated to scenes characteristic of the genre and in general to everyday life. Nevertheless, royal collections did possess some Dutch paintings originating from the Catholic city of Utrecht. Charles III bought *Artemisia* by **Rembrandt** harmensz van Ryn (1606-1669). Signed in 1634, it is the only work in the Prado by the leading exponent of this school. It constitutes one of his masterpieces. His subject is his own wife Saskia, who the master had married in that same year. According to some, it portrays Artemisa preparing to drink the ashes of her husband Mausolo. For others, the figure represents Sofonisba, the wife of Masinissa, doing the same with the poison sent by her consort so as not to fall into the hands of the Romans. A third interpretation is that the painting represents Cleopatra, about to consume the pearl. Whatever the truth, the straightforward composition is completed by a very dense atmosphere of golden shades that help to make this canvas one of the most outstanding paintings by Rembrandt.

Within this school, we should point out *Un filósofo* (A Philosopher). The painting has the initials of Salomon Koninck but in fact they belong to a pupil and imitator of his, Abraham Van Der Hecke, who was an active painter until 1655. From among the seascape painters of Amsterdam, **Hendrick Dubbels** (c. 1620-1676) presents a characteristic *Vista de un puerto de mar en invierno* (A Harbour View in Winter). In the same Amsterdam group, a prominent work is *Bendición episcopal* (Episcopal Blessing) by **Bartholomeus Breenberg** (1598-1657), a painter of historical themes who here presents the inside of a church during a service conducted by bishop Felipe Rovenius.

As we have said, there are a considerable number of works by the masters of Utrecht in the museum. Among these artists, whose work was linked to the style of Caravaggio, one of the most distinctive was **Mathias Stomer** (born around 1600, and still living in 1650). His painting *La incredulidad de Santo Tomás* (The incredulity of Saint Thomas) reveals the knowledge he had acquired in Italy, apparent in the solid drawing and striking illumination. Another member of the Utrecht group was **Jan Both** (1610-1652). He was very much influenced by the landscape artists then operating in Rome. His *Bautizo del eunuco de la reina Candace* (The Baptism of Queen Candace's Eunuch) was commissioned by Philip IV around

Rembrandt. *Artemisia.*
Canvas. 142 χ 153 cm. Ref. 2132.

1638-39 as a decorative work for the Buen Retiro. The canvas *El Jardín Albodrandini en Frascati* (The Aldobrandini Garden in Frascati) clearly reflects his experience in Rome. Cornelisz Poelembourg was also from Utrecht and likewise an exponent of classical landscape painting in Italy. He was born sometime between 1586 and 1595, and died in 1667). His *Baño de Diana* (Diana Bathing) shows great technical mastery. Joost Cornelisz Droochsloot (1586-1666) painted *Paisaje invernal con patinadores* (A Winter Landscape with Skaters). It splendidly reasserts the skill of the Utrecht painters in this genre.

The Haarlem group included **Salomon de Bray** (1597-1664) who is represented by a panel portraying Judith and Holofernes for which there are preparatory drawings dating from 1636. **Willem Claesz Heda** (1594-1682) was from the same circle. His work is exemplified by three still lifes painted in 1657. Far from the Catholic concept of 'vanitas', they evoke the Protestant idea of enjoyment of beauty and harmony in the domestic setting. The most important painter from the Haarlem School and even from the whole of Holland was **Adriaen van Ostade** (1610-1685). The Prado holds four of his works including *Villagers Singing* (1632) from his first phase and *Peasants' Concert* (1638) which already shows the influence of Rembrandt in the contrasts of light. **Isaac van Ruisdael** was born in about 1628-1629 and died in approximately 1682. His signed painting entitled *Paisaje* (Landscape) is on display and projects the typical dramatic qualities and complexity of light of this supreme exponent of the genre, not only in Haarlem but also elsewhere. Philips Wouwerman belonged to the same movement. The Prado holds an important group of his paintings with his typical equestrian scenes.

As far as the Delft group is concerned, **Michiel Mierevelt** (1567-1641) is represented by three portraits, an area in which he specialized superbly well. **Leonard Bramer** (1596-1674) was also from this group. He was the creator of paintings with historical themes in a particular style. In 1630, he signed the small panel entitled *Abraham y los tres ángeles* (Abraham and the Three Angels). Likewise, he was the artist who produced the signed copper painting *El dolor de Hécuba* (The Pain of Hecuba). In the time of Charles IV, this work was attributed to Rembrandt. In both compositions, he set the scene with small figures against a vague background of ruins.

A very notable work form the Leyden group is *La vieja o anciana meditando* (An Old Woman Meditating) with the false signature of David Teniers but in fact produced by **Quringh Gerritsz Van Brekelenkan** (c. 1620-1668). The picture shows a typical scene from this genre, displaying the contents of a kitchen along the lines of realism and intimacy characteristic of the Dutch School. An extraordinary work to come out of the same circles in Leyden is *Vanitas* by Pieter Van Steenwijk. The most recent estimate of its date is 1654. Another exceptional work by a member of the Leyden group is *El gallo muerto* (The Dead Cock) by Gabriel Metsu (1629-1667). This picture constitutes one of the greatest Dutch paintings to portray nature in death.

Lastly, the group from The Hague is represented by the prominent picture *Paisaje con dos vacas y una cabra* (A Landscape with Two Cows and a Goat). It was signed in 1652 by **Paulus Potter** (1625-1654), the famous landscape painter who set the Dutch meadows to canvas.

FLEMISH PAINTING IN THE SEVENTEENTH CENTURY
Rooms 7a, 8, 8a, 8b, 9, 9a, 9b, 10, 10a, 10b and 11

Following the division of the Low Countries and the separation of the northern part, the southern area stayed under the auspices of Spain and the Catholic monarchy. Therefore, it is not surprising to find that the extraordinary upsurge in Flemish painting during the seventeenth century is appropriately reflected in the composition of royal collections and therefore in the Prado Museum itself. The paintings in the Prado belonging to this school and period undoubtedly make up the Museum's supreme display.

Rubens

Peter Paul Rubens (1577-1640) was the great master of Antwerp. He divided his time between painting and high– ranking diplomatic duties. As a painter, he was not only in the service of the court of Madrid and of the archduchy of Brussels but also the courts of Paris and London. He was the leading exponent of this school and in general of heroic Baroque from the first half of the century. A great many works by

Adriaen van Ostade. *Villagers Singing.*
Panel. 24 χ 29 cm. Ref. 2123.

Stomer. *The Incredulity of Saint Thomas.*
Canvas. 125 χ 99 cm. Ref. 2094.

Rubens are preserved in the Prado. They show his mastery of the most varied genres and also the peculiar system used by his studio. By employing numerous assistants, Rubens was able to deal with endless commissioned work. Even then, however, it was possible to distinguish the artwork created by the artist himself from the efforts of his associates.

El apostolado (The Apostolate) is a princely series believed to have been completed during the artist's first trip to Spain in 1603 although there is no documentary evidence to support this theory. Some analysts have put the date at around 1612-13 for reasons of technique and style. There are other versions of the series which consists of twelve panels. It is therefore incomplete as the panel corresponding to Christ is missing. The design of the series and its evocative expressiveness indicate that it derives from Renaissance engraving or Florentine sculpture from the fifteenth century. With regard to the near certainty that it was produced in Spain, it has been pointed out that the grandeur and deliberateness of the gestures as well as the marked sense of individualism provide evidence that Rubens had been in contact with Spaniards. Some have claimed to detect the influence of El Greco in the series. In response, however, it has been stated that there exist similar series in engravings and Belgian collections of the time. In spite of the traditional Flemish preference for a bright background and a local range, the chiaroscuro comes from Caravaggio. The series belonged to the royal favourite, the duke of Lerma, and, according to records, was kept at Philip V's palace of La Granja.

The figure of *San Juan Evangelista* (Saint John The Evangelist), reminiscent of initial designs from Bologna close to the work of Carracci, appears once again in another composition by Rubens. The painting of *Santiago el Mayor* (James the Elder) was joined to the *Incredulidad de Santo Tomás* (Incredulity of Saint Thomas). The engraving for the latter served as the basis for a canvas painting by Zurbarán on the same theme. *Santiago el Menor* (James the Younger), previously identified first as Saint Thomas and then as Saint Matthew, is reminiscent of a character from *La adoración de los Magos* (the Adoration of the Magi), also kept at the Museum. The painting of *Saint Thomas* was used by Rubens in other works, specifically for the figure of King Gaspar in the said Adoration. *San Mateo* (Saint Matthew), with a halberd, is believed by some to be

saint Thomas, whose sign of authority is the lance. He reappears in other early works by Rubens. The figure of *Saint Paul,* perhaps inspired by an engraving by Goltzius, is similar to that of *Saint Joseph* in the *Adoration of the Magi.*

The grand *San Jorge* (Saint George) is believed to have been made in approximately 1606 during the Italian period. It is composed of traditional medieval figures, namely the equestrian character, the dragon and the princess. In general, Rubens refers to a Milan fresco on the same theme by Bernardino Lanino although there are some elements of Leonardo da Vinci whose struggle for the banner is clearly perceptible in this picture. The expressiveness of the lady could come from a classic relief used as a source but others tend to think that the figure originates from an engraving made at the end of the sixteenth century and based on a sculpture of Leda.

La adoración de los Magos (The Adoration of the Magi) is a huge canvas painting and one of the most characteristic of Baroque art. Commissioned in 1609, it is on record as being in the Council of Antwerp one year later. This institution then gave it as a gift to Rodrigo Calderón. After his resounding fall, it came into the possession of Philip IV. In 1628, Rubens was once again in Spain and, displeased with the picture, he repainted and enlarged it, although the additions can be easily distinguished. Like other artists of the time in similar religious scenes, Rubens paints a self-portrait in this picture. He appears on horseback on the right with younger features than he would have had at that time. This indicates that he used a portrait from his youth. Italian influence has bee seen in the composition. This style includes a great deal of pontifical ceremony as well as the dramatic qualities of Tintoretto. The lavishness of Veronés can be observed to an even greater extent. However, the traces of Caravaggio in the background of the original version are far from insignificant.

Guirnalda con la Virgen y el Niño (Garland with the Virgin and Child) is dated around 1614-18. In the picture, Mary bears a perfect resemblance to the artist's first wife. Rubens repeats the face of the Virgin and the angel on the right in other canvas paintings. This one is a unique example of the collaboration of the master with Jan Brueghel, who was the creator of the elaborate garland motif.

The *Acto de devoción de Rodolfo I de Habsburgo* (Act of Devotion by Rudolph I of Hapsburg) dates,

Peter Paul Rubens. *The Adoration of the Magi.*
Canvas. 346 χ 488 cm. Ref. 1638.

Peter Paul Rubens. *Saint Peter.*
Panel. 108 χ 84 cm. Ref. 1646.

according to some, from 1618-1620. For others, it was made in about 1636, the date when it was recorded as being in the Alcázar in Madrid. It had a particularly symbolic significance for the Spanish Austrian royal family as it evoked a supposed devotional act by the founder of the dynasty. This proved an inspiration for the conduct of his successors. In accordance with the statutes of the order of Saint George, which Rudolph himself had helped to draw up, on finding himself with the priest bearing the viaticum, he accompanies His Holiness like a humble anonymous servant.

The *Sagrada familia con Santa Ana* (Holy Family with Saint Ann) was painted in about 1626-1630. It shows the fine completion and subtle transparency Rubens' mature work. His Raphaelite borrowings had already been pointed out by the nineteenth century.

The identity of the painter of *La Virgen rodeada de Santos* (The Virgin Surrounded by Saints) is a matter of debate. First, it was understood to be a copy and later it was attributed to Van Balen. It is an actual reduction of the canvas painting commissioned in 1628 by princess Isabel Clara Eugenia for the Augustinians of Antwerp. The picture has also been called 'The Militant Church' or, taking things as a whole, the theme is a part of the complex composition entitled *Los desposorios místicos de Santa Catalina* (The Mystic Betrothal of Saint Catherine). Although Rubens takes great care over interrelations among the saints, he gives each one an independent existence.

The *Inmaculada Concepción* (Immaculate Conception) was commissioned by the marquis of Leganés in 1628. Rubens has recently been reconfirmed as the artist responsible for the picture after it had been mistakenly attributed to Erasmus Quellinus. The painting shows how the theme was approached by Spanish Jesuits at the time. Also apparent is the iconographic encoding of Pacheco. Specific additional touches, freely applied and of great quality, have prompted speculation that Velasquez contributed to this canvas painting when it was at the Escorial.

Around 1628, princess Isabel Clara Eugenia commissioned the famous series of eucharistic tapestries intended for the Descalzas Reales convent in Madrid. The series is still preserved there but the distribution and arrangement of the items continues to pose a serious problem. The Prado holds six panels with Rubens' preparatory sketches for the respective cartoons. One cannot discount the possibility that Spanish theologians participated in the process of creating the series nor that the artist was very much aware of *Triunfos Divinos* (Divine Triumphs) by Lope de Vega. According to some analysts, the princess wanted to emulate the series completed by Rubens a short time before for Maria de Medici, but with the emphasis on monarchic apotheosis or glorification. Designed as spectacular Baroque compositions, these scenes express with the utmost intensity the Counter-Reformation ideals current in Spain at that time. However, these ideals are conveyed in the form of a heavily detailed ostentatious style that only Rubens could provide.

In *Santa Clara entre los doctores de la Iglesia* (Saint Clare among the Fathers of the Church), the face of the protagonist is perhaps that of princess Isabel Clara Eugenia herself while that of Saint Buenaventura could be Cardinal Prince Ferdinand of Austria. *Abraham ofrece el diezmo a Melquisedec* (Abraham offers the Tithe to Melquisedec) can be seen from a low angle and with a certain exaggerated effect. The architectural background is the gateway to Rubens' own house. It is possible that Rubens knew the engraving by Martin de Vos on the same theme, a piece which also served as a source of inspiration for Velasquez in *Las Lanzas* (The Lances). The liveliest composition in the series is entitled *El triunfo de la eucaristía sobre la herejía* (The Triumph of the Eucharist over Heresy) in which Luther and Calvin are presented as desperate and distraught in the face of doctrinal truths. These direct references are supplemented by other more metaphorical elements of a secular nature such as Time and *Truth* with their respective attributes, and a lion and a fox, symbols of strength and cunning.

In *El triunfo de la Iglesia sobre la furia, la discordia y el odio* (The Triumph of the Church over Fury, Discord and Hatred), the main personification carries the monstrance. Behind come Blindness and Ignorance while the others are left between the wheels of the cart. Rubens took old Roman victories as a source of inspiration. He used colours according to their dramatic significance in a similar way to Venetian painters. Following designs by Raphael, *El triunfo de la eucaristía sobre la idolatría* (The Triumph of the Eucharist over Idolatry) is set among Solomonic columns. The panel depicts the sudden appearance of an angel in a pagan temple where the

Peter Paul Rubens. *The Holy Family with Saint Anne.*
Canvas. 115 χ 90 cm. Ref. 1639.

sacrifice of a bull is going to take place. The inscription on the altar reads Jovis, Jupiter. The figure of Zeus is an exact copy of the one created by Fidius for the temple of Olimpia. *El triunfo del amor divino* (The Triumph of Divine Love) contains a female figure who also symbolizes charity. Rubens' mastery is evident in the way he paints the chariot drawn by two lions, a symbol of the authority of the goddess *Cibeles* (Cybele). The small wood painting *San José adorando a la Virgen y al Niño* (Saint Joseph Adoring the Virgin and Child) dates from about 1631-32. It is based on a canvas painting from Antwerp, a source of inspiration for some of his other pictures. Long thought to be the work of studio artists, the painting is now once again considered to be from the brush of Rubens without any doubt. *Descanso en la huida a Egipto con Santos* (Rest During the Escape to Egypt with Saints) is a panel from his later years, about 1632-35, and entirely in the artist's own hand. An outstanding feature is the poetic vision of the landscape. While the figure of Saint George is repeated in the painting of his own sepulchre, the Virgin represents an idealized portrait of his wife, Elena Fourment.

La cena en Emaus (The Supper in Emaus) is a picture of notable quality. Its date is a matter of debate, varying between 1635 and 1638. The background made up of nature cannot be attributed to an associate. It has been mistakenly ascribed to Frans Snyders. Rubens reproduced the theme in another version.

As a portrait painter, Rubens displays undoubted mastery in capturing the features and even the personality of the subjects in spite of the Baroque grandeur with which he sometimes envelops them. The paintings of *El archiduque Alberto y la infanta Isabel Clara Eugenia* (The Archduke Albert and Princess Isabel Clara Eugenia) form a matching pair. The protagonists appear against real rather than idealized landscapes. These canvas paintings were sent to Rodrigo Calderón, marquis of Siete Iglesias, in 1615. Although the approach shows little innovation and follows artists like Sánchez Coello, the pictures constitute an accomplished portrayal, more private than official, of these subordinate Belgian sovereigns, reliant on the Spanish crown to all intents and purposes. The background in the first of these paintings presents the forests of Voer and the castle of Tervueren, a country residence near Brussels. Jan Brueghel is deemed to have painted the landscape and

flowers although there is insufficient evidence for this. However, studio artists seem to have collaborated in painting the garments and decorations. The portrait of the princess is based on a previous engraving. Against a background containing the castle of Mariemont, she displays the medal of *Nuestra Señora del Buen Socorro* (Our Lady of Good Assistance).

It has been said that the portrait of María de Medici, dated around 1622, has a certain indefinable quality in accordance with her destiny. A possible natural portrait, it was a particular 'type' of picture for the great allegorical series in the Parisian palace of Luxembourg. It dispenses with all artificial devices in favour of spontaneity in the face. Thus, with an economy of resources, Rubens manages to fully convey the complex psychological make-up of the subject.

Another portrait of the Queen of France, Ann of Austria, dates from the same time and forms a matching pair with the previously described painting. However, it does not have the same depth of perception. The queen was the daughter of Philip III of Spain, the wife of Louis XIII and the mother of Louis XIV. From a current perspective, it is difficult to see the magnificent beauty that contemporary chroniclers ascribed to her. An informal picture, the only symbolic detail is the curtain with fleurs-de-lis.

The panel with the portrait of Thomas More is from 1629. It was created by Rubens during a diplomatic mission in England. He copied this well-known work by Holbein the Younger, using baroque techniques and a baroque setting and not without significant changes to the original.

El duque de Lerma (The Duke of Lerma) is an extraordinary equestrian portrait from 1603. It represents a turning-point in the subgenre and one of the peaks in Rubens' career. From a low perspective taken from Mannerism and associated with the conventions of Spanish etiquette, Rubens portrays the proud favourite of Philip III, approaching the observer in the Venetian mode or perhaps in the style of El Greco. The slight wandering look shown in the subject's eyes is one of the most characteristic features of this intense psychological portrait. Perhaps it also reveals his extremely bad physical and mental state at that time. The background with a battle scene comes from an engraving.

The retrospective portrait of *Felipe II a caballo* (Philip II on Horseback) is from 1628. The style is very classical and therefore contrary to heroic

Peter Paul Rubens.
The Triumph of the Eucharist over Idolatry.
Panel. 63 χ 91 cm. Ref. 1699.

Peter Paul Rubens. *The Duke of Lerma.*
Canvas. 283 χ 200 cm. Ref. 3137.

baroque. This could reflect a deliberate intention to return to the restrained formal guidelines current during the reign of the subject of the painting. Nevertheless, the theme of the winged victory with a laurel crown flying on high becomes the artist's own through his brush-strokes rather than being presented as a Renaissance subject. This composition is reminiscent of an engraving by Stradanus. The monarch's face is based on a painting by Titian. On the other hand, the horse moving at a slow pace seems like Gatamelata painted by Donatello. For the completion of this canvas produced in Madrid, Rubens had at his disposal whatever he might have needed from the stables and the armoury of the Alcázar. Even so, the armour and the sword also originate from Titian.

Rubens painted *The Cardinal Prince* in 1634, the year in which he entered the service of the subject of the portrait. In the picture, the Prince appears on horseback as the victor at the battle of Nördlingen, with the same sword carried by Charles V at the battle of Mühlberg. A long emphatic inscription at the foot of the painting manifests the triumphalist ideology present in this equestrian portrait. The allegorical decoration displays the eagle of the Austrian dynasty and the embodiment of Fame which unleashes bolts of lightning against the enemy. Rubens again used this design for the portrait of the Duke of Buckingham.

La muerte del cónsul Decio (The Death of the Consul Decio) dates from around 1618-20 and can be categorized in the classical history genre. It is part of a series of tapestries planned some years before. A sketch, or rather a reduction of the original from Vienna, it reveals the influence of Leonardo, from whom the artist takes the horse rearing up and the dead warrior. It has been said that in the deliberate diagonal pattern, there prevails a clear balance of masses.

The small panel **Danza de aldeanos** (Villagers Dancing) is proof of Rubens liking for portraying everyday life as a genre painter. These preferences were very important in the Flemish school. The date of this picture is a matter of debate and has been put between 1627 and 1639. The collaboration of Lucas Van Uden in creating the background landscape has now been discounted. This work was inspired either directly or indirectly by Pieter Brueghel. Not only is there a mythological undercurrent, as indicated by the Bacchic signs from one of the dancers and of course by the figure of the faun, but there is also a certain esoteric feeling that is difficult to unravel. Both the apparel and the Palladian architecture show Italian influence.

Rubens not only reinterpreted Holbein but he also stood out as an imitator of Titian, with whom he had so many links, perceptible or otherwise. *Adán y Eva* (Adam and Eve) is a version of the painting by the Venetian master which is exhibited in this very same museum. Rubens' version was produced during his second trip to Madrid in 1628-29, according to information from Velasquez conveyed to him by his father-in-law Pacheco. In this copy, he freely modified the colour and the composition of the picture, giving the child serpent a diabolic appearance, involving a qualitative leap from the Renaissance mentality. In fact, this version was so successful that Spanish critics considered it to be better than the original. Rubens had already approached this theme in 1620, bringing forward the head of Adam, a modification that he would later apply to the copy. This canvas painting was not commissioned work. Rather, the artist painted it for himself.

El rapto de Europa (The Abduction of Europe) painted in 1628, also resulted from the artist's second stay in Madrid, again according to information from Velasquez gathered by Pacheco. Unlike *Adam and Eve*, this picture is a literal copy of a work by Titian presented as a gift by Philip V in 1704. The original is now in Boston.

Far from representing Titian's methods from a heroic Baroque standpoint, Rubens here reproduces the master's technique and range of colours with superb perfectionism. Rather than an academic exercise, the copy is a complete tribute to the original artist. As in the case of *Adam and Eve*, Rubens painted the canvas for himself, away from the commercial circuit of patronage.

Without doubt, mythology is the most appropriate genre for Rubens' glowing expressive solutions and his splendid use of colour. *Ceres y Pan* (Ceres and Pan) was brought to Madrid by the artist in 1628. However the complete artwork and classical structure would tend to indicate that the picture was painted around 1612-15. For this painting, Rubens could count on the collaboration of Fran Snyders for the fruits. A contribution to the landscape work by Jan Brueghel cannot be discounted.

Peter Paul Rubens. *The Garden of Love.*
Canvas. 198 χ 283 cm. Ref. 1690.

Peter Paul Rubens. *A Village Dance.*
Panel. 73 χ 106 cm. Ref. 1691.

Aquiles descubierto por Ulises y Licomedes (Achilles Discovered by Ulysses and Licomedes) had already been recorded in 1618. It was also brought to Madrid by Rubens ten years later. The architectural background reveals the influence of Venice. This canvas painting is an eloquent example of the way in which Van Dyck collaborated with his master. Some critics have overstated this collaboration and have even suggested that the pupil had a hand in this composition. But the picture is clearly and exclusively the work of Rubens. When they worked together, the otherwise distinctive and individual Van Dyck went along with the style of his master. According to some, the assistant here displays his superior skill in the human figures but the truth is that he restricts his personal style in favour of a more traditional technique.

Diana cazadora (Diana the Huntress) is a high-quality painting from about 1620. It is the liveliest of the various exultant versions on this theme produced by Rubens. The portrayal of the dogs has been ascribed to his associate Paul de Vos.

The three panels depicting the history of Achilles belong to a series of designs for tapestries. Whether they were commissioned by Philip IV or Charles I of England is a matter of debate. In any case, they were donated by the duchess of Pastrana at the end of the nineteenth century. The paintings could have been in her family since the seventeenth century itself. The actual date of the pictures is subject to controversy but it is put at between 1625 and 1635. They are freely painted works of considerable quality. Framed by two caryatids that represent Esculapio and Terpischore, garlands, and hunting implements, *La educación de Aquiles* (The Education of Achilles) corresponds to Hellenistic sculptures, probably through Roman copies of the Centaur and Cupid.

Achilles Discovered by Ulysses and Licomedes returns to the theme developed in collaboration with Van Dyck. The picture is framed in by two caryatids presenting Palas and Talia with their symbols. There are numerous copies of the painting. *Briseida devuelta a Aquiles* (Briseida Returned to Achilles) closely follows *La Ilíada* (The Iliad). In the former, the dead body of Patroclo lies in the background and the caryatids depict Mercury and Paris with their emblems.

El jardín del amor (The Garden of Love) was called *La conversación a la moda* (Fashionable Conversation) in the time of Rubens. For the setting, the artist evokes an idealized image of his princely mansion in Antwerp, a residence that he very proudly saw as a symbol of his high status as a painter. In Spain, the picture has traditionally been interpreted as a representation of the family, a domestic concept that is perhaps out of step with this ambitious view of modern middle-class reality and classical placidity. In any case, numerous mythological or allegorical references seem to indicate a symbolization of marriage. For obvious reasons, this canvas painting anticipates the eighteenth-century world of rococo. This type of episode provided one of the clearest sources for rococo. It has been claimed that the gentleman with the broad-brimmed hat is in fact a self-portrait by the master and that all of the women are rerepresentations of Elena Fourment. For the sculpture of the fountain, Rubens copied a design by Juan de Bolonia.

Between 1635 and 1640, Rubens painted *Ninfas y sátiros* (Nymphs and Satyrs). In the picture, he probably emphasizes the fertility of the land through an earthly song to Nature and fundamental life. Inspired by classical sculpture, perhaps by a Roman relief, it presents a beautiful landscape with a golden atmosphere that cannot be the work of an associate.

Atalanta y Meleagro (Atalanta and Meleagro) was previously regarded as a copy by Lucas Van Uden with a contribution by Rubens himself. However, it is now acknowledged to be the artist's own work. According to the records, it been already completed by 1636. The mythology of the piece, taken from Ovidio's *Metamorphoses*, is used as a pretext to display a vast panoramic view of the fields of Flanders. As we have said, however, the landscape is not a passive copy of nature but instead holds a living pulsating organism which bursts out in an orgy of rhythm and colour. Wisely, Rubens traces receding diagonal lines so as to make the scene as dynamic as possible.

The great panel of **Las tres gracias** (The Three Graces) dates from between 1636 and 1638. The first sketch for this work seems to have come from a symbolic drawing about the vanity of life belonging to *Los horrores de la guerra* (The Horrors of War) by Rubens himself. Ancient sculpture is once again used as a creative source, perhaps this time by means of Renaissance engravings. Rubens may have drawn inspiration too from a Hellenistic collection in the Cathedral of Siena, a collection already copied by

Peter Paul Rubens. *The Three Graces.*
Panel. 221 χ 181cm. Ref. 1670.

Raphael. Rubens' picture has recently been restored and shows a high quality incompatible with claims that his pupils collaborated in the work. As a piece belonging to Rubens' 'secret museum', it evokes his two wives although the occasional critic has seen the face of Elena Fourment repeated in the Graces. The picture was acquired by Philip IV and enjoyed great recognition in Spanish royal collections as the Flemish epitome of the female nude.

Rubens painted *El juicio de Paris* (The Paris Trial) between 1638 and 1639, a panel based on the texts of Homer. In this work, he repeated the approach to earlier versions on the same theme and followed an engraving with designs by Raphael. Perhaps Rubens was influenced by classical sculpture. Although some have claimed to identify weaknesses in the completion of the two male figures and in the landscape (the latter supposedly the work of Lucas Van Uden), the freedom of the brush-strokes and the freshness of the colours confirm that this is a picture in the artist's own hand.

Diana y sus ninfas sorprendidas por sátiros (Diana and her Nymphs Surprised by Satyrs) was created in the latter stages of Rubens' career. It is a canvas painting with a dynamic pattern of diagonal lines, free brush-strokes and successful chromatic fusion. According to some analysts, Rubens achieves harmony between painting and musical values in this work. Probably through engravings, Rubens referred to the sleeping Hermaphrodite from the Alexandrian School as the basis for the young girl in the same situation with her back turned away from the observer. Jan Wildens collaborated in the painting of the landscape.

Perseo y Andrómeda (Perseus and Andromeda) was an unfinished work at the time of Rubens' death. Some have unjustifiably interpreted the work as the story of Rugiero and Angelica. In fact, it is the last version of a theme repeated by Rubens and also well known by the Spanish Court. It is no coincidence that Lope de Vega devoted one of his plays to this subject. In order to complete the work, the artist considered a number of artists in succession – Gaspar de Crayer, Van Dyck and Jordans. It was the latter who finally carried out the work, a very difficult task given the delicate bush-strokes of Rubens already present on the canvas. The figure of Andromeda is a direct portrait of Elena Fourment, not an idealized portrayal as on other occasions.

In 1636, Philip IV commissioned Rubens with the substantial project of decorating the tower of Parada on the estate of El Pardo. This immense scheme was based on the Metamorphoses of Ovidio although the mythological series alternated with hunting scenes and animals, arranged on lintels. This work was assigned to Snyders and his pupil Paul de Vos. In general, Rubens was aided by his large and highly-skilled group of studio artists during this project. To achieve a classical effect, the influence of Ovidio was reinforced by Renaissance engravings from the sixteenth century. Martínez del Mazo made copies of the series. While for the English and French monarchies, Rubens set about making allegorical compositions with a clear political content encoded as monarchic glorification, for the Spanish monarchy, more reluctant to accept explicit symbolic displays of power, the artist had to be content with this series in which the reference to the king is indirect.

From this collection of paintings, the museum holds canvases from Rubens himself and also from his associates. Of the fifteen pictures considered to be by the master himself, *El rapto de Deidamia* (The Abduction of Deidamia) shows the strong forceful touch characteristic of his later works although a lack of care in the drawing has prompted speculation that his studio may have participated in the work to some extent. This painting has consistent links with a print by Tempesta and even ties in with a design by Michelangelo.

If Rubens' assistants had participated in the production of *El rapto de Proserpina* (The Abduction of Proserpina), Rubens would have totally rearranged the picture. As it is, the intensity and dramatic quality of the chromatic effect totally rules out any contribution by his pupils. For this composition, the master had to refer to a Roman relief. He approached *El banquete de Tereo* (The Banquet of Tereo) with the same light touch and mastery of colour. This work was the subject of literary coverage in Spain by Lope and by Rojas. Suggestions of Tintoretto and links with replicas of the chaste Venus have been pointed out in connection with *Orfeo y Eurídice* (Orpheus and Eurydice), whose structure derives from the Rospigliosi sarcophagus, perhaps through an engraving.

La creación de la Vía Láctea (The Birth of the Milky Way) deals with a theme that is rare in art. A previous picture on this subject had been painted by

Peter Paul Rubens. *Diana and her Nymphs surprised by Fauns.*
Canvas, 128 χ 314 cm. Ref. nº 1665.

Peter Paul Rubens. *The Birth of the Milky Way.*
Canvas. 181 χ 244 cm. Ref. 1668.

Tintoretto. In the Rubens painting, the figure of Jupiter with the appearance of an eagle and the ray of light could have been painted by studio artists on account of the lower quality. Emphasis has been placed on the discontinuous technique with which Rubens sets out the golden light in *Diana y Calixto* (Diana and Calixto). According to some, the landscape in this picture was painted by Lucas Van Uden. The face of Calixto may be that of Elena Fourment. It was also thought that a Lucas Van Uden landscape, with finishing touches by Rubens, formed a part of *Mercurio y Argos* (Mercury and Argos), a theme dealt with by the master on previous occasions. Here, the work is influenced both by a Tempesta engraving and Hellenistic sculpture.

Demócrito y Heráclito (Democrito and Heraclito) form a matching pair and represent optimism and pessimism. They are believed to have been made during Rubens' first visit to Spain in 1603. The obviously poor completion has been ascribed either to Venetian influence or to the difficulties inherent in fast work, without the benefit of designs. Inspired by sculptures of Roman philosophers, Democrito takes on additional significance from a Christian viewpoint as a reference to the vanity of life. Also previously thought to have been made in 1603, the *Satyr* reflects an engraving by Goltzius and uses designs by Praxiteles.

In accordance with the theme, an atmosphere of fire and shadow predominates in *Vulcano* (Vulcan), regarded by some as the work of a pupil with finishing touches by the master or alternatively as a canvas painted entirely by Jordaens. The composition entitled *Fortuna* (Fortune) stems from *Los emblemas* (The Emblems) by Alciato. The iconography approaches that of The Truth as described in the compendium of Ripa. *El rapto de Ganimedes* (The Abduction of Ganimedes) covers a theme that Rubens had already tried out in 1615. The picture draws inspiration from Perino de Vaga as well as the Laocoonte group. It expresses a complex Christian pagan syncretism which, although very dear to Rubens, was widely practised in European art at that time.

Mercurio (Mercury) was an original work by Rubens with some assistance from the studio. The painting refers to praxitelic sculptures through a print by Goltzius. This picture is reminiscent of Belvedere's Apollo and the Meleagro in the Vatican. **Saturno** (*Saturn devouring his son*) could be based

on Michelangelo's Saint Bartholomew in the *Juicio final* (Final Judgement), without wishing to reduce the importance of a certain Mannerist influence. This picture was the probable source of Goya's Saturn in the black paintings.

We will look at four of the makers of the series for the tower of Parada who followed the designs set out by Rubens. This list excludes Jordaens who is described later.

Firstly, Erasmus Quellinus, the creator of *La muerte de Eurídice* (The Death of Eurydice), *Cupido sobre un delfín* (Cupid on a Dolphin), *La persecución de las Arpías* (The Pursuit of the Harpies), *Baco y Ariadna* (Bacchus and Ariadne), *Jasón y el vellocino de oro* (Jason and the Golden Fleece) and a fragment of *Psiquis y el Amor* (Psiquis and Love).

Secondly, Cornelius de Vos, with *El nacimiento de Venus* (The Birth of Venus), *El triunfo de Baco y Apolo* (The Triumph of Bacchus and Apollo) and *La serpiente pitón* (The Python Serpent). Then, Theodore Van Thulden, the creator of *El descubrimiento de Púrpura y Orfeo* (The Discovery of Purple and Orpheus). Finally, Jan Cossiers who made *Narciso, Júpiter y Licaón* (Narcissus, Jupiter and Licaon) and *Prometeo con el fuego* (Prometheus with Fire).

The museum holds several of the master's extraordinary sketches for this gigantic royal series. Regarded as the best example of Rubens' style during his later years, they were designed with amazing force and spontaneity. In *Apollo and the Python Serpent*, developed as a definitive canvas painting by Cornelis de Vos, the god is portrayed according to Belvedere's canonical design, without forgetting the influence of an engraving by Tempesta. *Deucalión y Pirra* (Deucalion and Pirra), apparently inspired by an Italian fresco, provided the basis for a painting by Jan Cossiers which is now lost. *Prometeo* (Prometheus) boldly depicts the story narrated by Hesiodo and Esquilo. It was used as a design for the Cossiers canvas painting preserved in the museum.

Rubens set out to paint *Hércules y el Cancerbero* (Hercules and Cerberus) with powerful dramatic effect and unprecedented forcefulness in the engraved fountains. The definitive version of this picture by Jan Boskaert is thought to have disappeared. *Vertumno y Pomona* (Vertumno and Pomona) is based on prints by Tempesta and works by Perino del Vaga. The large-scale version of the painting is now in a Portuguese collection. Erasmus

Peter Paul Rubens. *The Abduction of Europe.*
Canvas. 181x 200 cm. Ref. 1693.

Quellinus carried out other large-scale versions for the pictures entitled *In Pursuit of the Harpies and The Abduction of Europe*, the latter lacking the power with which Rubens took the same theme from Titian. Rubens used engravings to develop the figures of Cefalo and Procris, the second of which he later repeated. Peeter Symone was entrusted with the task of creating the definitive product, now kept in the Museum. *La muerte de Jacinto* (The Death of Jacinto) was apparently created by Cossiers whose canvas painting has been placed in the royal palace in Madrid. This piece was probably inspired by a Michelangelo drawing.

Also a native of Antwerp, **Anton van Dyck** (1589-1641) developed a distinctive personality at an early stage. His role in relation to Rubens was not so secondary as traditional opinion has maintained.

Van Dyck was the favourite painter of Charles I of England. There, he established a type of portrayal that would largely determine British elegance. In fact, when Rubens died, Van Dyck could have succeeded him as the favourite painter of the King of Spain but Van Dyck's character thwarted this plan by Cardinal Prince Ferdinand of Austria. Although Van Dyck pursued religious and mythological themes in his youth and exceptionally during his mature years, his special area was portrait painting, an activity that he developed with a hitherto unknown refined sophistication that has never since been equalled.

As far as holy or sacred themes were concerned, Van Dyck created *La Piedad* (Devotion) in about 1618-20. It was a composition very much in the mode of Rubens for whom he was the best associate painter at that time. Mistakenly attributed to the master, the picture has been reconfirmed as undoubtedly the work of Van Dyck. Although being in the service of Rubens restrained his nervous technique, the young Van Dyck is shown here to be a fully distinctive painter. This picture ties in with another by Rubens which was inspired by a Goltzius engraving containing retrospective medieval iconography. In line with Germanic tradition and the preference of Michelangelo, Jesus is half supported on the knees of the Virgin.

Around the same time, Van Dyck completed *La serpiente de metal* (The Metal Serpent). There have been unjustified claims that Rubens collaborated in this picture. It is no coincidence that you can see the artist's signature on the bottom strip of the picture. In fact, the painting is a re-presentation of a previous version on the same theme, one attributed to the master. Van Dyck was in touch with Rubens' studio at that time. In spite of this possible influence, Van Dyck also incorporated specific characters from the work of both Caravaggio and Raphael. On the other hand, Van Dyck repeated some of the designs that galvanize this painting throughout his career.

Another work from his youth painted in about 1618-20, is *Los desposorios místicos de Santa Catalina* (The Mystic Betrothal of Saint Catherine), a picture that has been highly debated until recently. As the preparatory drawings show, the process of developing this painting was particularly complex. In line with techniques that were very common in the world of Rubens, hints of classicism can be detected in some of the figures. That of the angel bearing a palm branch reappears in bust studies, usually for apostolates.

San Jerónimo (Saint Jerome) is from the same period of 1618-20. The artist's free and forceful technique, then alien to Rubens, can be explained by his links with Jordaens. Up until this time, Van Dyck had been inspired by the work of Titian but had replaced Titian's diagonal outline plan with an upright vertical one. Van Dyck painted with agile brush-strokes and a wealth of colours. In *La coronación de espinas* (The Coronation of Thorns), changes to the picture can be detected, thus indicating a conscientious approach to work, all this in spite of the long series of studies and versions going to make up the canvas. One of the warriors comes directly from a print by Dürer. As usual in the case of Van Dyck, some of the designs are repeated in other works by the artist.

El prendimiento (The Capture), also dated around 1618-20, closes the display of this first phase of the artist's religious output. This composition was not influenced by Rubens, as has been suggested, but instead by the Venetian School, possibly through drawings or prints by Martin de Vos although the technique once again reveals contact with Jordaens. The face of an armed warrior has again been taken from Dürer.

The style of *Santa Rosalía coronada* (Saint Rosalia Crowned) pertains to Van Dyck's Italian period and the date can therefore be put at between 1621 and 1627. Confirmation that the picture had been painted

Peter Paul Rubens. *Saturn Devouring his Son.*
Canvas. 180 χ 87 cm. Ref. 1678.

Van Dyck. *The Capture.*
Canvas. 344 χ 249 cm. Ref. 1477.

entirely in the artist's own hand came up against an old contribution by Carreño de Miranda who restored the canvas in 1686. The composition was repeated in another recorded piece in 1624 when the artist was in Genoa. Van Dyck made fresh use of the design for an Ascension. According to some critics, the Santa Rosalia Picture was used by Claudio Coello as a basis for his Saint Catherine of London.

San Francisco de Asis (Saint Francis of Assisi) belongs to the artist's Antwerp period, between 1627 and 1632. It is a symbol of meditation about death. There is an exact replica in Vienna with slightly smaller dimensions. Curiously, the painting was taken to be an anonymous work from Seville when it formed a part of the royal collection. During the early years of the Museum's existence, it was attributed to Mateo Cerezo.

Diana y Endimion sorprendidos por el sátiro (Diana and Endimion surprised by the Satyr), illustrates the work of Van Dyck as a painter of mythology. Based on texts by Luciano and Safo, it is a painting from his Italian period, between 1622 and 1627. Compositively, it may go back to Tintoretto or to an engraving by Goltzius about *Jupiter and Antiope*. Claims of collaboration by Frans Snyders have now been discounted.

As a portrait artist, Van Dyck reaches unsurpassable heights of distinction. In *Policinela Spinola*, he paints a full-figure Marchioness of Leganes with the characteristic approach of the Genoese School. Taken from a low angle with a clear emphasis on the upright body, the appearance of this lady does not reflect the "manly woman and great landlady" spoken of by contemporaries. According to some critics, the elegant laziness of her bearing is a tribute to the artist. It is no coincidence that it has been suggested that the distant sophistication with which he portrays Charles I of England is more of the artist's own making than an inherent quality of the royal figure himself.

Both the date and the identity of the subject are a matter of great debate with regard to another portrait, the one supposedly of *Jacob Gaultier*. Whereas one critic has suggested that it was painted between 1622 and 1627, another has categorised it in the second Antwerp period, in 1627-32 and a third has stated that it dates from the artist's second trip to London i.e. not before 1632. As far as the subject of the portrait is concerned, equal mention has been made of Jacob Gaultier, who was a lord from the English Court and Nicolas Laniere although he was a flautist.

The signed portrait of *Conde Enrique de Bergh* (Count Henry of Bergh) belongs to the second Antwerp period from 1627 to 1632. In the picture, Van Dyck captures the versatile personality of this general who was so worthy of praise according to his contemporaries. This, in spite of the fact that he enlisted on the Dutch side. ***The portrait of Martin Ryckaert***, also signed and from the same date, presents the said painter in strange attire, namely a gown and a Turkish sable cassock. There is a replica of the painting in Vienna. A print by Neeffs based on this same picture has enabled it to be identified. A portrait from the same time is that of *El músico Enrique Liberti* (The Musician Enrique Liberti). A good replica exists in Munich although the quality is lower. The text of an engraving by Pedro de Jode confirmed the identity of the artist.

In 1628, Van Dyck painted a portrait of *Federico Enrique de Nassau* (Frederick Henry of Nassau) and at the same time produced a picture of a female figure from The Hague in order to create a matching pair. The portrait of Henry presents a half-length view of a heroic figure in armour with a general's flare and his helmet on a desk. Three years earlier, Henry had been chosen as a 'stathouder', a great fighter for Dutch independence.

The picture of *Sir Endimion Porter and Van Dyck* is dated around 1623 although its style is typical of the artist's work in his last decade, between 1632 and 1641. The painting follows a formula established for Venetian families in which the double portrait contains one subject facing the observer and one in profile. Critics have pointed out the subtle way in which one of the figures is dominated by the other within tight formal cohesion. Van Dyck turns towards the observer as if interrupting the dialogue. The artist has painted himself as a discreet background figure in comparison with his protector and patron, secretary to the Duke of Buckingham and a great lover of art.

In 1634, Van Dyck painted the portrait of *El cardenal infante don Fernando de Austria* (The Cardinal Prince Ferdinand of Austria), the hero of the victory at the battle of Nördlingen. He is dressed in splendid clothes for the reception held in Brussels after his triumph. For such an auspicious occasion,

Van Dyck. *The painter Martin Ryckaert.*
Panel. 148 χ 113 cm. Ref. 1479.

Van Dyck. *Sir Endimion Porter and Van Dyck.*
Oval canvas. 115 χ 141 cm. Ref. 1489.

the prince carries the same sword that Charles V wore in the battle of Mühlberg, a detail also brought out by Rubens. Some analysts have doubted whether Van Dyck was responsible for the picture, putting forward instead the name of his former master, but the very precise preparatory drawing eliminates this possibility.

El grabador Paul de Pont (The Engraver Paul de Pont) is a picture that probably belongs to the artist's second Antwerp period, between 1627 and 1632. It was identified through its similarity to another image. The subject collaborated both with Rubens and with Van Dyck. The display of portrait painting by Van Dyck is completed by *Diana Cecil, the Duchess of Oxford* and wife of Robert de Vere. This piece dates from his final English period. A replica of this work is known. The rose, in the subject's right hand, possibly symbolizes fertility. As some commentators have emphasized, the superior air of the aristocratic lady is a requirement of the English code of conduct.

The third member of the group of seventeenth century Flemish painters was **Jacob Jordaens** (1593-1678). He was also from Antwerp and like the other two he had close ties with the Spanish royal family. His **Retrato de familia** (Portrait of a Family) from around 1623 is considered to be one of the most beautiful portraits from the whole century. It is an outstanding illustration of this genre within the varying collective whole. The picture is interpreted as a self-portrait by Jordaens with his family. The informal elegance with which the figure of the artist appears, holding a lute, apparently suggests that he has musical knowledge and may be the result of hints from his contemporary Dutch colleagues. This painting is a typical middle-class group portrait showing the social and professional self-satisfaction of the Flemish painters.

The panel *Tres músicos ambulantes* (Three Roving Musicians) is a genre painting evidently created as a preliminary study for another work. It has given rise to the most contrasting opinions. The artist makes a great show of virtuosity with strong strokes making up the sketched artwork. One critic has expressed doubts about the originality of the work while another assumed that it was a youthful piece by Van Dyck and a third even questioned the generally acknowledged quality of the picture. Although analysts have pointed out the absence of

similar designs during the course of Jordaens' artistic development, the postures visible in the picture are at least his.

La ofrenda a Ceres (The Offering to Ceres) is a notable example of the artist's mythological output. The figure of the goddess links up with Titian's picture *La ofrenda a Venus* (The Offering to Venus) which is also kept at the Museum. Other characters are based on figures in works by Jacobo Bassano. Previously interpreted as a tribute to Pomona, the goddess of gardens, the current image created by the picture stems from the attributes of the fruits and the locks of hair. This canvas painting was produced between 1618 and 1620 and shows the artist's initial style. It is characterized by a strong tighttly technique. Some historians have wondered whether the child figure in the foreground resulted from the influence of Caravaggio.

Meleagro and Atalanta was based on *The Metamorphoses* by Ovidio. The picture was painted at some time between 1617 and 1630 but the exact date is a matter of debate. There is a replica of the painting in Naples and many other versions also exist. In this one, the hero adopts a heroic posture which is conspicuous by its absence in the other versions. All versions of the picture prominently display Jordaen's preference for the expressive style of Caravaggio.

In approximately 1630, Jordaens painted *Diosa y Ninfas después del baño* (The Goddess and Nymphs After Bathing). The picture is set against a background of a garden with baroque architecture, namely ringed columns identical to those of Rubens' mansion. Incidentally, Van Dyck also used this mansion as the basis for one of his portraits. The flirtations of the characters in this painting by Jordaens are repeated in a similar way in *The Offering to Venus* by Brunswick. The uncertain iconography has been interpreted as Juno with the nymphs, given the emblem of the peacock.

For the series pertaining to the tower of Parada, Jordaens took on the task of producing four canvas paintings while working under the orders of Rubens. *Las bodas de Tetis y Peleo* (The Wedding of Tetis and Peleo) or *Banquete de los dioses* (Banquet of the Gods) are pictures which so closely follow the sketchwork of Rubens that it has become difficult to distinguish the characteristic style of his assistant. The shortened signature on *The Banquet of the*

Jacob Jordaens. *The Jordaens Family in a Garden.*
Canvas. 181 χ 187 cm. Ref. 1549.

Gods is reminiscent of the one used by Jan Van Reyn but it is in fact the same as Jordaens' signature in other works.

This time, the composition does not originate from *The Metamorphoses* by Ovidio but instead from Catulo. It derives directly form Raphael. *La Caída de los Gigantes* (The Fall of the Giants) or *La derrota de los titanes* (The Defeat of the Titans) is a painting that was mistakenly ascribed to Jacob Peter Gowhy. The theme very much suits the grandeur of Rubens' art in that it lends itself like few others to his dynamic foreshortening and to the effects of his receding diagonal lines. This painting comes from a mural by Giulio Romano in the palace of Te in Mantua.

Although loyally continuing with the sketchwork of his master, Jordaens set out his own personal style in the scene entitled *Apolo vencedor de Pan* (Apollo the Victor over Pan). Here, the reference to Belvedere's Apollo alternates with echoes of Tempesta. As the painting was then in Velasquez's studio, it is reproduced in *Las Meninas* (The Maids of Honour). The high quality of *Cadmo y Minerva* (Cadmo and Minerva) led to the painting being attributed to Rubens himself. With few variations, it keeps to the design of a Renaissance engraving from the end of the sixteenth century which depicts the same theme.

Jan Brueghel de Velours, the son of Pieter Brueghel the Elder was a court painter for Archduchess Isabel Clara Eugenia and Archduke Alberto. He worked with the most outstanding painters of the time, in particular with Rubens, and covered such diverse genres as landscape, still life and the allegory. *La visión de San Humberto* (The Vision of Saint Humberto) was produced by him in collaboration with Rubens around 1620 although Rubens took the leading role. This panel shows the saint kneeling against a background opening onto a vast plain. In front of him, there is a deer from whose horns a cross emerges.

Between 1617 and 1618, Brueghel produced the series of allegories of the five senses in collaboration with Rubens. They were on record at the Alcázar in Madrid in 1636, fourteen years after the artist's death. A study of the designs and an analysis of the style indeed indicate this collaboration. Several copies, some of them painted in a particularly free style, followed on from this princely series. The panels can be spread out as typical Flemish painting cabinets representing interiors where real pictures by various artists are reproduced with greater or lesser detailed precision.

Signed and dated in 1617, *La vista* (The View) presents a porch leading to the gardens of the castle of Mariemont behind. The picture shows diverse reproductions of sculptures by Michelangelo and of well-known ancient sculptures. We can also see a large number of pictures that are not only Flemish. The identity of these pictures has been the subject of exhaustive study. The figures were previously attributed to Henry Van Balen or to Brueghel himself but they have now been reconfirmed as the work of Rubens, as is the case in the whole series. *El oído* (The Ear) is also set at the castle of Mariemont and displays pictures with themes alluding to music, including one by Jan Brueghel himself. *El olfato* (The Sense of Smell) contains a great variety of flowers as is appropriate to this sense. In the painting, a nymph, logically enough Flora, waits to be admired by a lover in the garden. Signed in 1618, *El gusto* (Taste) has abundant supplies of food. In the foreground, a number of food items are pictured together in an approach that was also used by Frans Snyders in many of his still lifes. On this occasion, the background landscape behind the series of arches shows the valley of Voer with the castle of Tervueren. For the fifth allegory, *El tacto* (Touch), Brueghel uses as his setting the cavern of Vulcan where the god and his minions are forging weapons. In keeping with the theme of war, the artist includes diverse pictures with violent themes.

A specialist in hunting scenes and still lifes, **Frans Snyders** (1579-1657) came to prominence through the teachings of Jan Brueghel de Velours. However, he performed at his best when working in collaboration with Rubens. One of his most successful concepts, in spite of the limitations of the vertical plane, is *Aves acuáticas y armiños* (Water Birds and Stoats). The picture shows a magnificent landscape and perhaps belonged to a series of four pieces. *La gata y el zorro* (The She-cat and the Fox), illustrates an Aesop fable. The landscape is painted in the style of Jan Wildens while the picture as a whole creates a beautiful effect from the balance of masses.

The art of **Paul de Vos** (1595-1678) emerged from the work of Snyders. In fact, de Vos shows superior technique and also compares favourably in freedom of composition although he still imitates the back-

Brueghel de Velours. *The Sense of Smell.*
Panel. 65 χ 109 cm. Ref. 1396.

Paul de Vos. *A Deer Hounded by a Pack of Dogs.*
Canvas. 212 χ 347 cm. Ref. 1870.

ground landscapes of Jan Wildens. A major work recently reconfirmed as that of de Vos is *Animales y aves* (Animals and Birds), a great canvas painting in which the separation of the figures probably reflects the aim of portraying three different Aesop fables.

The existence of numerous copies indicates the notable success achieved by *Ciervo acosado por la jauría* (A Deer Hounded by a Pack of Dogs). The artwork is more advanced than that hitherto carried out by Snyders and this enables us to set the date at around 1637-40. Forming a matching pair with the previous picture and likewise displaying high quality, *Cacería de corzos* (A Roe Deer Hunt) surpasses other similar scenes by Snyders in terms of the quality of the drawing and the dramatic tension.

Among painters of architectural interiors, **Peter Neefs the Elder** stands out in the Flemish context. He was born about 1578 and died at some time between 1656 and 1661. Today, he is credited with painting *Interior de Iglesia* (The Inside of a Church), a picture traditionally ascribed to Frans Francken the Elder. The figures are characteristic of Frans Francken the younger. In 1636, Peter Neefs signed *El viático en el interior de una Iglesia* (The Viaticum Inside a Church). In this painting, the delicate figures also reflect the work of Francken II.

The Prado holds a considerable collection of Flemish landscape paintings from the seventeenth century. **Joost de Momper** (1564-1635) created *Paisaje con patinadores* (A Landscape with Skaters). With free artwork and a simplified perception, the painting shows the influence of Pieter Brueghel. **Martin Ryckaert** (1587-1631) painted *Un paisaje* (A Landscape). Signed in 1616, it is his oldest work. Its conception corresponds to the tastes of the beginning of the century and also provides evidence of contact with Paul Bril. Following his personal Italian apprenticeship, **Paul Bril** (1554-1626) made a substantial contribution to the modern definition of the genre of landscape painting. He is believed to have painted *Un paisaje con Psiquis y Jupiter* (A Landscape with Psiquis and Jupiter), dating from 1610 and previously ascribed to Uden and Jordaens with the possible collaboration of Rubens. **Jan Peeters** (1624-1677) is credited with painting *Un puerto de mar* (A Harbour), a picture that shows his careful technique and drawing. Until recently, this piece was understood to be the work of a Dutch seascape painter, thus emphasizing the similar approach taken by artists towards this genre in the northern and southern parts of the Low Countries.

This display of painting by the Flemish school from the seventeenth century is completed by the prolific **David Teniers** (1610-1690). Following in the footsteps of Adriaen Brouwer and Frans Francken the Younger, his extremely delicate artwork and palette created scenes from this genre. *Fiesta campestre* (A Countryside Party) was signed in 1647 and shows a folk wedding. However, the scene also includes a group of high-ranking dignitaries among whom we can distinguish the Governor of Flanders himself, Archduke Leopold William, who is acting on behalf of the King of Spain. *Fiesta y comida aldeana* (A Village Festival) was painted in about 1650 and again presents contrasting social classes, perhaps with the presence of the archduke once more.

El rey bebe (The King Drinking) is one of several versions in which Teniers deals with this theme from Flemish folklore. The same subject was also taken up by Jordaens. In this picture, designs for the grotesque jester were in fact based on the work of Jordaens. *El mono pintor* (The Monkey Painter) exemplifies Teniers' simian pictures, several of which are housed in the Prado. They also provide evidence of the attraction for genre painters of this type of satire or parody.

A remarkable array of Flemish pictures dates from about 1647. It is entitled *El archiduque Leopoldo Guillermo en su galería de pinturas* (The Archduke Leopold William in his Art Gallery). The piece was certainly commissioned so that Philip IV would get to know the governor's fantastic collection. In fact, the governor appears in one of the scenes. He is showing the collection to the Count of Fuensaldaña and a priest. In addition, Teniers portrays himself in their company. It is no coincidence that he signs as a court painter for His Most Serene Highness. Most of the pieces reproduced here have been identified. They consist of Italian and Flemish works and they make up the basis of the Vienna museum collection.

SPANISH PAINTING IN THE SEVENTEENTH CENTURY
Rooms 18, 18a, 29, 28, 26, 25, 24 and 1

Spanish pictorial naturalism from the seventeenth century owed its existence to a greater or lesser extent

David Teniers. *The King Drinking.*
Copper. 58 χ 70 cm. Ref. 1797.

David Teniers. *A Village Festival.*
Canvas. 120 χ 188 cm. Ref. 1788.

to the tenebrism of Caravaggio. It basically developed in three main centres – Seville, Valencia and Madrid, the latter being the venue for court painting. The Dominican friar from Toledo, **Juan Bautista Maino** (1578-1649) was close to the Madrid circle of painters. He applied the knowledge he had acquired during his trip to Italy by developing a very personal style with strange matching colours. In 1614, he painted the famous *Cuatro pascuas* (Four Festivals) for the main reredos of the Dominican conventual church of *San Pedro Mártir* (Saint Peter the Martyr) in Toledo. The artist uses great contrasts of light and has a strong interest in capturing the qualities of multicolour fabrics. Two typical examples of Counter-Reformation naturalist art are *La adoración de los pastores* (The Adoration of the Shepherds) and *La adoración de los Magos* (The Adoration of the Magi), both by Juan Bautista Maino. These paintings were orientated towards popular devotion. For the general decoration of the *Salón de reinos* (The Hall of Kingdoms) in the Retiro park, the artist painted an untypical war scene in 1634. In this sense, it ranks alongside *Las lanzas* (The Lances) by Velasquez. Using unprecedented light shades and a strange, almost pointillist, technique, the foreground presents the theme of the anonymous fall while the glorification of the general and the king takes place behind. Here too, the humiliated Dutch kneel down in front of a tapestry bearing an allegorical portrait of Philip IV accompanied by the Count-Duke Olivares. Right in the background, we can see the landscape of La Ensenada.

Juan Sánchez Cotán (1560-1627) was from Toledo but moved to Granada. From his work, the Museum houses the extremely important **Bodegón** (Still Life) signed in 1602. Although the composition is balanced and routine within the framework of a food cupboard, it constitutes one of the leading works in the genre in terms of Spanish painting. In this picture, Sánchez Cotán uses solid corporeity to express the poetic nature of the humility present in everyday life. This painting has recently been acquired with funds from the Villaescusa bequest.

Francisco Ribalta (1565-1628) brought realist art to Valencia and acted as head of the local Baroque School. His **Cristo abrazando a San Bernardo** (Christ Embracing Saint Bernard) is a very tenebrist work in which two angels can hardly be distinguished against the shadowy background. *San Francisco confortado por un ángel músico* (Saint Francis Comforted by an Angel Musician) dates from about 1620 and is a mature painting. In spite of the mannerism of the heavenly messenger, Naturalist work is plainly visible.

It may be said that the Valencian School culminates in the work of **José Ribera "El Españoleto"** (1591-1652). Nevertheless, he lived in Naples from 1616 onwards and there he stood out as the head of the local art school. Even so, he had direct contact with Spain, the destination for much of his most important work. As a result, it is no exaggeration to regard him as the leading exponent of baroque art in the eastern provinces of Spain. The Prado Museum houses notable canvas paintings by Ribera. They provide evidence of his relations with the court although many of the paintings were acquired later i.e. in the eighteenth century. His debt to Caravaggio does not take anything away from the fact that as a classicist and a great colourist, his style of art in synthesis has tremendous character.

La Trinidad (The Trinity), from around 1635-36, is one of his most beautiful works from this period. Perhaps it is a second version of the canvas painting kept at the Escorial. Although the figure of Christ is still very tenebrist, the fabrics is striking on account of the rich colouring. Iconographically, the picture derives from the design by Dürer but it also seems to have links with *The Trinity* by El Greco.

The canvas paintings of *San Roque* (Saint Rock) and *Santiago el Mayor* (James the Elder) come from the Escorial. The pictures form a matching pair signed in 1631. Painted on a large scale and containing similar compositive elements, both paintings present the protagonist on foot emphasized by a rounded upright support. In *Saint Rock,* the realism with which the dog is portrayed gives proof of Ribera's great expertise as a painter of animals. The background in *James the Elder* is not so tenebrist. Neither is the iconography very clear, as the apostle, when appearing as a pilgrim, does not wear a scallop shell. As some analysts have suggested, he is probably portrayed in his role as an evangelist.

The canvas painting *San José y el Niño Jesús* (Saint Joseph and the Boy Jesus) dates from the early 1630s. The picture involves the reassessment of the patriarch during the Spanish baroque period although some historians have expressed surprise at the portrayal of Christ in a submissive stance, humbly carrying the carpenter's tools. Whereas the

Sánchez Cotán.
Still Life with Poultry, Vegetables and Fruit.
Canvas. 68 χ 89 cm. Ref. n° 7612.

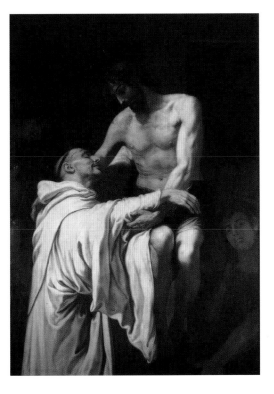

Juan Ribalta. *Christ Embracing Saint Bernard.*
Canvas. 158 χ 113 cm. Ref. n° 2804.

painting still displays tenebrism in the style of Caravaggio, it already shows a move towards the bright mellow artwork characteristic of Ribera.

Signed in 1632, *Ixión y Ticio* (Ixion and Tityus) form one of the two series of *Furias* (Furies) completed by Ribera in a similar way to those of Titian. Ixion is one of his most violent works both in composition and in concept. Whereas in this canvas painting, the artist dramatically highlights the satyr or devil who makes the wheel of the storm go around, in Tityus, we can hardly see one of the vultures that pulls at the liver of one of the damned.

Also signed in 1632, *El escultor ciego* (The Blind Sculptor), who is touching a head of Apollo, has been the subject of considerable iconographic debate. The sculptor Giovanni Gomelli, 'The Blind Man of Gambassi', has been discounted as the subject of the painting. Perhaps the picture represents the philosopher Carneades distinguishing the bust of Panisco by touch. Another possibility is that it personifies the sense of touch, not according to conventional allegorical guidelines but by following a harsh Baroque realism so characteristic of Ribera's demythologizing style. In bad condition, the painting is nevertheless illuminated by bright light channelled towards the protagonist who is still claimed to be the work of Caravaggio.

At some time between 1630 and 1638, the artist painted *La visión de San Francisco de Asís* (Saint Francis of Assisi's Vision). Controversy about the date arises from doubt as to what degree the style of Caravaggio had given way to a more free-flowing approach. The angel displays a flask or decanter with water as the symbol of the purity of the priesthood. The hitherto unsure Saint Francis definitively renounces the priesthood.

Signed in 1633, the painting of *San Sebastián* takes up a common theme in Ribera's work. He sometimes represents it in this way with the right arm raised and tied. As usual, the topic is a pretext for an anatomical study of the male body. Although the predominant colours are rather dark, the picture presents beautiful shades of blue in harmony. The painting contains compositive elements which are characteristic of this phase in Ribera's artistic development such as the diagonal structure and the placement of the human figure on a thick trunk in search of solidity in addition to the contrast of chiaroscuro.

La cabeza de anciano (The Head of an Old Man) and *La cabeza femenina* (The Female Head) –belonging to Dionysius, Bacchus and Sibyl respectively- are fragments of a great canvas painting which has been destroyed. A Third Chird painting from this *Triunfo de Baco* (The Triumph of Bacchus) is still preserved away from the museum. Some believe that this work dates from 1629-30 while others put the date at 1634-35. Judging by the technique, the paintings probably belong to the latter of these two periods. There exists an old copy of the whole composition which shows that Ribera drew inspiration from a classical relief.

La Trinidad (The Trinity) is from about 1635-36 and is one of the artist's most beautiful works from this period. Perhaps it is a second version of the canvas painting kept at the Escorial. Although the figure of Christ is still very tenebrist, the picture has a striking wealth of colours. Iconographically, it derives from the design by Dürer but there also seem to be links with *The Trinity* by El Greco.

Signed in 1637, *Isaac and Jacob* depicts the Biblical scene in which the former deceives the latter in order to receive a blessing as the first-born son. It is one of Ribera's masterpieces. The colouring is undoubtedly in the Venetian tradition. The painting reveals that the artist has assimilated the lessons of Venice but also that he is familiar with Flemish art of the time, specifically the work of Van Dyck.

El sueño de Jacobo (Jacob's Dream) was signed in 1639 and also shows that the tenebrism from his early period has been refocussed towards Venetian colourism. Instead of the material staircase that other painters used to present this theme, Ribera settles for a golden sky in which the figures of the angels almost lose their form. Recent cleaning of the picture has revealed the extraordinary brilliance of the sky. This, together with the pleasant artwork, explains why the painting found its way into the royal collection in the eighteenth century as the work of Murillo.

La liberación de san Pedro (The Release of Saint Peter) forms a matching pair with the previously-mentioned canvas painting. The plan is almost exactly repeated. Ribera's familiarity with the work of Van Dyck is illustrated by the angel on the right painted with beautiful foreshortening and refined artwork. The picture is seen from a high perspective. The lighting still harks back to Caravaggio but both

José de Ribera. *The Magdalene or Saint Tais.*
Canvas. 182 χ 149 cm. Ref. 1103.

the colour and the technique show how much 'El Españoleto' has developed in his own right.

El martirio de San Felipe (The Martyrdom of Saint Philip) is an extremely well-known canvas and is representative of the supposed realist cruelty in certain Spanish baroque painting. The painting was apparently created in 1639 and the saint was previously thought be Saint Bartholomew. It is one of Ribera's masterpieces. The portrayal is very vivid but the artist refrains from showing the martyrdom itself. Instead, we see the preparations. A prominent aspect is the light almost 'impressionist' touch with which the artist paints the ordinary people in the middle distance. This canvas painting is definitely baroque. Noticeable is the free approach to the elements making up the picture and the dynamic use of diagonal lines in the composition.

La Magdalena Penitente (The Penitent Magdalene) is a mature work signed in 1641. For the subject of the painting, the artist perhaps used his daughter, kidnapped in 1649 by the illegitimate royal son Juan José of Austria. It forms part of a series of four canvas paintings featuring the contrast between youth and old age. It is one of the most beautiful portrayals of this penitent saint in Spanish art, which abounds in this type of painting. The light is markedly tenebrist and reinforces the sculptural appearance of the figure.

San Jerónimo (Saint Jerome) was signed in 1644 and is usually considered to be unfinished. Indeed, it was painted when Ribera was ill. This picture is a masterpiece with the mellow style of his last period.

Although he was not born in Seville, the Extremaduran Francisco de Zurbarán (1598-1664) received his artistic training in that Andalusian city and became the most important exponent of the Seville School of art during the first half of the seventeenth century. Nevertheless, he had contact with the Madrid court, mainly through his friend Velasquez. Zurbaran was a 'gothic' and conventual painter without a great capacity for composition, which he based on prints. However, his standing increased enormously in the nineteenth century. The Prado Museum holds important works by Zurbaran but not enough to give an overview of his artistic output.

His *Inmaculada* (The Immaculate Virgin) is a small canvas painting dating from 1628-30. It is his earliest portrayal of this theme, so characteristic of the Seville School. In painting the picture, he adheres to the design by Pacheco although not without repeating a northern European print. Zurbaran's rigidity meant that he created the portrait as a polychromatic sculpture.

La aparición de San Pedro a san Pedro Nolasco (The Appearance of Saint Peter to Saint Peter Nolasco) was signed in 1629 and intended, together with the following picture, for the cloister of La Merced Calzada in Seville. The composition derives from a print, given the limited inventiveness of Zurbaran. In a sharp visual impact, we see the apostle crucified and head-down and, following iconographic convention, immersed in an incandescent cloud that breaks up the neutral background. *La vision de San Pedro de Nolasco* (Saint Peter Nolasco's Vision) is a canvas painting with very clear masses in light shades. A salient feature is the brilliant effect caused by the folds in the clothes. The angel shows the heavenly Jerusalem to the protagonist by way of an opening on high and to one side. Reflecting the Apocalypse, the phantasmagorical city gives out a strong light which, on the other hand, is the only one that illuminates the cell.

The enigmatic *Crucificado con San Lucas* (Crucified with Saint Lucas) dates from around 1630-35. A small and sombre canvas painting, it undoubtedly comes from a private chapel. This would explain the poignant iconography, a new development. Indeed, the painting presents an uprecedented dialogue between the painter evangelist and Christ, still alive, although the figures are not on the same scale as if the saint were in front of a sculpture. Some analysts have interpreted the figure with the palette as a self-portrait by Zurbaran but if this were the case, he would have to look as he did around 1660. Perhaps this composition derives from a German print.

Without discounting the influence of the Count-Duke of Olivares, who was so closely connected to Seville, it was probably at the suggestion of Velasquez that Zurbaran was summoned to Madrid to collaborate in the decoration of the new palace of the Buen Retiro. Once again, he showed a serious lack of creativity. He painted a series of ten pictures on the theme of Hercules, the "Hercules Hispanicus", a reference to the monarch. These pieces were intended for the *Salón de Reinos* (The Hall of

Francisco de Zurbarán. *Still Life.*
Canvas. 46 χ 84 cm. Ref. 2803.

Francisco de Zurbarán. *Saint Isabel of Portugal.*
Canvas. 184 χ 98. cm. Ref. 1239.

Kingdoms). The receipts for these paintings are dated 1634. He also painted *La defensa de Cádiz contra los ingleses* (The Defence of Cadiz Against The English). This great picture of contemporary history is included in a series with contributions by several artists, among them Velasquez with *Las lanzas* (The Lances). Zurbaran's picture shows little inventiveness and an archaic concept of the landscape. In the foreground, we can see Francisco Girón, the local governor, giving orders to repel the English landing of 1625 led by Lord Wimbleton. The melodramatic figures in the foreground appear as if in a frieze. This area of the picture reveals some borrowings by Velasquez. Although Zurbaran assimilated the motives and even the stylistic features of the Madrid painters who took part in this series, the scene was undoubtedly painted in his own hand.

The small painting entitled *Agnus Dei* was produced, according to some experts, in about 1635-40 although other analysts believe it to be earlier. There are several versions of the picture. Perhaps the refined brushwork in this picture is better than that in the others. Here, Zurbaran re-established a medieval theme which had already reappeared in mystic literature, that of the lamb tied up for sacrifice as a symbol of the sacrifice of Jesus Christ.

El Bodegón (The Still Life) is a small canvas painting from his last period in Madrid at the end of the 1660s. The picture was a gift from Cambó in 1940. There is an almost identical version in the Catalonia Museum of Art. Against a neutral background, the painting shows several pots placed in a solemn line, reminiscent of the ritual arrangement of liturgical items on altars.

Throughout the Central Gallery, two large tables are set out. They are called by the name of Saint Pius V because it has traditionally been considered that he gave his great panels to Philip II as a gift. They are magnificent Florentine pieces from the grand ducal hard stone workshops and were produced at the end of the sixteenth century. In addition, they are supported by seven of the twelve lions ordered by Velasquez during his second trip to Rome as consoles for the Hall of Mirrors in the Alcázar in Madrid. The sculptural design was the work of Giuliano Finelli. It was inspired by the marble lions which were then in the Roman Villa Medici and are now to be found in the Loggia dei Lanzi,

Florence. Matteo Bonarelli was responsible for the moulding in bronze. Another four lions are in the throne room at the royal palace in Madrid. One was lost and has been replaced in the Prado by a copy from the nineteenth century.

VELASQUEZ
Rooms 27, 12, 14, 15, 15a and 16

The Prado houses fifty of the approximately one hundred and twenty pictures known for certain to have been painted by Diego de Silva Velasquez. For more than a century, they have occupied the great central hall and the immediate surroundings, thus symbolizing their role as the focal point of the collection. This is due not only to the numerical and qualitative importance of the pictures but also to the contribution of the master to the Spanish art movement. In the artistic output of Velasquez, we can see the influence of the artists admired by the Spanish monarchs, especially Titian but also Rubens and contemporary Italian painters. This influence helped in the development of a genius who not only reflected his time but also anticipated the future. The impressionists considered him to be a pioneer. In fact, Manet's visit to the Prado was a kind of revelation for the French artist.

Velasquez was born in Seville in 1599 but left for Madrid in 1623. Protected by the all-powerful Prime Minister, the Count-Duke of Olivares, he entered into the king's service as a painter. His success was meteoric. Philip IV never again posed for another painter, with the exception of Rubens. For almost forty years until his death in 1660, Velasquez's life involved a palace career comparable to that of other masters of his time, such as Van Dyck and Rubens. By means of painting, declared a "liberal art", an intellectual profession, not a mechanical job, artists reached a high social status and achieved personal aggrandisement. This was brought about by a tenacious decision whose importance should be seen in the context of the stately and rigid hierarchical structure of the baroque age. Velasquez crowned his professional career as a confidant of the king by acquiring the post of Master of the Chamber, a position that made him largely responsible for decorating the building. His ultimate triumph was his appointment as a knight of the Order of Santiago in 1658.

Diego de Velasquez. *The Adoration of the Magi.*
Canvas. 203 χ 125 cm. Ref. 1166.

Three trips shaped Velasquez's artistic development: the move to Madrid and the two journeys that he made to Italy in 1629 and 1649-51. But after the first time he returned from Italy, it becomes difficult to put his paintings in chronological order with the technique as the only criterion. Moreover, as a court painter, with a studio in the palace itself, he was continually confronted with his own pictures and it was therefore impossible for him to repaint or correct them. This makes it even more complicated to work out a chronological order. Therefore, it is more straightforward to categorize them by themes, even though the precise dates of some of the pictures are known, particularly in the case of his portraits of members of the royal family. Among these portraits, some of the most outstanding are those of Philip IV who reigned between 1621 and 1665, Philip's first wife Isabel de Valois, and his niece Mariana of Austria with whom he entered into matrimony for the second time in 1649.

Almost all of the Velasquez paintings on display come from the Royal collection and have been in the Museum since it opened, except as indicated.

The Seville period and the first journey to the court

At the beginning of the seventeenth century, the influence of Flemish painting was predominant in Seville. It was characterized by lingering attention to individual detail. This proved decisive for Velasquez as did the works of Caravaggio brought back by traders. So, for Velasquez, these influences were greater than that of local predecessors such as Pedro de Campaña or Luis de Vargas, although the work of Roelas may have attracted him more on account of the Venetian-style colouring. *La adoración de los Reyes Magos* (The Adoration of the Magi) from 1619 s very typical of Velasquez's early style. It is full of the naturalism with which he reflects everyday objects and people. The characters in the picture are obviously the subjects of portraits and it has even been thought that they are a family group, perhaps members of the artist's own family. However, the resemblance is dubious. The picture originally came from *San Luis* (Saint Louis), the Jesuit noviciate in Seville and was later owned by Francisco de Bruna who presented it as a gift to Ferdinand VII.

Velasquez was a pupil of Francisco Pacheco from 1611 onwards and in fact he married Pacheco's daughter, Juana, in 1618. On the other hand, Pacheco was one of the painters that least influenced Velasquez although he must have been impressed by his master's artistic discipline and his interest in the great Italian painters of the sixteenth century and his study of the natural state. It has been claimed that the subject of *Retrato de Caballero* (The Portrait of a Gentleman) is actually Velasquez's master. However, there is not a great deal of resemblance to the self-portrait by Pacheco in the Museum of Seville. In any case, it is a portrait characteristic of the middle class or minor aristocracy intended for private use. The picture must have been painted no later than 1623 as the type of ruff, displayed by the subject in the portrait, was prohibited in that year. This portrait comes from Philip V's collection al La Granja.

La venerable Madre Jerónima de la Fuente (The Venerable Mother Jerónima de la Fuente), signed and dated in 1620, reflects a very different spirit: a nun of the order of St. Clare, full of "a certain determination", prepares to set sail for Manila at 65 years of age in order to found a convent of her order there. This will give impetus to the drive to evangelize the Philippines. The crucifix that she holds up reminds us of the devotion to the cross that characterizes her piety. The "vera effigies" (true image) of this potential saint was painted at the request of her colleagues at the convent from which she came, Santa Isabel la Real in Toledo. The picture was kept there until Fernández de Araoz bought it and donated it to the Prado in the 1940s.

Velasquez's Early Years at the court: *El retrato de hombre* (The Portrait of a Man) was painted later than 1623, judging by the new collar, a new kind of ruff established by law. The picture therefore belongs to the beginning of the artist's Madrid period. The supposed resemblance to the features of *San Juan Evangelista en Patmos* (Saint John the Evangelist in Patmos) (The National Gallery, London) have led to the belief that it is a self-portrait or that of a member of the painter's family. In any case, the picture is a good example of the expertise shown by Velasquez in this particular field when he arrived in Madrid. He enjoyed great success in spite of the jealousy of those who branded him as a painter who only knew how to paint heads.

Diego de Velasquez. *The Drunkards or the Triumph of Bacchus.*
Canvas. 165 χ 188 cm. Ref. 1170.

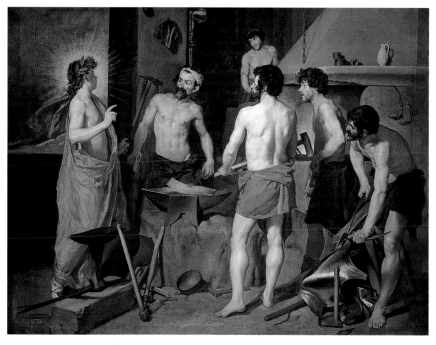

Diego de Velasquez. *Vulcan's Forge.*
Canvas. 222 χ 290 cm. Ref. 1171.

A portrait of the young Philip IV standing brought about the fulfilment of his ambition to enter the service of the king. This picture apparently dates from the last quarter of 1623. Velasquez later repainted the portrait. This has been verified from some old copies and from X-ray pictures which show that he corrected the position of the legs and the cloak and that he repainted the face. Velasquez had assimilated with astonishing speed the lessons provided by Titian in his portraits of Philip II, the grandfather and the political and moral role model for the young king. Velasquez evokes the distant unruffled dignity personifying the majestic royal figure. With the Golden Fleece as the only insignia, the monarch's measured posture while granting an audience next to a desk, having just received another request, convens the simplicity that for the Austrian royal family was the supreme sign of absolute power.

Felipe IV con Armadura (Philip IV in Armour) was painted around 1626-1628. It is a military portrait. This is borne out by analyses which show that the picture is a fragment of a larger canvas, produced in two very different stages. Several theories have been put forward suggesting links with the portrait of the king standing and also with the great equestrian portrait that brought the artist so much fame in 1626 when it was exhibited in *La calle Mayor* (The High Street) in Madrid.

The portrait of Prince Carlos was painted when the subject was twenty years old. Therefore, the picture dates from approximately 1626. Prince Carlos was the younger brother of Philip IV. His most memorable gesture before his early death in 1632 was the one he made to hold up a glove. As well as the virtuosity that Velasquez shows in depicting a figure almost from nothing, in this picture he begins to display his mastery in using fewer resources to suggest space. To do so, he only needs shadow on the ground, shades of grey and just a few colours.

With apparently effortless ease, Velasquez displayed the skill of portraying very different types of objects as if they were real. At the same time, he always kept within an earthy range. He utilized this and indeed all of his resources in **Los borrachos o la fiesta de Baco** (The Drunkards or The Festival of Bacchus). It seems that Velasquez devised the painting in answer to critics who accused him of not being able to paint anything other than portraits. This picture was intended as a real demonstration of his competence. It was painted in about 1628 and he was paid in the following year. At the Alcázar in Madrid, Velasquez saw a bacchanalia by Ribera and another by Stanzione. The paintings had recently arrived from Naples. Velasquez must have studied the well-worked compositions carefully, aware that he was starting out in the most noble artistic genre, the painting of history, in this case mythological. This was a new field for Velasquez. The approach to this theme is characteristic of the way in which seventeenth-century Spanish culture regarded the mythological fable, interpreting it with mock sarcasm but not discounting a serious meaning. Reality, here mixed in with the classical fable, holds in its appearance many levels of meaning for the idealism and conceptism of the Baroque period. So, in this scene, whether it is bacchanalia in ordinary modern clothes or whether it is a group of rogues imitating paganism, we can interpret the picture as a eulogy of the goodness of wine, capable of providing people with consolation away from daily tribulations. The weather-beaten faces are reminiscent of those which characterize the artist's pictures form his Seville period while the compositive ambition and the introduction of nude figures anticipates his achievements during his first visit to Italy.

The first trip to Italy

Rubens' visit to Madrid influenced Velasquez in different ways. One result of this visit was that Velasquez was prompted to make an educational trip to Rome, thus indicating the special treatment that he received from the king.

La fragua de Vulcano (Vulcan's Forge) was made in Rome in 1630. It apparently forms a matching pair with *La túnica de José* (Joseph's Tunic), a work of similar dimensions also produced in Rome at the same time and which is now kept at the Escorial. It seems that the pictures were painted on Velasquez's own initiative. They were then sold to Philip IV in 1634. Although *Vulcan's Forge* presents a scene from mythology and *Joseph's Tunic* depicts a passage from Biblical history, both express the power of the word over men. Another common factor is that they both study the various human reactions and emotions in

Diego de Velasquez. *A view of the Garden at Villa Medici in Rome.*
Canvas. 48.5 χ 43 cm. Ref. 1210.

response to a stimulus. When Apollo bursts into the forge where Vulcan and the Cyclops are working iron, he discovers the adultery of his wife Venus with Mars. Confronted with this disclosure, the lame god and his colleagues display the most diverse expressions. Unlike the mocking tone of *The Festival of Bacchus,* the story is here taken seriously. In general, the story symbolizes the superiority of the intellect over manual work whose cavern the god of Arts comes to illuminate. He is dressed in an orange tunic which in itself constitutes a tribute to Poussin, who was active in Rome at that time. This bright colour contrasts with the darker earthy colours predominant in the rest of the picture. As usual, these colours combine with Velasquez's confident brush-strokes to portray the most diverse characteristics of materials ranging from mud to iron. In addition, the modelling of the seminude figures reveals the study of ancient statuary and also of contemporary Italian painters such as Guercino or Reni. This modelling reflects consummate maturity. The basic elements in the composition are derived from a print by Antonio Tempesta.

Mary of Austria, Queen of Hungary, was born the year after her brother Philip IV. She passed through Naples on her way to Vienna where she was to marry her cousin Ferdinand of Hapsburg, King of Hungry and later Emperor. This marriage resulted in the birth of Mariana, the King's second wife. Velasquez painted a portrait of Mary there in Naples but this may be one of the pictures made before the departure of the princess in 1628.

The two **Views of the Villa Medici** estate in Rome form an essential part of any appraisal of Velasquez's sensitivity as a landscape painter and of his importance as a predecessor of the nineteenth-century artists. These pictures are outstanding works from their time as they were painted in the open air, not in a studio. Although nature is humanized, it is depicted as a changing reality which we only take in for a moment. Nature's interest lies in itself, without the need for stories or background information. These paintings do not seem to prepare the way for greater works. The light and shadow express the fleeting moment when two people exchange a quick word, in contrast with an isolated figure who is contemplating the view in the background. Each picture shows a different moment of the day, differentiated by the light. However, these moments are connected by the 'Serlian' arch, a common feature of both paintings. The date of these works is a matter of debate. The Roman fashion of the time with specialist landscape painters like Paul Bril helps to explain these two masterpieces which are surprising in the context of Velasquez's first trip to Rome. On the other hand, they could be related to some of the *"pasillos"* (sketches) bought by Jerónimo de Villanueva for Philip IV in 1634. Velasquez's technique in these pictures is highly developed and close to that used to paint landscapes in portraits of hunters. The paintings recorded in the cave at the beginning of the fifties lead us to believe that these pictures were in fact made during his second trip to Rome.

The religious compositions

After returning from his first trip to Rome, Velasquez evoked a meticulous study of human proportions in **El Cristo Crucificado** (The Saint Placid Christ) In this painting, the classical canon conveys a sense of balance and serenity in spite of the theme. The picture gets its name from the convent of Benedictine nuns situated next to the street called Pez in Madrid. The church here was built in the second half of the seventeenth century and is still one of the best preserved from that period. Apparently, this painting was commissioned for the convent around 1632 or 1633 by Velasquez's patron, Jerónimo de Villanueva. He was a good client of Velasquez's but was involved in dubious business as a link between the convent and Philip IV himself. Legend has therefore identified this picture with the sins and the repentance of the king. Iconographically, it follows the design of the crucified man with four nails depicted by Pacheco, with the precedent set by Dürer and the contemporary example from Seville by Martínez Montañés. At the start of the nineteenth century, the picture became a part of the Godoy collection, inherited by the Duke of San Fernando. He then presented it as a gift to the Crown in an attempt to ingratiate himself with Ferdinand VII.

Cristo en la Cruz (Christ Crucified) is a small painting, not considered by experts to be the work of Velasquez although it was signed and dated in 1631. It was put in the Museum after the Spanish

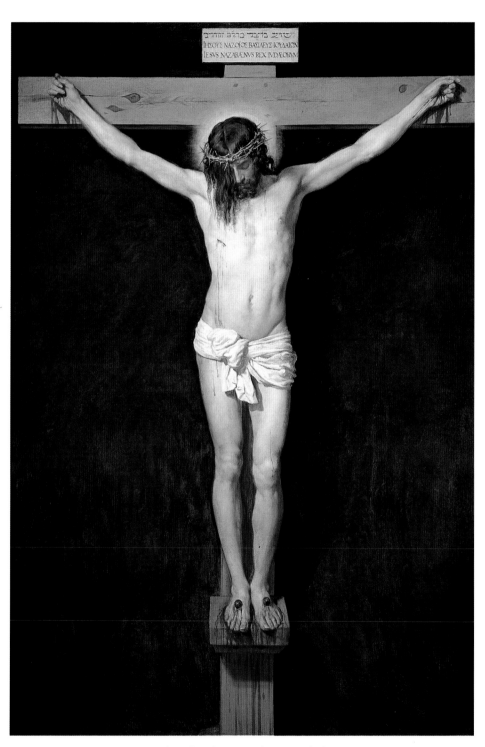

Diego de Velasquez. *Christ Crucified.*
Canvas. 248 χ 169 cm. Ref. 1167.

Civil War, having previously been housed in the Madrid convent of Las Bernardas del Sacramento.

San Antonio Abad y San Pablo, Primer Ermitaño (Saint Anthony Abad and Saint Paul, the First Hermit) is a religious picture which is at the same time a magnificent landscape painting. It was commissioned for one of the pavilions that decorated the gardens of the royal palace of El Buen Retiro. These pavilions were called "hermitages" because they had a chapel, thus giving a holy element to this Royal location. This reinforced the escape to nature as a means of searching for spiritual peace by retreating from the world. The episodes in the picture are set out with complex and subtle free-flowing artwork in a splendid landscape painting. They include Saint Anthony's complicated journey through the desert, guided by a centaur and a satyr, to reach the retreat of *San Pablo* (Saint Paul) where he had to knock at the door for a long time. The scenes also show the raven bringing the saint his daily food. After another raven arrived, he received a double ration. Following the death of Paul, we see how lions dig his grave. The magnificent brush-strokes are reminiscent of the landscapes on the Medici estate. The sense of reality is so well achieved that a later date for the painting has been suggested. Now, however, analysts tend to put the date at around 1634, when the hermitage was under construction.

La coronación de la Virgen (The Crowning of the Virgin) has been related with previous work by Dürer, El Greco, Martin de Vos or Rubens. If it is true that Velasquez used some of this artistic input in the creation of this picture, then he also demonstrated his skill in attaining a very personal interpretation of other influences. This painting was intended for the chapel in the Queen's Room at the Alcázar in Madrid. The French background of the sovereign who was then still on the throne, the reddish, violet and purple colours predominant in the group and the general outline which looks like a heart have all contributed to the belief that the picture refers to the devotion to the sacred hearts of Jesus and Mary, a religious practice promoted by the Jesuits.

Court paintings and other portraits:

Diego del Corral y Arellano was one of the high-ranking court officials whom Velasquez was to join. The cross of Santiago embroidered over his chest denotes his noble origin and the other adornments – the gown, the documents and the biretta –

reflect his position as Judge of the council of Castile, a professor in Salamanca. This portrait must have been painted shortly before he died in Madrid in 1632 at the age of 62. In 1627, he had married Antonia de Ipeñarrieta, whose bearing also indicates her social status. She is leaning on a chair, the usual posture for portraits of ladies of her social standing. These paintings came from the family mansion in Zarauz and were donated to the Museum in 1905 by the Duchess of Villahermosa.

El escultor Juan Martínez Montañés (The sculptor Juan Martínez Montañés) is a very different kind of portrait. The approach is indicative of an understandable proximity between the two artists while still emphasizing the intellectual rather than mechanical nature of the subject's art. He is perfectly dressed. This portrait was painted in about 1635-36. The bust sketched in clay is reminiscent of the one made in Madrid by Montañés and sent to Florence as a design for the equestrian statue by Pietro Tacca, now in *La Plaza de Oriente* in Madrid. Velasquez also made a joint study for the statue. This study is now kept at the Palazzo Pitti.

The painting entitled **La Sibila** (The Sibyl) undoubtedly merits this name on account of the uncertainty surrounding the identity of the protagonist. On the one hand, the small board that she is carrying appears to come from a scene of Old Testament prophecies and her gaze into infinity as if drawing inspiration is usual in this context. On the other hand, it has also been suggested that she represents Clio, the Muse of history, or perhaps also an allegory of painting. It was traditionally believed that she was "Velasquez's wife". This was certainly the interpretation existing on record in 1746 at the palace of *La Granja de San Ildefonso,* from where the painting came. Now, however, this explanation is not believed to be correct. Although the protagonist looks like one of the angels in *La imposición de la casulla a Saint Ildefonso de Sevilla* (The Placing of the Chasuble on San Ildefonso of Seville), she is not exactly the age that Juana Pacheco would have been around 1631-32, the appropriate date for this painting given its similarity to other works of an allegorical or historical nature which Velasquez produced at that time.

Velasquez painted numerous portraits of the all-powerful prime minisiter or favourite of Philip IV,

Diego de Velasquez. *The Sibyl (presumably a portrait of Juana Pacheco, the painter's wife).*
Canvas. 62 χ 50 cm. Ref. 1197.

Gaspar 'de Guzmán, Count-duke of Olivares and Duke of Sanlucar, an Andalusian gentleman whose support was decisive in the painter's court career from the beginning of the reign until the Count-Duke's downfall in 1643. In one particular portrait, the Count-Duke appears on horseback, his fall from grace already approaching but still at the height of his power. The favourite does not hesitate to adopt a very similar pose to the king in his equestrian portraits. The horse is prancing with its front feet in the air, a position effectively associated with the maximum expression of power. A whole range of symbolic, moral and political literature focussed on this image as the epitome of self-control and the domination which the prince was subjected to. Here, Olivares demonstrates his arrogance, apparent in the very expression on his face, and his power, on daring to be pictured on a more vigorous and more attractively-coloured horse than that of the sovereign himself. With complex foreshortening, the king's horse is thrust into the background where a distant battle has led to the belief that this is a reference to the battle of Fuenterrabía in 1638. This would therefore be the date of the painting. Alternatively, it could be a generic picture alluding to the Count-Duke's status as a general. On the advice of Mengs, the painting was transferred from the collection belonging to the Marquis of Ensenada to form a part of the collection owned by Charles III. Mengs hung the picture in the palace along with the other equestrian paintings by Velasquez.

El salón de reinos (The Hall of Kingdoms)

Before painting the above-mentioned portrait of Olivares, Velasquez had created several great equestrian portraits of the king. Of these, one survives. This one, together with another four equestrian portraits of the king and one of the main historical paintings by the master, made up an essential part of the *Salón de reinos* (Hall of Kingdoms) in the Palace of the Buen Retiro.

When creating *El real sitio del Buen Retiro* (The Royal Setting of El Buen Retiro), the Count-Duke of Olivares did not put a high priority on symbolic and political content except in one area: the main hall called the *Hall of Kingdoms* as a result of the

coats of arms from the various kingdoms which had merged into the Monarchy of Spain. On small canvases over the windows, there was a display of ten of the great deeds by Hercules painted by Zurbaran. They symbolized the heroic role of the sovereign while the figure of Philip IV and those of his parents, wife and heir, all on horseback in pictures positioned over the fireplace in the hall, lent a sense of dynastic glorification to the paintings. The other great pictures covering the walls were painted to order and represented a number of military victories achieved during the early years of the reign of Philip IV in line with the belligerent policy of the royal favourite. He understood the degree to which art could be used not only for the purpose of monarchic or national propaganda but also as a means of ideologically exalting his own image. In spite of its coherence and importance, this programme of embellishment lasted only a few years but the images that Velasquez created during the course of the project have proved enduring.

La rendición de Breda (The Surrender of Breda) or *Las lanzas* (The Lances) has become a symbolic image in the history of Spain. The painting depicts the handing over of the keys to the Flemish city of Breda by Justino de Nassau to Ambrosio Spinola, a Genoese general in command of the Spanish regiments. This event took place on June 5th 1625. The importance of this victory was reflected in a number of artistic and literary works. Outstanding among these are the prints by Callot, the paintings of Peter Snayers, the historical account Obsidio Bredana written by the Jesuit Hermann Hugo, the comedy by Calderón and *The Siege of Breda* first shown a few months after the event. The latter emphasizes the magnanimity of the victors:

"Honouring the vanquished
is an action worthy
of the noble victor.
He owes it to the defeated:
Losing is no disgrace...
As the bravery of the vanquished
Makes the victor famous."

Velasquez the court painter took the same view of events when he painted this canvas, no later than April 1635. Unlike other pictures that his colleagues produced for the Hall, he did not portray the battle

Diego de Velasquez.
The « Lances » or The Surrender of Breda.
Canvas. 307 χ 367 cm. Ref. 1172.

Diego de Velasquez. *Philip IV, The Hunter.*
Canvas. 191 χ 126 cm. Ref. 1184.

itself although the smoky background evokes the destruction of war. Within the code of contemporary values, he focuses on the sense of honour as the basis for promoting a "just war" and also a just peace. This begins with the actual ceremony portrayed in the picture and is to be based on the mercy shown by the victor towards the loser, an image previously developed by the emperor Augustus. The scene is set out with objective realism on the part of the artist. The expressions of the main characters and the skill involved in creating the composition convey the content with a much greater degree of efficiency than in the case of rhetorical allegories. In grouping the two semi-circles of Spanish and Dutch soldiers around the central embrace, Velasquez took up hints by other artists who had dealt with themes from the Old Testament in a similar way. However, he created a highly individual painting in which he deployed all the facets of his artistic style – the open air, light and landscape, the science of perspective and the immediacy of the portrait.

Two of the five equestrian portraits that occupy the two short spaces above the fireplace in the *Hall of Kingdoms* are purely the work of Velasquez whereas in the other three he corrected and enriched compositions by other painters from Madrid. These three comprise a pair of portraits of the parents of the monarchs, Philip III and Margarita, and one of Queen Isabel. In the pictures, very detailed clinical artwork characteristic of painters such as Bartolomé González exists alongside magnificent touches by Velasquez which give the paintings enormous value. Moreover, Velasquez seems to have made contributions at different times, both before and after his first trip to Italy. A picture that can be attributed to González is the portrait of *Philip III* who is wearing the type of wide ruff fashionable during his reign. His prancing horse represents authority and majesty. The painting can be ascribed to González because it fairly accurately matches the description of a portrait of the King with a *"traje rozagante"* (striking costume) that he used for his arrival on the banks of the river Tagus in Lisbon in 1619. This city actually appears in the background of the picture. However, the surface areas have been brightened up by Velasquez. With magnificent flourishes of artwork, he completely repainted the heads and the manes of the steeds on which *Margarita of Austria* and Isabel de Valois ride. In fact, González painted *La casa de campo* (The Country House) estate in Madrid deep inside the steeds.

The other two equestrian portraits are entirely the work of Velasquez. In the portrait of Philip IV on horseback, Velasquez has, without imitating, assimilated the lessons learnt from Titian's picture of Charles V and the lost portrait of Philip IV painted by Rubens in Madrid in 1628 and which served as a replacement in the *Hall of Mirrors* at the Alcázar for Velasquez's portrait of the King in 1626. Without the grandiloquence of Flemish painting but instead with realism, Velasquez portrays the majestic upright serenity of the king and conveys the concept that like an armed general, he will take the reins of the state and of his own character with as firm a hand as the one he uses to restrain the onrush of his prancing horse. Never was a portrait as flattering without appearing so.

The portrait of Baltasar Carlos on horseback represented an optimistic projection of the dynasty into the future. It occupied the space over the door between the portraits of his parents. This high position explains the unusual foreshortening used in painting the small horse whose outline stands out against the Sierra del Guadarrama mountains in the background. The free-flowing brush-strokes and the attractive shades of blue are characteristic of Velasquez's most exquisite works.

Decorating *La Torre de la Parada* (La Parada Tower)

In *La Parada Tower,* one room differed from the others in that it was decorated only with paintings containing hunting scenes. There were works by Snayders together with one by Velasquez which is now in the National Gallery, London. In addition, the room held three portraits of male members of the royal families pictured during a break in the hunt. Since the Middle Ages, hunting had been regarded as a suitable preparation for war on the part of the high classes. In itself a reflection of war, hunting necessitated the application of useful qualities such as patience, guile, and sound judgement. It also had the effect of strengthening the body and sweeping away the melancholic feelings brought on by leisure. Therefore, the room constituted a peaceful and intimate, albeit exclusively masculine, version of

Diego de Velasquez. *Philip III on Horseback.*
Canvas. 300 χ 314 cm. Ref. 1176.

Diego de Velasquez. *Queen Margarita of Austria on Horseback.*
Canvas. 297 χ 309 cm. Ref. 1177.

the dynastic display presented in *Salón de reinos* (The Hall of Kingdoms).

The portrait of *Philip IV,* the hunter, is usually considered to be from the beginning of the 1630s. In the painting, some objects in fact have a very similar colour and are only highlighted by lighter shades at the points which stand out most. Velasquez appears to revel in overcoming these self-imposed limitations and achieves an extremely stylish result.

El cardenal-infante don Fernando (The Cardinal-Prince Ferdinand) was born in 1609 and was the younger brother of the king. He became Governor of Flanders from 1634 to 1641, thus succeeding his aunt Isabel Clara Eugenia. Therefore, it is usually thought that Velasquez painted a portrait of him in the period immediately before i.e. between 1632 and 1634. However, it has also been suggested that the painting was made later and based on the portrait of a bust.

The portrait of *El príncipe Baltasar Carlos* (Prince Baltasar Carlos), the hunter, was painted when he was six years old in 1635-36. It portrays an active and intelligent child on whose shoulders rested hopes for a very capable successor to take charge of such a vast kingdom. These expectations were dashed by his premature death at the age of sixteen. In the picture, the dogs represent loyalty. One of them was cut out, since the canvas was originally wider on the right-hand side, allowing the subject of the portrait to occupy a more central position. His relaxed pose matches the open-air feeling of the landscape. Velasquez portrays *El Monte del Pardo* (The Prado Hillside) in a new light. In the distance, we can see the Sierra del Guadarrama mountains where *La torre de la Parada* (The Parada Tower) is located.

For other rooms at *La torre de la Parada,* Velasquez produced pictures that complemented some of the aspects developed by Flemish painters, specifically, the mythological god Mars and two ancient philosophers, Aesop and Menipo, who appear to correspond to Rubens, Heraclito and Demócrito.

Esopo (Aesop), a figure with basic human dignity, was one of the paintings that had the most influence on nineteenth-century painters, from Goya onwards. Velasquez adopts Ribera's idea of updating the image of the poor ancient philosopher with wretched modern rags, suiting his independent detached outlook, away from wealth. The attitude

of the painter towards the resourceful character has been the subject of numerous and varying interpretations. Analysis focusses on the ambiguous expression and the structure of the face, bovine according to contemporary essays on facial features. The bundles and the pail of water refer to incidents in his life.

Menipo, another of the "Simple Greek philosophers" and originally a slave, uses his sly smile to express a less equivocal attitude to reality, one which apparently does not deserve to be taken seriously. These two paintings can be categorized together, along with the pictures of Mars and another two philosophers, *Heraclito* and *Demócrito,* created by Rubens for the same tower. All of these paintings are of a similar size. It is attractive to think that they constitute a reflection on the vanity of the world and of authority. They provide suitable decoration for a museum in the middle of a plain Castilian oak wood used as a winter hunting ground by the Spanish monarchs. As such, they must have been painted by the artist from Seville around 1639-1640 in response to works by Rubens.

In this context, Velasquez painted **Mars,** a flabby soldier with a floppy moustache who had seen better days. His melancholic tiredness does not indicate victory. It does, however, tie in with the critical and personal view that Velasquez took of mythological themes in *Baco and Vulcano* (Bacchus and Vulcan). There is also a link with his portraits of jesters. In fact, one of them, Antonio Bañules, was painted in a mythological style. Although it is risky to assume that this is a portrayal of a monarchy in decline, the fact is that it was painted around 1640 at the time of the serious crisis involving Catalonia and Portugal. This led to the downfall of Olivares and initiated a decade of serious disillusionment. Velasquez utilized prestigious cultural references associated with a military image, such as the Ares Ludovisi and Michelangelo's Pensieroso. He then combined them with unprecedented masterful artwork. Velasquez displays wisdom and independence from Rubens in giving form and shape to the figures. The result is a work of art with deep significance that has led to a great deal of written analysis in terms of the decline of Spain and the picaresque genre.

The head of the deer is a 'portrait' of an animal pictured at a moment of suspended movement, full of life. This hunting theme of "the prize catch" was

Diego de Velasquez. *Mars.*
Canvas. 179 χ 95 cm. Ref. 1208.

the subject of other paintings made for the tower and even formed the basis of literary works at the time of Philip IV. The history of this particular painting is not known but it must have come from a Royal House. In 1920, it was acquired by the Marquis of Casa Torres who donated it to the Museum in 1975.

Dwarves, jesters and entertainers

The portrait of **Pablo de Valladolid** displays this self-imposed limitation of resources and colour. There is, however, a wealth of shades. The result is amazing. The space, suggested only by the shadow, highlights the presence of the subject, a comic character already in the service of the court in 1632 and who died in 1648. The date of this painting is generally thought to be 1632-35. Manet admired the picture and drew inspiration from it in order to paint the fife.

Barbarroja (Redbeard) is a portrait of the jester Cristobal de Castañeda y Pernia, who was at the court between 1633 and 1649. His quarrelsome character perhaps justified the pose Velasquez assigned him in the portrait by setting him against **Don Juan de Austria** (Juan of Austria) whose obviously shy character makes his assumed role as the hero of Lepanto seem grotesque. Both portraits are supposed to have been painted between 1632 and 1634 in order to decorate the Palace of El Buen Retiro where there existed a staircase called "de los bufones" (of the jesters) on account of its decoration. But the free-flowing brush-strokes, particularly in the background to the battle featuring Juan of Austria, have led to suggestions that the pictures were painted at a later date. Barbarroja was apparently left unfinished, as the quality of the artwork on the cloak is certainly much less impressive than for the very expressive face.

The portrait of *Diego de Acedo, "el primo"* seems to have been made for *La torre de la Parada* (The Parada Tower). He was an Official of the Royal Seal, the reproduction of the King's signature with a stamp. As such, he is surrounded by volumes and inkwells that give an idea of his small stature.

Sebastian de Morra is a portrait that can be dated between 1643 and 1649, the years when he served

prince Baltasar Carlos. This picture of a jester is one of the most evocative by Velasquez. We can see the contrast between the reflective seriousness of his expression and the deformity of his body, the rotundity with which he occupies the foreground, and the contrasts between the red and green of his clothes. It is therefore not surprising that Wilde used this type of image as a basis for a story on the theme of man's inhumanity to man.

Francisco Lezcano was called The Child of Vallecas in eighteenth-century records and has been described as a mentally retarded cretin by modern science. The portrait is no less impressive with the protagonist's rounded and deformed presence in the foreground, his ambiguous face and his hands holding a pack of cards. The painting enjoyed great literary attention in Spain in the twentieth century. It comes from *La torre de la Parada*.

Juan Calabacillas, whose surname or nickname was not unheard of among court jesters and referred to his lack of sanity, is one of Velasquez's most surprising portraits in terms of technique and composition. This is evident in the indefinable nature of the space and the extravagant pose of the subject together with his perturbing smile. The portrait must have been painted in 1639, the year of his death.

The royal family

The last decade of Velasquez's life coincided with the king's second marriage. At this time, the aged and disillusioned king had to endure speculation about the Monarchy's huge inheritance, to be divided between a prince, Felipe Próspero (who died prematurely) or one of the two princesses whose marriages therefore became a matter or the greatest political interest in Europe. As a result, their portraits also became extremely important.

Felipe IV (Philip IV) in black and in the form of a bust represents the official likeness of the king in the last ten years of his life. It was made between 1653 and 1657, when it was circulated in print. With the male heirs to the throne dead – the future Charles II was not born until 1661 – and the international influence of Spain diminished, the monarch took refuge in his collection of paintings. He fell into disillusionment, a spirit also reflected by contemporary writers such as Barrionuevo. An analysis of the

Diego de Velasquez. *Pablo of Valladolid.*
Canvas. 209 χ 123 cm. Ref. 1198.

Diego de Velasquez.
The Jester Called Don Juan de Austria.
Canvas. 210 χ 124.5 cm. Ref. 1200.

king's state of mind focuses on his facial features, ignoring all other aspects. This is in total contrast to customary practice in Baroque portraiture.

Queen Mariana of Austria had been the intended bride for her cousin Baltasar Carlos. Finally, however, she got married to her uncle Philip in 1649. Her portrait could not be painted by Velasquez until he returned from his second trip to Italy, where he stayed between 1649 and 1651. Even then, Queen Mariana was not well enough to have her portrait painted and so this caused a further delay until 1652 or 1653. In a very narrow space, there is ample room for all the elements of a royal portrait- the chair, the curtains, the symbolic clock, the costume itself. The symphony of red, grey, black and white colours has been composed with fresh free-flowing brush-strokes. This masterpiece was intended for the Escorial and formed a matching pair with the portrait or Philip IV in armour with a lion at his feet, certainly a studio piece, in which a previous portrait of the king was reproduced against a well-constructed background. The grandiloquence of the symbolic attributes was never a feature of Velasquez's work, even less in his last decade.

The portrait of *La infanta Margarita de Austria* (Princess Margarita of Austria) is much more surprising in terms of the master's process of self-limitation, and it is now attributed to his pupil and son-in-law Juan Bautista Martínez del Mazo on the basis of technical aspects and a study of the composition where incoherence and variations in quality appear. There are some admirable sections such as the neckerchief and her costume in general. Traditionally, therefore, it was thought that this had been the last painting by Velasquez with finishing touches by Mazo.

The last great compositions

Following his second trip to Italy, the last ten years of the painter's life were taken up by his duties as the king's Master of the Chamber, responsible for decorative paintings in El Alcázar and the Escorial, and by definitive success in his court career. Consequently, the pace of his creative output declined although his most universally famous compositions date from that time.

Las hilanderas o la fábula de Aracne (The Spinners or Aracne's fable) is apparently an every-day scene from the Santa Isabel upholstery workshop in Madrid but in fact deals with a mythological theme, The Fable of Aracne. In this story, the legendary Greek weaver was so confident in her skill that she challenged Minerva to a competition. The result was a tie but the goddess turned the mortal into a spider on the pretext of having dared to include the love life of Jupiter, the goddess's father, in her work. Indeed, in the background, we can see in the form of a tapestry *El Rapto de Europa* (The Abduction of Europe)by Titian which was then a part of Philip IV's collection (now it is in Boston but the Prado holds the copy made by Rubens in Madrid). Confronted by the woven scene, the helmeted Minerva strikes Aracne with lightning as three personifications of the Arts look on. And in the workroom, apparently so ordinary, the three main figures, for whom Velasquez was inspired by some of Michelangelo's figures in the Sistine Chapel, represent the Three Fates who interweave the strands of human life. The overall purpose of the picture, therefore, is to create an allegory of the dignified nature of plastic arts and in a subtle way to demonstrate the success of the painter in emulating his two main masters, Titian and Rubens. Technically, it is a fully mature work by Velasquez although it is not clear whether it was produced immediately before or just after his last trip to Italy. It belonged to the king's huntsman, Pedro de Arce, and then to the Duke of Medinaceli. Since 1711, it has formed a part of the Royal Collection. In approximately 1765, the picture was enlarged by Calleja so as to make it suitable for decorating Charles III's royal chamber at the Royal Palace in Madrid. He added strips at the top and on the sides, seriously impairing the overall effect of the composition. It is essential to visualize the picture without these added strips.

Las Meninas o la familia de Felipe IV is another picture in which latent allusions and complex meanings underlie the realistic appearance of the visible story line. There is room for diverse interpretations. Moreover, they are not incompatible. In a room of the prince's royal chamber at the Alcázar in Madrid, Velasquez is working on a large picture, perhaps a portrait of Philip IV and Margarita, who occupy the place where the observer would be, given that their faces are reflected in the background mirror. Perhaps the portrait is of princess Margarita, the girl served by

Diego de Velasquez. *The Spinners or Aracne's Fable.*
Canvas. 220 χ 289 cm. Ref. 1173.

Diego de Velasquez. *Mercury and Argos.*
Canvas. 127 χ 250 cm. Ref. 1175.

two of her young ladies or meninas María Agustina Sarmiento, who is offering her a jug of water, and Isabel Velasco, who is making as if to curtsy. Everything in the picture moves smoothly, bearing in mind how difficult it was to be sure who should inherit the throne of Spain then, in 1656. This five-year-old girl was the presumptive heir and the subject of complicated dynastic intrigues. Fifty years later, following the reign of the unfortunate Charles II who was born in 1661, a war of succession set the descendants of this future empress against those of her sister, who was married to Louis XIV. The grandson, Philip V, became the first Spanish King from the House of Bourbon. Going back to the picture, we can see other palace servants like the Master of the Chamber José Nieto on the staircase, a bodyguard talking to lady Marcela de Ulloa, and the dwarves María Bárbola and Nicolasito Pertusato who, perhaps personifying rebellion, is harassing the dog, the image of loyalty. The artist, who had been decorated with the Cross of Santiago, filled in this detail two years after finishing the picture. Here, he expresses the dignified nature of his art by openly pursuing it as he thinks in the presence of the monarchs. The concept of art is reinforced by the mythological stories portrayed in the pictures in the background – Minerva and Aracne, and Apollo and Marsias – copies of Rubens and Jordaens by Mazo. But the supreme demonstration of the dignity of his art is the mathematical construction of space in perspective, the masterly touches and the expertise used in the composition, whose complex equilibrium does not deprive it of a natural appearance.

Mercurio y Argos (Mercury and Argos) seems similarly fortuitous but the theft of the cow by the god of eloquence and commerce who lulls the hundred-eyed guard to sleep with his flute in order to kill him is an allegory about the need to constantly be on the alert. The picture was painted in 1659 (one year before the artist's death) together with three other mythological and symbolic scenes. It was intended for the Hall of Mirrors where ambassadors were received in the Alcázar. It was designed to be placed above a window, thus necessitating a difficult format from a low perspective with light entering from below for the chiaroscuro of the composition. Very skilfully completed with bold and fluent brushwork, the picture shows the extent to which Velasquez developed the techniques learnt from the masters of Venice and Flanders.

SPANISH PAINTING IN THE SEVENTEENTH CENTURY (continuation) Rooms 16a, 17 and 17a

Alonso Cano (1601-1667) was born in Granada and worked as a sculptor and an architect as well as a painter. He was educated in Seville where he was a fellow pupil of Velasquez. A great traveller, he also became familiar with the court. Although not many of his works are on display in the Prado Museum, some very characteristic ones can be seen. His tightly-packed brush-strokes combine with a balance almost in the Renaissance style. The canvas paintings *Un rey* (A King) and *Dos reyes* (Two Kings) date from around 1645. They were intended for *El salón de comedias o dorado* (The Comedy or Golden Hall) at the Alcázar in Madrid. In the pictures, we can see medieval monarchs who are seated and wearing apparel appropriate to the theatre. Their appearance is histrionic. The exaggerated foreshortening contributes to a strange image, similar to that of the jesters. This is partly explained by the very high position of these pictures, placed on a frieze. Technically, they are works of the highest quality with skilful touches of white light.

El milagro del pozo (The Miracle of the Well) was painted in approximately 1648. It portrays the well-known incident when a child was saved by *San Isidro Labrador* (Saint Isidro the Ploughman), the patron saint of Madrid. A picture from the artist's Madrid period, it displays traces of Titian in a warm range attributable to Cano's knowledge of the royal collection. This lends distinctive features to the canvas and is significant in terms of his artistic development taken as a whole.

Cristo muerto sostenido por un ángel (The Dead Christ Held up by an Angel) is a signed painting from around 1646-1652. There exist other versions on this theme, inspired, like this one, by Mannerist prints in the style of Michelangelo. In the picture, the angel is holding a burning candle in his right hand. This candle appears from behind the head of Christ in a strange effect of the light and acts as a substitute for the halo. The painting has always been very well received by the critics due to the excellent drawing and the strong but delicate modelling.

The canvas *San Bernardo y la Virgen* (Saint Bernard and the Virgin) was painted in Madrid around 1658-1660 for a monastery in Toledo. The

Diego de Velasquez. *Las Meninas or the Family of Philip IV.*
Canvas. 220 χ 289 cm. Ref. 1173.

overall cold and stiff impression makes it one of Cano's less attractive works. Mention has been made of the pleasing colour scheme although this proves to be somewhat anomalous. The iconography must seem surprising to any mentality other than the Spanish devotional baroque mind. The kneeling saint receives into his mouth a stream of milk arising from the Virgin's bosom. In the foreground, a cardinal witnesses the marvel with his back turned towards us.

The Seville School of painting again achieved maximum prestige with the advent of Bartolomé Esteban **Murillo** (1618-1682). He escaped the attentions of the court but became universally well-known as a result of coming into contact with contemporary painting from the most diverse origins. Initially tenebrist, following in the footsteps of Zurbaran and Ribera, Murillo later achieved a very original range of light resulting from his assimilation of masters such as Van Dyck and Velasquez. The basis for Murillo's universal reputation was established at the beginning of the eighteenth century and his fame lasted until the middle of the nineteenth century. At this time, wholesale changes in art trends meant that his work gave way to more expressive forms. A pleasant painter, full of domestic mysticism, he anticipated eighteenth-century rococo sensitivity, the key to his subsequent success. In Spain, Isabel de Farnesio made a decisive contribution to a revival of Murillo's art. During the *"lustro real"* (royal lustrum) when the court resided in Seville, she searched for his canvas paintings and collected them. As a result, the Prado Museum holds an important selection of his work although not one which is comparable with the collection of his paintings at the museum of Seville.

La Sagrada Familia del pajarito (The Holy Family of the Little Bird) dates from before 1650 and is therefore a relatively youthful work. In the painting, the aesthetics of naturalism combine with a still tenebrist lighting technique. However, the picture already shows his characteristic Seville theme of popular devotion, soft and direct. It was painted in the context of a reassessment of the patriarch Saint Joseph that was then taking place in Spanish Baroque devotion. Here, the artist connects this theme with family values that are especially dear to him.

Santa Ana y la Virgen (Saint Ann and the Virgin) was painted around 1650. The picture expresses a theme which is common in work by the Seville School although perhaps this piece was inspired by a composition from Rubens. The influence of the Flemish painter can be seen in the background architecture and in the portrayal of the two angels descending over the girl with a crown of roses. But with his delicate shades, Murillo here anticipates his subsequent artistic style, moving increasingly away from naturalism.

The two semi-circular arches are exceptional works originating from the church of Santa María la Blanca in Seville. They were made in 1650 and display magnificent Neo-classical frameworks added by Percier in Paris, where they had been taken as a result of the French invasion. These expressive and mature paintings undoubtedly constitute two of Murillo's most important works of art. They depict the fourth century legend concerning the foundation of the basilica of Saint Mary the Elder in Rome. *El sueño de Patricio* (Patrick's Dream) presents a large-scale domestic scene with the emergence of the Virgin to ask the protagonist to construct the temple. The extraordinarily vivid portrayal of this tightly-packed interior setting contrasts with the way that the landscape is broken off at the side. In conclusion, the painting anticipates Murillo's late vaporous style, the culmination of his artistic development. *La visita de Patricio al papa Liberio* (Patrick's Visit to Pope Liberius) is a similar composition, also with a diminishing effect but the other way round. The landscape is the scene of a procession while, on the other side, great structural complexity is evident in the arrangement of the group presided over by the Pope against a magnificent architectural background with superb resplendent tapestry. This backdrop shows strong Venetian influence.

Murillo specialized as a painter of children and varied his pictures according to the type of genre setting required by his middle-class clientele made up of foreign merchants resident in Seville. Due to the nature of this commissioned work, the Prado Museum does not possess any of these child portraits produced without a religious pretext. *El Buen Pastor* (The Good Shepherd) was certainly painted later than 1655 and comes from the artist's mature period. The artist uses restraint in painting the elegant melancholic figure. This softness of style later proved detrimental to Murillo's fortunes following changes in art trends. *Los niños de la concha* (The Children of the Shell) dates from about 1670 and is

Bartolomé Esteban Murillo.
The Holy family and the little Bird.
Canvas. 144 χ 188 cm. Ref. 960.

Bartolomé Esteban Murillo.
Saint Anne and the Virgin.
Canvas. 219 χ 165 cm. Ref. 968.

one of his most popular pictures. It can be interpreted in two ways, either at face value, close to the genre, or in religious terms. The latter view is reinforced by the outburst of glory with angels. Here, Murillo displays the pleasant religious forms demanded by his devotees. However, he uses a golden colour scheme and vaporous brush-strokes which go beyond all conventional concepts of piety. The composition derives from Guido Reni.

If there is a type of painting by Murillo that quintessentially expresses the aspirations of Seville baroque devotion, then it is undoubtedly his portrayal of *La Inmaculada* (The Immaculate Virgin). This genre had already been perfectly defined in this Andalusian city but Murillo definitively reinterpreted the theme. However, his excessive use of reproductions and the eighteenth century turnround in artistic taste made it difficult for Murillo to tune into contemporary sensitivity with these works. The Prado Museum contains four versions. The so-called *Inmaculada de El Escorial* (The Immaculate Virgin of the Escorial) dates from about 1660-65. It was previously called the Immaculate Virgin of La Granja as it was thought to have come from that palace. The subject is extremely young. Murillo carefully prepared the composition. For the first time, he presents angels in an open arrangement instead of drawing a "pedestal" under the protagonist. The truly distinguished colouring is an outstanding feature of this canvas painting.

Among more than thirty versions on this theme produced by Murillo, the most prominent is *The Inmaculada de Soult* (The Immaculate Virgin of Soult) named after the French major-general who took it out of a hospital in Seville called *Los Venerables*. The picture is remarkable not so much because of its artistic expression but more on account of the quality of the painting itself together with the variety of detail and the magnificent angelic choir. Everything is subject to a greater awareness of space. Painted around 1678, the picture also stands out due to the wealth of colours on the children's bodies and the interplay of whites and blues on the Virgin.

Juan de Valdés Leal (1622-1690), a painter from Seville, is hardly represented in the museum. Nevertheless, two pictures provide evidence of his unusual and very individual style of art. The signed canvas painting of San Jerónimo (Saint Jerome) dates from around 1656-57. It comes from the sacristy of the monastery in Seville belonging to the order. There, it formed part of a series on saints and friars also pertaining to the order. All this influenced the composition and meaning of the painting. The full figure of the saint is visible. He has a pen in his hand. Standing next to an office and against an architectural background with a thick curtain, he appears to be searching for inspiration for his writing.

Cristo camino del calvario (Christ on the Road to Calvary) is a signed painting form 1661. Very close up in the foreground, we can see the impressive but strange figure of Christ bent under the weight of the cross. The figure is illuminated from the front. In contrast with the direct and intense drama of the situation, the background landscape is painted with extremely free-flowing brush-strokes dispelling all explicit indications of the place. There exists another version with a different format.

Francisco de Herrera (1622-1685) was born in Seville but he trained as an artist in Italy. He was nicknamed *"el joven"* (The Youngster) or *"el mozo"* (The Young Lad). He brought back decorative baroque from Italy and applied it to tremendously successful altar pictures. He had a great influence in redirecting Spanish painting towards this new language of triumphalism. To this effect, he found more suitable scope in Madrid than in the now decadent Seville. His *Triunfo de San Hermenegildo* (The Triumph of Saint Hermenegildo) was painted in 1654. It returns to a characteristic theme of Seville devotion in evocatively anti-traditional terms. The protagonist appears in magnificent flight, confusing the Arian authorities whose large-scale figures can be seen in the foreground. This canvas painting was bought for the museum by Ferdinand VII.

Friar Juan Rizi (1600-1681) from the Madrid School is represented by the portrait of General Tiburcio of Redin. The picture was painted before 1637, the year when the subject of the portrait became a Capuchin friar. This canvas, with a technique that is firm but at the same time mellow and rather free-flowing, shows the influence of Velasquez, Rizi's contemporary. It is no coincidence that it was attributed to Martínez del Mazo. Although the picture is very noteworthy as a portrait, Friar Juan Rizi rarely developed this type of painting.

Antonio de Pereda. *Saint Jerome.*
Canvas. 105 χ 84 cm. Ref. n° 1046.

Antonio de Pereda (1611-1678) is a very important figure in the Madrid School of the seventeenth century. In 1634, he produced his only work that can really be classified as a court painting. This was *Socorro de Génova por el segundo marqués de Santa Cruz* (The Relief of Genoa by the Second Marquis of Santa Cruz), an episode that had taken place in 1625. This picture was designed to form a part of the great battle series in *El salón de reinos* (The Hall of Kingdoms) at the palace of El Buen Retiro. The painting is a youthful work, achieving a limited impact. The Spanish general and the doge merge into the large group or frieze in the foreground. The afore-mentioned battle appears in the background. However, the city in the picture bears no resemblance to Genoa at all and furthermore, appears to be Antwerp.

In 1643, Pereda signed *San Jerónimo escuchando la trompeta* (Saint Jerome Listening to the Trumpet). In the immediate foreground, we can see an open book with the Last Judgement from the small Passion by Dürer as well as other objects that make up the moral death of nature, the genre in which Antonio de Pereda excelled.

An extraordinary work from the artist's best period is *San Pedro liberado por un ángel* (Saint Peter Released by an Angel), also signed in 1643. Whereas the design of the Saint is reminiscent of Ribera, the figure of the angel shows northern European influence, specifically the Dutch pupils of Caravaggio from the first naturalist wave. But Pereda reinterprets these borrowings with his own indistinctive colouring derived from Venetian influence and his characteristic frothy brush-strokes.

One of the most prominent works by the prolific Madrid painter Francisco Rizi 1614-1685) is *La Anunciación* (The Annunciation). It was painted in about 1662 during his most advanced phase. The picture is along the lines of some of his previous compositions but the technique is more progressive and is characterized by free artwork, brightness, the striking colour and the width and clarity of the background. The painting was probably intended for the top of a reredos. A picture with a very different significance is the enormous *Auto de fe* (Auto-da-fé), signed in 1683. It portrays the great inquisition ceremony held in *La Plaza Mayor* (The Main Square) in Madrid on June 30th 1680 and presided over by Charles II. A work of far-reaching importance from a historical and descriptive point of view, it makes us regret the loss of so many other paintings with the same scope. In spite of its inherent limitations, the picture individually depicts the most varied characters from society within the crowd setting.

Velasquez was such an exceptional genius that he could not be, categorized strictly speaking, within a particular school. Apart from the artistic output of his son-in-law and pupil Martínez del Mazo, there exists a series of paintings displaying considerable quality which can be generically ascribed to Velasquez's studio. The canvas painting *La fuente de los tritones* (The Fountain of the Tritons) was first attributed to Velasquez himself and later to Mazo. The date 1657 which appears on the fountain refers to the working of the material, not to the actual picture. The fountain in question was previously in the gardens of Aranjuez and is now in the Campo del Moro in Madrid. Seen from a high perspective against a background of poplar trees forming a kind of green blanket, this scene has strong evocative power apart from its obvious artistic value.

Juan Bautista Martínez del Mazo (c. 1615-1667) not only displayed the knowledge acquired from his father-in-law but he was also the fortunate imitator of Titian and Rubens. In addition, he was very familiar with the work of Claudio de Lorena. Besides one or two other works that are described as pertaining to Velasquez owing to the recency of their assignation, it is appropriate to point out **Vista de Zaragoza** (A View of Saragossa). This painting was commissioned by prince Baltasar Carlos who died in Saragossa in 1646. Apparently, he decided the location where the view of the city should be painted. Signed in 1647, the picture constitutes an extremely important iconographic legacy as well as being an excellent painting, amply demonstrated by the numerous small figures filling the foreground in the Velasquez style. In fact, until recently, the figures were attributed to the master himself. In the middle of the nineteenth century, a part of the picture was removed, namely the Virgin of the Pilar held up by angels floating in heaven. As a result, the view took on an unreligious or secular character which is unusual in Spanish painting.

The portrait of *La Emperatriz Margarita de Austria* (The Empress Margarita of Austria) was painted in 1666, the year of her wedding. The mistaken inscription confuses her with princess Maria

Martínez del Mazo.
A view of the city of Saragossa.
Canvas. 181 χ 333 cm. Ref. n° 889.

Francisco de Herrera.
The Triumph of Saint Hermenegild.
Canvas. 328 χ 229 cm. Ref. n° 833.

Teresa. Following court convention, she is resting her right hand on the back of an armchair and carrying some gloves in her left hand. Without diminishing the obvious artistic interest of the painting, it serves the additional purpose of providing a curious illustration of palace life as, in the background, we can see Charles II the boy with the female dwarf Maribarbola, a lady and a lady in waiting.

Juan Carreño de Miranda succeeded Velasquez as the royal portrait painter and partially adopted his artistic style. Miranda's portrait of *Carlos II* (Charles II) has given us a vivid impression of the personality of the last member of the Austrian royal family. Here, the king is standing in front of one of the consoles in the *Hall of Mirrors* at the Alcázar in line with court etiquette for audiences with ambassadors. This canvas painting is part of a series whose leading work is the version housed in *El museo de Bellas Artes* (The Museum of Fine Arts) of Asturias. This version dates from 1671.

El duque de Pastrana (The Duke of Pastrana) is a superb portrait from around 1665-70. Its composition and colouring make it one of the paintings with the most restrained magnificence in the whole of Spanish art. The picture shows obvious connections with Van Dyck who was in the service of Charles I of England. This can be seen in the generic concept of portraying an aristocrat in an informal style within a landscape setting. The influence of Van Dyck can also be observed in particular aspects of the composition.

The portrait of Pedro Ivanowitz Potemkin, the Russian ambassador, is an equally important work of art. It was painted in 1681, the date of his second trip to Spain. Carreño depicts his eastern ceremonial splendour with magnificent red and gold effects reminiscent of the spent palette of the last Titian. Nevertheless, we cannot discount direct traces of Van Dyck in this canvas painting.

Between 1667 and 1668, **Juan Antonio Escalante** (1633-1669) produced a series of eucharistic allegories for the sacristy of the monastery of La Merced Calzada in Madrid. The series was always highly praised. Two outstanding canvas paintings both signed in 1667 are *La prudente Abigail* (Prudent Abigail) and *Triunfo de la fe sobre los sentidos* (The Triumph of Faith over the Senses). Due to the subject matter, the second picture involves a type of symbolic iconography which is unusual in

Spanish painting although it is common in emblematic prints. The personifications of the five senses are put into focus by the Chalice with the sacred form sustaining Faith and also projecting light onto the background blue.

A characteristic canvas painting by **José Antolínez** (1635-1675) is *La Inmaculada Concepción* (The Immaculate Conception) signed in 1665, contains beautiful blue colours. There are two other versions dating from the following year. The picture shows a crown of stars and the essential little angels bearing emblems.

The ill-fated **Mateo Cerezo** (1637-1666) painted *El juicio de un alma* (The Trial of a Soul). Perhaps this is not a genre painting but instead a reference to a specific story. The personification of the spirit is portrayed as a very small-scale nude figure kneeling down between Saint Dominic and Saint Francis. These two intercessors are joined by the Virgin who is pictured above, addressing Christ. This is a work of art displaying great technical quality and splendid colouring. It is very close to the style of Carreño and some analysts have even attributed the painting to him.

Claudio Coello (1642-1693) provided a fitting climax to the work of the Madrid School. *El triunfo de San Agustín* (The Triumph of Saint Augustine), signed in 1664, is a magnificent composition with brilliant colouring. It is very evocative of the baroque decorativism of the time. Against a background partially made up of architecture, the saint, who is dressed in pontifical vestments, flies among clouds and angels while below to the right, we can see an infernal dragon and the statue of a classical god. These represent absolute evil and pagan religion respectively. Their inclusion is a typical Catholic triumphalist gesture.

The great canvas painting *La Virgen y el Niño adorados por San Luis rey de Francia* (The Virgin and Child Adored by Saint Louis, King of France) was signed by the artist in approximately 1665-1668. It is a variation on the theme of holy conversation, a very unusual type of painting in Spanish art. This picture was based on a piece by Mateo Cerezo and indirectly derives from Rubens.

Santo Domingo de Guzmán (Saint Dominic of Guzmán) was painted around 1684-85. It came from the Madrid monastery of El Rosario. In the picture, the very low perspective reinforces the enormity of

Juan Carreño de Miranda. *Charles II.*
Canvas. 201 χ 141 cm. Ref. nº 642.

the figure. Saint Dominic has a globe at his feet and, to one side, his symbol of a dog with a burning lamp. The concept is similar to that used for reredos sculptures and it is therefore housed in a kind of side-chapel.

SPANISH PAINTING IN THE EIGHTEENTH CENTURY
Rooms 19, 20, 21 and 22

Eclipsed by the genius of Goya, eighteenth-century Spanish painting was the object of regular reassessment. Whereas art from the first half of the eighteenth-century showed low-key links with the traditional art of the seventeenth, the second half of the century was characterized by the work of foreign masters active in Spain such as Guiaquinto, Tiepolo and Mengs. In this latter period, styles ranged from the latest international baroque to academic classicism, whose restrictions very few artists apart from Goya managed to elude.

The Saragossa painter **Francisco Bayeu** (1734-1795) who was actually related to Goya, pursued several genres. Influenced by Mengs and also by Guiaquinto, his frescoes are represented here by a number of important sketches that illustrate his compositive skill. They are the following: *La asunción de la Virgen* (The Assumption of the Virgin), made in about 1760 for a section of the dome at the monastery church of Santa Engracia, Saragossa; *El Olimpo o La caída de los gigantes* (Olympus or The Fall of the Giants) made in 1764 for a vault at the royal palace in Madrid; *La creación de Adán* (The Creation of Adam) for the now destroyed decoration of the vault and the supports at the collegiate church of La Granja, and *La monarquía española con las órdenes* (The Spanish Monarchy with the Orders) in chiaroscuro, begun in 1794 for another ceiling in the palace.

Among his portraits, that of his daughter, Feliciana Bayeu, was painted in about 1788 and is on display in the Prado. The painting has a certain expressive intensity that is rather inappropriate for this thirteen-year-old youngster. There are also strange blue-pink touches.

Regarding his work for the Royal Tapestry Factory, so much a result of Goya's initiative, we can highlight the sketches for the festive cartoons entitled *Merienda en el campo* (The Picnic) and *El Paseo de las Delicias* (Delicias Avenue), created in 1784 and in about 1785 respectively. Both were connected with the decoration programmes for the Pardo palace. The second cartoon constitutes a vivid image of Madrid at that time. Interesting on account of the system of working in collaboration that these decoration companies sometimes followed, one of the most prominent pictures has thirteen small sketches for the same number of cartoons. The designs were previously attributed to Ramón Bayeu, who was responsible for the definitive canvas paintings. Now, however, they have been reconfirmed as the work of his brother Francisco.

The above-mentioned series of thirteen sketches by Francisco Bayeu included one of the paintings entitled *El choricero* (The Crook). This picture exemplifies the skills of the ill-fated **Ramón Bayeu** (1747-1793) in portraying this type of popular scene. As the cartoon for a famous tapestry intended for Aranjuez, it shows the artist's preference for one main character to the detriment of the traditional group.

José del Castillo (1737-1793) was very closely connected to Ramón Bayeu. He was the designer of four cartoons from 1780 which were intended for the same number of tapestries at the Pardo palace. The cartoons show pleasant well-produced scenes that can also be considered as authentic genre paintings. They are entitled *Muchachos jugando al peón* (Boys Playing with a Top), *Muchachos solfeando* (Boys Singing a Tune), *Muchachos jugando al boliche* (Boys Playing Skittles) and *Tres muchachos jugando al chito* (Three Boys Playing with Hoops).

The work of the prolific **Mariano Salvador Maella** (1739-1819) is very well represented in the Prado. Pictures including several of his main themes are on display. *La Inmaculada Concepción* (The Immaculate Conception) was a sketch made in 1784 for the enormous canvas painting intended for the Madrid church of San Francisco el Grande. In a departure from the encoded formula used during the seventeenth century, the sketch gives equal prominence to the outburst of glory with God the Father and to the glory accompanying the angelic figures, one of whom is wearing the chain of the order of Charles III which is linked to this Marian dedication.

As far as portraits are concerned, the one of Carlota Joaquina, infanta of Spain and princess of

Claudio Coello. *The Virgin and Child adored by Saint Louis, King of France.*
Canvas. 229 χ 249 cm. Ref. nº 661.

Bayeu. *Olympus, The Battle of the Giants.*
Canvas. 68 χ 123 cm. Ref. nº 604.

Portugal, has been praised due to the substantial and precise brush-strokes. The picture was painted in 1785, the year of the princess's wedding to Juan de Braganza. There is another version of the painting in the Moncloa palace.

In 1785, Maella made ten sketches with maritime themes. These were used as designs by Zacarías González Velázquez in order to create the corresponding cartoons for tapestries. *Marina* (A Seascape) shows fishermen against a background of ruined buildings. The studied brightness highlights Maella's interest in sky scenes characteristic of the genre. Attention has been drawn to the French rococo style of *El embarque* (The Embarkation), whose charm and picturesque qualities were unusual in Spanish art at that time, except in the case of Paret. In approximately 1795, the artist created his allegories of the four seasons as canvas paintings with a vertical format. *La primavera* (The Spring) is undoubtedly the most accomplished. *La primavera* (The Spring), *El verano* (The Summer) and *El otoño* (The Autumn) are represented by Flora, Ceres and Bacchus respectively. However, *El invierno* (The Winter) shows two old men inside a hut. This is a reversion to genre painting.

The work of the less famous **Agustín Esteve** (1753-1820) sometimes receives indirect praise in the sense that it can be confused with paintings by Goya. Esteve's portrait of Doña Joaquina Téllez-Girón, the daughter of the dukes of Osuna, displays great elegance in both the concept and the artwork. The portrait may have formed a matching pair with that of the subject's sister. As the portrait was painted when the subject was thirteen years of age, the date of the picture can be put at 1798. The portrait of Don Tomás de Iriarte by Joaquín Inza (c. 1736-1811) is a typical portrait of an intellectual. In the picture, the famous fable writer is portrayed with his hand on his poem entitled *La música* (Music).

Camarón, Carnicero and Paret are inseparable painters in terms of being influenced by French and Flemish styles. Regrettably, they were not called upon to serve in the Royal Factory of Tapestries. *Parejas en un parque* (Lovers in a Park) is as sensual as it is imaginary and exemplifies the very individual path taken by the Valencia painter **José Camarón Boronat** (1731-1803) towards a rococo pastoral approach with 'majista' touches. This com-

bined a stylized version of typical popular cartoon designs with references to an evanescent world that had little or nothing to do with Spanish culture. The artist's "gallant" style is also demonstrated in *Una romería* (An Open-air Dance) featuring a couple dancing and characterized by the painter's very slender and graceful figures.

Antonio Carnicero (1748-1814) painted the portrait of Tomasa de Aliaga, lieutenant governess to princess Maria Amalia. The picture was made in approximately 1778-91 and shows the artist's customary meticulousness. Mariano Sánchez was commissioned to paint a series of pictures with harbour scenes. However, he was not able to complete the series before his death. *La vista de la Albufera de Valencia* (The View of the Valencia Lagoon) is attributed to Sánchez. It picturesquely combines farm workers with small sailing boats. An extremely beautiful documentary painting with a variety of animated groups can be seen in *La ascensión de un globo Montgolfier* (The Ascent of a Montgolfier Balloon). The picture is based on a balloon flight made by the Frenchman Bouclé at the royal location of Aranjuez in 1784.

Many works of art provide evidence of the high degree of specialization exercised by **Luis Egidio Meléndez** or Menéndez (1716-1780) in the still life genre. In this context, he showed a great deal of skill in combining all kinds of inanimate objects. His oldest work in this sense is *Manzanas, nueces, tarro y cajas de dulce* (Apples, Nuts, a Jar and Boxes of Sweets) signed in 1759. The bodegón (Still Life) signed in 1760 and entitled *Peritas, pan, jarra, frasco y tartera* (Small Pears, Bread, A Jar, A Flask and a Cake Tin) has enabled analysts to establish the dates of other similar paintings which are obviously linked to this one in terms of the content and artwork. The last *Bodegón* (Still Life) from 1774 is entitled *Pepinos y tomates* (Cucumbers and Tomatoes).

The work of **Luis Paret y Alcázar** (1746-1799) has undergone continuous reassessment. His colourful life led to exile for acting as a procurer on behalf of his master, prince Louis. Claimed to be the Spanish Watteau, he is almost alone in representing the potential of non-academic painting. The picture entitled *Baile en máscara* (A Masquerade) actually came from Louis of Bourbon. Made in about 1767, it is a type of graphic representation of the Casanova stories and in an unparalleled elegant rococo style

José Camarón Boronat. *Lovers in a park.*
Lienzo, 83 χ 108 cm. Ref. nº 6733.

Luis Paret y Alcázar. *A Masquerade.*
Tabla, 40 χ 51 cm. Ref. nº 2875.

portrays a carnival apparently held at *El príncipe* (The Prince) theatre.

In approximately 1770, Paret painted the picture entitled *Carlos III comiendo ante su corte* (Charles III Dining in Front of His Court), signed humorously in Greek. This piece is in total accordance with everything conveyed by the royal biographer, Count Fernán Núñez. The artist uses a dry flecking technique. *Las parejas reales* (The Royal Couples), signed in 1770, is also a documentary painting but on a larger scale. The scene is portrayed with total accuracy. There exists a superb replica of the painting in England. Against an evanescent tree-filled background, Paret orchestrates a large number of figures in depicting the equestrian festival held in Aranjuez at that time. The participants included the future Charles IV accompanied by his august father.

Ensayo de una comedia (A Rehearsal for a Comedy) dates from around 1772-73. It is a very informal scene without daylight. In the foreground, we can see a man and a woman in sixteenth-century apparel, linked together at different levels. There are several other characters adopting suspect postures, tending towards villainy. The portrait of the artist's wife, **María de las Nieves Micaela Fourdinier** was painted in about 1782-1785. In this picture, Paret painted in a framework in the form of a window with climbing plants on top. This involved a tightly-packed virtuosity in the deployment of intermediate shades that created a sense of unreality. Perhaps this picture forms a matching pair with his previous work, the *Autorretrato* (Self-Portrait) from about 1786. Nevertheless, the identity of the painter of this picture is a matter of debate. It shows a man dressed as a rich 'majo' (a popular Madrid figure) together with two classical busts against a background formed by an oval picture in which a shipwreck can be glimpsed. Judging from the posture of the subject, who is resting his head on his hand, this canvas painting can be seen as a characteristic melancholic portrait by the artist.

La jura de Fernando VII como Príncipe de Asturias (The swearing of the Oath by Ferdinand VII as the Prince of Asturias) portrays an exceptional event from the history of that period. The ceremony took place in the Madrid Church of San Jerónimo on September 23rd 1789, and was presided over by the monarchs accompanied on the throne by prince Carlos María Isidro. Two consecutive moments from the ceremony are shown. The heir takes the oath in front of cardinal Lorenzana but, when the painting is spread out in two, he is also seen to be kissing the hand of Charles IV. The whole monarchical set-up of the old regime shines through in agonizing solemnity.

El paseo ante el Jardín Botánico (A Stroll in Front of the Botanical Gardens) is assumed to be from about 1790 or a little later. It although unfinished, it is the first version of this lively scene from Madrid life in which fashionable people of the time stand out, either in carriages or on foot. The picture may be related to a series of views of the court and royal locations as well as public events.

GOYA
Rooms 32, 35, 34, 36, 37, 38 and 39

"Given the structure of the Museum, it is not easy to arrange Goya's pictures so as to reflect the different phases of his artistic output. In order to appreciate his work with a certain degree of chronological and artistic coherence, the visitor showed first proceed to Rooms 85-94, on the second floor, begining with the cartoons for tapestries, and then enter rooms 32 to 39 on the first floor, finally arriving at the *Pinturas Negras* (Black Paintings)".

When the museum was inaugurated in 1819, only two works by Francisco de Goya (1746-1828) were registered among the exhibits. The artist was still alive at that time. Nowadays owing to continual acquisitions, the latest addition being the portrait of *La condesa de Chinchon* (The Countess of Chinchón) the Prado possesses the most important collection of pictures by Goya, both in quantitative and qualitative terms.

Following his early apprenticeship in Saragossa, Goya arrived at the Madrid royal court in 1763 as a candidate for a grant to study in Italy where he stayed between 1770 and 1771. Goya began to establish the basis for a very individual style, far removed from academic stereotypes, that found distinctive expression after he had made professional contact with the count of Floridablanca and Prince Louis in 1780. Goya's most successful period started in 1785. Four years later, he attained the position of royal painter. Although Goya's work revealed borrowings from Giaquinto, Tiépolo and Mengs and therefore

Luis Paret y Alcazar.
Doña María de las Nieves Micaela Fourdinier,
the Painter's Wife.
Copper. 37 χ 28 cm. Ref. n° 3250.

Luis Paret y Alcazar. *The Avenue opposite the*
Botanical Gardens.
Panel. 58 χ 88 cm. Ref. n° 7661.

overlapped with prevailing academic trends, he began to develop a freedom of technique and style that reached a peak at the end of the century. Goya's opposition to absolutism led to his exile in France although the flexibility of this situation meant that he sometimes returned. The artist died in Bordeaux in 1828 after completing a series of paintings ranging from, on the one hand, his conventional late-baroque Italianesque style pertaining to the first phase of his career to, on the other hand, fragmented revolutionary painting beyond impressionism and linking up with expressionism.

The great equestrian portraits of Charles IV and Maria Luisa have been present in the museum since its inauguration. *La reina María Luisa a caballo* (Queen Maria Luisa on Horseback) from 1799 shows a return to the designs of Velasquez although on a simplified basis and merged with a new concept of light and colour. For some analysts, the painting is not simply an expression of monarchical power but also a measure of her affection and gratitude to her favourite Godoy. It is no coincidence that she is wearing the uniform of colonel in 'Las Guardias de Corps", the unit in which the royal favourite had begun his meteoric career, and that she is riding 'Marcial', a gift from him.

Afterwards, in 1800-01, Goya painted the portrait of *Carlos IV a caballo* (Charles IV on Horseback), inspired by the portrait of Margarita of Austria by Velasquez. As the rear feet of the animal were not visible in this previous portrait by Velasquez, Goya did not know how to fit the horse's feet into the later work. Following logical modifications, he reduced them to shapeless marks. The two equestrian portraits taken together show that they were not designed to be hung on the same wall but, instead, opposite each other.

The large canvas painting of **La familia de Carlos IV** (Charles IV's Family) dates from 1800-01. It is outstanding due to its artistic qualities and also because of its historical or documentary significance. Although the painting is vaguely reminiscent of *Las Meninas* (The Maids of Honour), prompting Goya to portray himself on one side behind a sewing frame, here lacking all compositive justification, the structure relinquishes former designs for pictures of the royal family in favour of a mere frontal approach. Some critics have seen this as a kind of Neo-classical frieze, in tune with the pre-

dominant aesthetic climate. However, it was the artist's intention that the mirror from *Las Meninas* (The Maids of Honour) should indeed be here opposite the subjects of the portrait. In this way, Goya is able to paint the reflected image. The free-flowing brilliant touches reach sublime quality as they illustrate the array of insignia and jewels on the lavish costumes. The purpose of the picture is a matter of considerable doubt. From the perspective of romanticism, it was understood to be a cruel satire. But the hypothetical attempt at caricature does not tie in with the actual circumstances in which the painting was created.

The Prado holds a number of preparatory sketches for this large family portrait. All of them date from 1800. They are of the following members of the royal family: *La infanta María Josefa* (Princess Maria Josefa), *El infante Antonio Pascual* (Prince Antonio Pascual), *El infante Carlos María Isidro* (Prince Carlos Maria Isidro), *Luis de Borbón, príncipe de Parma* (Louis of Bourbon, Prince of Parma) and *El infante Francisco de Paula Antonio* (Prince Francisco de Paula Antonio). The latter is one of the most marvellous child figures by Goya. In the definitive canvas painting, he appears less spontaneous and fresh-faced.

Isidoro Máiquez, a signed portrait from 1807, shows the best actor in Goya's time. Here, the subject is presented as a member of the emerging middle class without any indication of his profession. Goya used a limited range of colours and sketchwork while focussing on the face.

El retrato equestre del general Palafox (The Equestrian Portrait of General Palafox), signed in 1814, comes from the period after the Peninsular War. The subject of the portrait had been a leading figure in the legendary defence of Saragossa. Palafox is not shown taking charge of the siege but instead we see him on an undefined battlefield. Although Palafox himself commissioned the painting, he never paid for it, perhaps due to financial difficulties arising from his constitutionalist stance. In this equestrian portrait, Goya breaks away from Velasquez's comfortable approach in favour of a more dynamic and modern image of war.

Fernando VII en un campamento (Ferdinand VII at a Military Camp) dates from the same time. This portrait was not commissioned by the king but instead by a teaching institution. For some, the pic-

Francisco de Goya. *The Family of Charles IV.*
Canvas. 280 χ 336 cm. Ref. n° 726.

Francisco de Goya. *Self-portrait.*
Canvas. 46 χ 35 cm. Ref. n° 723.

ture once again has a critical or satirical element. Others, by contrast, see it as a flattering picture. If this adulation is actually present in the painting, then it may come from the portrayal of the king as a general amid a battle scene. This background contrasts with the neutral or empty scenery providing a background to other portraits from the same period.

The artist makes use of an identical figure and pose in the portrait of *Fernando VII con manto real* (Ferdinand VII in a Royal Robe). The painting was probably made in 1815. In this case, the mellow intermittent brush-strokes do not match the subtle results achieved by Goya. The way in which the royal emblems of authority are arranged does not tie in with traditional Spanish approaches to portraying monarchs.

Autorretrato (Self-Portrait) dates from around 1815 and is considered to be one of Goya's most sincere and uninhibited works.

Goya was not very keen on pure allegory. From about 1801 to 1805, he made four allegories for Godoy's palace. Of these, three survive. Perhaps on the instructions of the favourite, the allegories reflected the reformist programme of the Enlightenment, then paradoxically in terminal crisis. Whereas *La agricultura* (Agriculture) is represented by the goddess Ceres, *La industria* (Industry) is personified by a spinner along the lines of conventional realism rather than symbolism. *El comercio* (Commerce) presents a simple office with two employees. So then, with the exception of the first, the other allegories in accordance with Spanish tradition would break up the genre. The allegories can only be interpreted on a deeper level through a second reading going beyond the immediate or obvious message.

Aves muertas (Dead Birds) and *Pavo muerto* (Dead Turkey) were both painted at some time between 1808 and 1812 although the exact date is uncertain. In these pictures, Goya provides evidence of his very original way of re-creating the still life. Here, the painting reaches an unusual dramatic intensity apart from the attention to detail, which had been a feature of the genre.

El coloso (The Colossus) from 1812 is a type of symbolic or imaginary composition in which the horrible nature of the theme is reinforced by the dramatic effects of light. Analysed iconographically in the context of the Peninsular War, the painting may be based on the myth that Hercules founded the

Spanish monarchy. Alternatively, it may refer to a contemporary literary source in expressing national resistance against the Napoleonic invaders.

Two large canvas paintings commemorate the Madrid uprising against the French. They are very closely connected with the previous series of engravings about the same events. Some analysts have considered that the pictures must have formed part of a series consisting of four scenes. It has also been suggested that they could have been intended for a temporary monument. El *Dos de mayo de 1808* (May 2nd, 1808) presents a tremendously violent and cruel moment from the popular struggle against the invaders. The nature of some of these invaders explains the title *La carga de los mamelucos* (The Charge of the Mamelukes). They were Egyptians serving in Bonaparte's army. In this picture, the location of the battle cannot be identified. Presumably, it is *La Puerta del Sol* (The Gate of the Sun). This picture saw the rise of the anonymous hero as a protagonist in history. Both on a popular level and a collective one, the anonymous hero acquired fundamental importance in subsequent nineteenth century painting.

El tres de mayo de 1808 (May 3rd, 1808) depicts a nocturnal scene. In doing so, the artist makes similar vibrant brush-strokes but applies a much more restrained colour scheme. In order to create the picture, the artist undoubtedly utilized contemporary prints and not only those dealing with the theme of French repression. The setting for the event is thought to be the mountain of Príncipe Pío, behind the hermitage of San Antonio de la Florida. But both in this canvas painting and in the previous one, Goya moves away from his customary descriptivism towards abstract formulas that take the mere chronicling of contemporary events into the realms of absolute symbolism. In *Los Fusilamientos* (The Executions by Firing Squad), Goya created a whole subgenre that provided a benchmark for painters such as Manet as he approached his painting of the Emperor Maximilian of Mexico.

La lechera de Burdeos (The Milkmaid of Bordeaux) is evocative of Goya's last phase but, on the other hand, it has received little attention. Painted in 1825-27, this work has been interpreted as a kind of advance display of impressionism. Indeed, it heralds the movement's new achievements in light and colour without any traces of the ugliness or austeri-

Francisco de Goya.
May 3rd. 1808 in Madrid. The executions by
Firing Squad on the Prinicipe Pio Hill.
Canvas. 268 χ 347 cm. Ref. nº 749.

Francisco de Goya. *The Milkmaid of Bordeaux.*
Canvas. 74 χ 68 cm. Ref. nº 2899.

ty that had characterized his work following his "pinturas negras" (black paintings). The picture in question may be a portrait but it immediately gives the observer a striking impression with all the spontaneity and freshness of a genre painting.

The Black Paintings

Around 1820-23, Goya set about producing his most personal, original, symbolic and revolutionary series. He was clearly beyond the conditioning factors imposed on him by his clientele. He also showed little regard for taste or fashion, for example in decorating his suburban Madrid house called *La quinta del sordo* (The Deaf Man's Residence). This highly distinctive decoration programme went against the prevailing court fashion in both formal and conceptual terms. Goya carried out the decorative work on both floors of his house, taking advantage of previous paintings which must have influenced his art. In 1873, this house was bought by baron D'Erlanger. After entrusting Salvador Martínez Cubells with the task of transferring the murals to canvas, the new owner tried unsuccessfully to sell them at the Universal Exhibition in Paris in 1878. But the international art climate was not yet ready for this kind of work performed out of context, a forerunner of expressionism. Three years later, D'Erlanger donated the series to the Prado Museum.

El Aquelarre (The Witches' Gathering) was one of the seven scenes that decorated the dining room on the ground floor, known as Saturn's hall because of its general themes. This painting was one of the most seriously altered as a result of restoration. The picture has the additional modern title of *Escena sabática* (A Sabbatical Scene) and may refer to a passage from a book by Cadalso that describes a general assembly of all the noble and ordinary members of witchcraft. In this sense, the scene must be a portrayal of an initiation ceremony for a young witch. Experts have also pointed out links with the symbolism of Saturn as the god of melancholy. Contrary to this type of interpretation, however, some experts have discerned in *El aquelarre* the work of a man expressing disapproval of the prevailing politics of the time.

The same room housed *La romería de San Isidro* (San Isidro's Fair), a picture also very badly affected by restoration work. In terms of descriptive interpretation, this painting has once again been regarded as alluding to the theme of Saturn, specifically to the festivities in honour of Saturn in ancient Rome. By contrast, another school of thought discounts all narrative or allegorical motivation in the production of this work. Here, Goya presents the less substantial dream-like opposite side to the happy conventional figures at the outdoor party celebrating San Isidro. Among these figures, the artist himself is the most prominent.

A number of other pictures completed the decoration of the dining room on the ground floor. *La Leocadia*, identified as such by the painter and friend of Goya, Antonio Grugada, is actually Leocadia Zorrilla y Galarza, who accompanied the Aragonese artist following the death of Josefa Bayeu in 1812. Her posture, as she lays one arm on a rock and rests her head in the appropriate hand, has been interpreted as a sign of melancholy. In view of the fact that the large rock in question holds a tomb, this painting has been associated with specific symbolization on the theme of the intercession between the world of the visitor and the world of the past.

There is disagreement as to whether *Dos viejos comiendo* (Two Old Men Eating) was included in this room. The scene from the painting is ambiguous, even as regards the gender of the characters. Once again, they come under the influence of Saturn, namely the forces of old age and annihilation. The figure on the right who is reading a piece of paper must represent death with his macabre list. For others, the scene expresses the bad habit of greed. Those who are most reluctant to see hidden meaning in the picture prefer to focus on the supposedly humorous direct message unless they interpret the painting as a reference to the poverty prevalent at that time. In other words, this could be seen as a combination of a protest painting and a genre picture.

Of the seven motifs in the dining room on the ground floor, el *Saturno* (Saturn) is prominent as a painting representing the horrible. It is probably the best known work in the series and in any case it holds the key to the artistic explanation. Although the theme might be developed by many other illustrations, the most evident and unavoidable example is provided by Rubens with his **Saturno devorando a su hijo** (Saturn Devouring his Son), a picture from the royal collection and one which Goya must have

Francisco de Goya.
El Aquelarre (El Gran Cabrón). (The Witches' Gathering. The Great Bastard).
Mural painting placed on canvas.
140 χ 438 cm. Ref. nº 761.

Francisco de Goya.
Saturn devouring his Son.
Mural painting placed on canvas.
143 χ 81 cm. Ref. nº 763.

known. However, as experts have pointed out, the Flemish painter presents the god as the initiator of chaos from the standpoint of heroic baroque whereas Goya portrays him as the devil or absolute evil. Here, Saturn has a satanic image in keeping with *El aquelarre,* the gathering of witches around the devil. But once again, political interpretations emerged from the allegorical ones. For one analyst, Saturn represented the Inquisition. Another critic identified Saturn with Ferdinand VII, who did not hesitate to destroy his own subjects in order to maintain his privileges.

Unlike the previous paintings, there are no doubts about the iconography in Judith and Holofernes. For this picture, Goya revived an old mythological theme that has given rise to numerous works in the Prado Museum. Goya reassesses the shape and content from the standpoint of drastic deconsecration. The association between this theme and that of Saturn, and indeed more generally the links between the Biblical and pagan worlds, has been a commonplace concept in modern European art. Curiously, some analysts have suggested that the picture of *Judith and Holofernes* came straight from the theatre and that even the distribution of light is reminiscent of that in plays. In this sense, Judith must be trying to persuade Spaniards to rise up against the power of Satan which is a threat to the country, personified by Saturn the neighbour.

The series of pictures on the ground floor concludes with **Dos viejos comiendo** (Two Old Men). This painting was seriously altered during restoration work. As a description of decrepitude and consequent melancholy, it fully enters the world of Saturn. According to some experts, Goya's old age, reflected in the main characters from the picture, was precisely the reason why the artist symbolically gave his house an additional role as the home of Saturn. The most important figure in the picture is not a self-portrait but, instead, simply a reference to the artist's advancing years, including his deafness. That is why the other old man, who is playing a secondary role, shouts into the ear of the first.

In the room on the upper floor, Asmodea, as she was already called by those close to Goya, seems to match a character from Golden Age Spanish literature. Indeed, this is a female version of the name Asmodeo, the devil in the Book of Tobias who reappears in *El diablo cojuelo* (The Lame Devil) by Vélez

de Vergara. On the other hand, the flying figures have been interpreted as Minerva guiding Prometheus to Mount Caucasus whereas the fusiliers on the right-hand side must be the angry gods. Nevertheless, the modern appearance of the fusiliers points to a more congruent explanation. It is no coincidence that the painting was known by the title of *Fusilamientos* (Firing Squad Shootings). In this sense, the picture would contain a constitutionalist political metaphor, with the large hillside representing the Rock of Gibraltar, a refuge for liberals and the bastion of their resistance to Ferdinand VII. Taking this allegory to more abstract or ideological conclusions, some have seen Asmodeo as the Fury and his female companion as War. At the same time, the rock would represent Reason and the building completing it would symbolize Peace.

On record as being in the same room, *El paseo del Santo Oficio* (The Holy Office Avenue) is very closely connected to the picture of the outdoor fair on the ground floor. In spite of bearing this title since being in Goya's circle, the painting was later interpreted as a pilgrimage to the miraculous fountain of San Isidro. It was badly damaged during restoration work. In the foreground, we can see a figure with a ruff and wearing a chain who undoubtedly exemplifies the political and ideological machine of reactionary Spain. The picture is usually interpreted as a comical portrayal of the Inquisition but it is unclear whether the artist is commemorating its extinction or warning about its re-establishment along with the threat from absolutism.

Opposite the Holy Office Parade we can see **Duelo a garrotazos** (A Duel Fought with Cudgels). This picture was considerably altered under the pretext of restoration work, which seriously affected its meaning. The legs of the brutal fighters were formerly completely present in the picture. Now, they are only included from the knees upwards. A green field previously occupied a space which has now been filled in. After the protagonists have been brought to a standstill, the scene acquires dramatic symbolic qualities, not so much on account of the fratricidal violence but more as a result of the contrast between the two opposing Spains. In any case, the final result is a scene expressing the definitive nature of death regarded by some as a portrayal of a form of combat characteristic of Aragon and Catalonia. Specifically it has been suggested that the painting is a mythologi-

Francisco de Goya. *Two Old Men eating.*
Mural painting tranferred to canvas. 53 χ 85 cm. Ref. n° 762.

Francisco de Goya. *A Duel Fought with Cudgels.*
Mural painting tranferred to canvas. 125 χ 261 cm. Ref. n° 758.

cal depiction of short-term political aims. The theme deals with the intervention by Hercules in Spanish affairs in relation to some particular events that would put the date of the picture between November 1821 and the end of the summer 1823.

Las parcas (The Parcae or Fates) is a variation on this mythological theme which reveals Goya's scant respect for genre conventions, especially in the present series. On the right, Atropos can be seen with his emblem, the scissors, leaving us in no doubt about the iconography. Cloto, on the other hand, does not display any cloth, but instead a small statue, perhaps of Pandora. In the centre, Laquesis is observing a round object that is just as likely to be a mirror representing transience as a snake biting its own tail, the symbol of eternity. In addition to the image of the scissors, we can also detect the existence of a magnifying glass enabling us to better appreciate the delicate thread of life.

On account of the disastrous restoration work, *Dos mujeres y un hombre* (Two Women and a Man) has been interpreted as an act of onanism with regard to the myth of Vulcan. Consequently, from a contemporary point of view, the picture has been as symbolizing the barren nature of political discussion. However, both X-ray analysis and old photographs confirm that the man had been carrying a kind of book in his hands, making this picture a comic version of the painting described next.

La lectura (The Reading or The Interpretation) is also to be found on the upper floor. It was very much altered during restoration work. The picture presents the serious side of the world of culture, perhaps from the viewpoint of clandestine political activity, the result of absolutist repression. It has also been stated that the scene emphasizes the sad truth about the extent of illiteracy among the populace, victims of obscurantism. Significantly, the man who is reading is a friar. But Goya offers a glimmer of hope in terms of the posture of the subject in the background who is looking upwards while ignoring the message from the friar.

This series of decorative pieces on the upper floor concludes with an enigmatic painting – *El perro semihundido* (The Semi-buried Dog). The animal has buried itself so deeply in the sand that only its head emerges. The fruitless debate about the meaning of the picture has seen two opposing groups arguing with each other once more. On the one hand, there are those who sought to discover a narrative link in this series. On the other hand, the proponents of a new artistic sensitivity have avoided intellectual analysis. Whereas the dreams of some romantic foreigners were based on literary material, those of Goya may well have been solely visual without any support from texts. Perhaps the large stain on the right-hand side conceals the key to this gratuitous theme. The mythological elements point to the presence of Cerberus. It has been suggested that a possible source for the painting was an emblem in which a dog observes the abduction of Ganimedes. The theory has been put forward that the animal represents the people who are shocked by the spectre of violence.

Francisco de Goya.
The Parcae or The Fates (Atropos).
Mural painting tranferred to canvas. 123 χ 266 cm.
Ref. nº 757.

Francisco de Goya. *Semi-buried Dog* .
Mural painting tranferred to canvas.
131 χ 79 cm. Ref. nº 767.

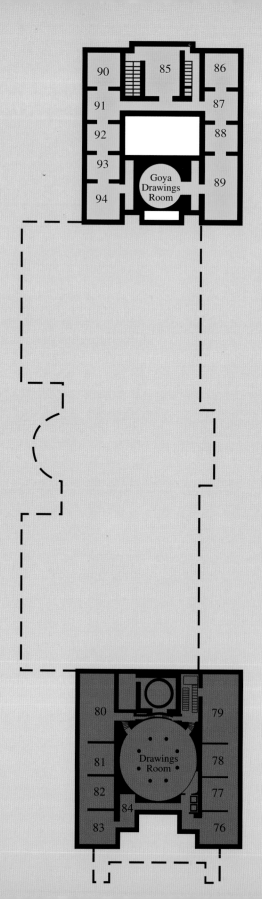

SECOND FLOOR

	ROOMS	PAGES
Goya	. . . .(85, 90, 91, 92, 93, 94, 86, 87, 88, 89 and drawings)	. .158
European painting in the XVIII century	. . . .(79, 78, 77, 76, 84, 83, 82, 81, 80 and drawings)	170

The Cartoons for tapestries

One of the most characteristic aspects of Goya's duties in the service of the court was his role as the designer of cartoons for the Royal Tapestry Factory, founded by Philip V. At the suggestion of Mengs, this factory underwent an appreciable change in terms of the themes promoted. Scenes of local customs and manners imitating the Flemish style were replaced by others directly inspired by the reality of daily life in Madrid.

The first series of cartoons made by Goya dates from 1775 and is composed of nine scenes. It was intended for the dining hall belonging to the princes of Asturias at the Escorial Palace. *Perros y útiles de caza* (Dogs and Hunting Implements) has been considered as one of his least individual paintings. Like the whole series, this picture seems more reminiscent of Francisco Bayeu than of Goya himself even though documentary evidence proves that Goya was indeed the artist. However, in *Caza con reclamo* (Hunting with a Decoy), some analysts have claimed to have seen the exceptional powers of observation that were a feature of Goya's art from the outset. In *Cazador cargando su escopeta* (A Hunter Loading his Gun), only half of the canvas painting was the work of Goya, as the background landscape forms part of a cartoon by Matías Téllez. Some critics have pointed to **Cazador con sus perros** (A Hunter with his Dogs) as the most distinctively characteristic painting by Goya in the whole of this first batch, not only due to the realism with which the character is portrayed in a style that is reminiscent of the 'majos' and 'chisperos' (popular figures from Madrid) in subsequent pictures but also on account of the contrasts of colour and the quality of the distant landscape. It could be argued that the conventional discretion shown in the series is the result of Goya's commitment to meeting the demands of the weavers.

Pescador con caña (A Fisherman with his Rod) from 1775 was commissioned along with another three cartoons in order to complete this first series of nine. In the subsequent collection, this is the only canvas painting that lacks a reference to hunting.

Like the previous painting, *Partida de caza* (A Hunting Party) is influenced by the style of Francisco Bayeu. In general, the picture follows the guidelines applied at that time for arranging these decorative compositions. Goya's personal situation together with the conditions of employment in which he joined the factory (where his protector was his brother-in-law Francisco Bayeu) and the demands arising from the themes and decoration of the tapestries probably prevented him from developing a distinctive style that would come later with maturity. As some critics have pointed out, Bayeu's work goes deeper than is generally believed, as the formulas he used correspond to his artistic ideals. These were Flemish in origin and involved a commitment to frontal views and a dramatic use of space in which the figures are not individuals but character types.

La merienda (The Picnic) from 1776 belongs to a second series of ten cartoons for the dining hall belonging to the Prince of Asturias at the Pardo palace. In this picture, we can clearly see how Goya began to break free from the influence of Bayeu. At the same time, Goya incorporated a new social phenomenon, the 'majo', whose significance in the work of Goya and other artists of his time has been the subject of reams of analysis. Some believe to have discovered in the role of the majo a focus for Goya's populism or popular sentiments, connected to a greater or lesser extent with his enlightened tropism. But the presence of the majo, both here and in subsequent paintings, was due to the nature of the commissioned work, ordered for objective reasons that had little to do with the hypothetical progressive or liberal message associated with the majismo phenomenon and which affected large sections of the aristocracy. The court wanted festive rural scenes full of humour, to be presented in updated versions of the already old Flemish tapestries. However, from the standpoint of enlightened despotism, there was absolutely no desire to use this artistic trend as a means of getting closer to the people.

From the same series, *Baile a orilla del Manzanares* (A Dance On the Banks of the Manzanares) dating from 1776-1777, presents a similar composition to the previous cartoon although the figures have been better incorporated into the picture. Instead of painting an imaginary landscape, Goya includes a well-known setting with the enormous dome of San Francisco el Grande in the background. *La riña en la venta nueva* (The Quarrel at the New Inn) from 1777 is, in all likelihood, based on a play or a sketch. The picture is apparently set in *Las ventas del Espíritu Santo* (The Espíritu Santo Inn). For some experts, the iconographic theme of gamblers

Francisco de Goya. *The Fisherman with his Rod.*
Canvas. 289 χ 110 cm.
Ref. nº 5542.

Francisco de Goya.
The Hunter with his Dogs.
Canvas. 262 χ 71 cm. Ref. nº 805.

fighting in front of an inn contains a moral element in terms of the portrayal of anger, a feature of northern European genre painting.

Like the previous accompanying canvas painting, *El paseo de Andalucía* (The Andalusian Parade) from 1777 seems to stem from a play, specifically a sketch by Ramón de la Cruz. Perhaps in accordance with this type of setting, the picture is reminiscent of the rococo structure of the dance scenes painted by Goya's contemporary, Camarón. Evidently, the Andalusia portrayed here by Goya who was still unfamiliar with that region, conveys no more than the popular image or stereotype view of the south of Spain.

In *El bebedor* (The Drinker), completed in 1777, the artist attempts to get away from Bayeu's designs in favour of his own inventive approach. To this effect, **El quitasol** (The Sunshade), from the same year, follows the guidelines set out by Mengs in organizing the figures according to a pyramidal pattern. Behind these figures, there appear others whose outlines are broken up by a mound. *El quitasol* (The Sunshade) is one of Goya's most famous cartoons. It shows French influence, no less controversial for all its clarity. This charming scene with a rococo background has regularly been interpreted as a moral allegory expressing vanity and pride.

La cometa (The Kite), painted in 1777-78 appears to be based on a print reflecting a painting by Lancret. At a symbolic level, the picture alludes to the futility of human knowledge. From the same time, *Los jugadores de naipes* (The Card Players) has been linked as much with the baroque story about the cheats as with a portrayal of boastfulness, thus complementing the previous cartoon.

Niños inflando una vejiga (Children Inflating a Bladder), painted in 1777-1778, is a possible reference to worldly glory, In the picture, Goya returns to a traditional theme that goes all the way back to sixteenth century Flemish work. *Muchachos cogiendo fruta* (Boys Picking Fruit) is a children's cartoon from the same time. The painting shows possible traces of the artistic knowledge that Goya had acquired through the royal collections and in particular by studying Murillo.

The seven scenes from his third series for the Royal Factory, intended for the bedroom of the Prince of Asturias at the Pardo palace, focus on a setting rich in subject matter, namely the Madrid fair. *El ciego de la guitarra* (The Blind Guitarist) from 1778

showed that Goya's art was incompatible with the technical demands made by the tapestry officials who imposed drastic alterations. The cartoon actually entitled *La feria de Madrid* (The Madrid Fair) made in 1778-1779 seems to be linked to a painting by Luis Paret – *El anticuario* (The Antiquary). One of Goya's best known works dating from the same time is *El cacharrero* (a kitchen utensil salesman). The painting shows how the artist has progressed in achieving greater spontaneity and vividness in comparison with the rigid dramatic style that the genre had become locked into. It has been said that the painting's dynamism makes us view the scene as an instant in time, something with a past and a future, pictured in all its transience.

El militar y la señora (The Soldier and the Lady) from 1778-1779 evokes the theme of the dandy ("la petimetra") with his lover, an ambiguous arrangement whose exact significance is still a matter of debate. From the same time and closely connected with the previous painting, La Acerolera (the fruit seller) creates a social contrast by turning the 'petrimetra' into a 'maja'. As in the previous series, Goya briefly enters the world of children, away from the Madrid fair, in his designs intended to decorate the lintels. The Prado holds one of the two cartoons on this theme that were painted for this series. It is entitled *Muchachos jugando a soldados* (Boys Playing At Soldiers) and dates from 1778-79. The series concludes with *El juego de la pelota a pala* (The Bat and Ball Game) from 1779, also away from the carnival world of the court. This picture shows a clear departure from traditional artistic conventions towards a dynamic unitary sense of structure.

El columpio (The Swing) from 1779 headed a new series of thirteen cartoons for tapestries designed to decorate the bedroom entrance of the Prince of Asturias at the Pardo palace. The picture has been interpreted in an allegorical sense as a representation of the three ages, thus linking it to a painting by Watteau. Nevertheless, some analysts have stated that its composition is contrary to the gracefulness of the rococo style. A symbolic image can also be discerned in *Las lavanderas* (The washerwomen), painted in 1779-1780. This time, it is one of female lasciviousness, although this fails to diminish the sense of melancholy expressed by the sleeping figure.

La novillada (A Bullfight with Young Bulls and Novice Bullfighters) is from the same time. Perhaps

Francisco de Goya. *The Blind Guitarist.*
Canvas. 260 χ 311 cm. Ref. nº 778.

Francisco de Goya. *The Sunshade.*
Canvas. 104 χ 152 cm. Ref. nº 773.

it includes a portrait of the artist, who was so enthusiastic about bullfighting. For some experts, the painting represents loyalty or, in the overall context of the programme, virility. *El resguardo de tabacos* (The Cigarette Receipt), painted in 1779-1780, has been interpreted as a defence of zealous civil servants who fought against smugglers through the checks made on this monopolized product. If this analysis were correct, then this would constitute one of the first canvas paintings to show an enlightened Goya, aware of national interests.

El niño del árbol (The Boy in the Tree) and *El muchacho del pájaro* (The Boy with the Bird), both painted in 1779-80, can also be seen in symbolic terms as references to the spring and to a strong-willed temperament. *Los leñadores* (The woodcutters) dates from the same time but has been regarded as backward-looking and of little interest. It supposedly consists of an allegorical reference to melancholy. *El majo de la guitarra* (The Majo Guitarist), also from 1779-1780, must be another metaphoric reference to the strong-willed temperament. Mention has been made of its similarities to a picture by Watteau. *La cita* (The Meeting) was completed in the same year and has been interpreted iconographically as a new portrayal of melancholy, brought on in this case by the influx of worldly pleasures.

Having become a royal artist, Goya resumed his duties as the creator of cartoons for tapestries with a series intended for the dining hall of the Prince and Princess of Asturias in the Pardo palace. The series consisted of thirteen identifiable units. *Las floreras* (The Flower-Sellers) or *La primavera* (The Spring) evidently refers to this season of the year. According to some critics, this picture from 1786-1787 is characteristically rococo on account of the variety of shapes and colours as well as the postures of the figures. It contrasts with the tough nature of the humble existence portrayed in other scenes from the series. *La era* (The Threshing Floor) or *El verano* (The Summer) was painted in the same period and was one of the largest cartoons undertaken by Goya. Its allegorical nature combined with its documentary value as a portrayal of rural life. *La vendimia* (The Grape Harvest) or *El otoño* (The Autumn), also from 1786-1787, is considered to be an actual review of Goya's artistic career up until that time in terms of his role as a tapestry designer. It has been pointed out that the arms of the figures show the same undu-

lations as the mountain range, a common feature of Goya's last cartoons.

La nevada (The Snowstorm) or *El invierno* (The Winter) was painted in 1786-1787. As in two other scenes from this series, Goya sharply alters his view of contemporary society. Already during the artist's lifetime, it was emphasized that this piece left iconographic conventions to one side in order to focus on the sublime. In fact, there are links with an undoubtedly Pre-Romantic approach to nature as an adverse and disastrous force.

None of the cartoons has given rise to so much discussion regarding its possible ideological function as **El albañil herido** (The Injured Bricklayer) dating from 1786-1787. The picture is usually viewed from the standpoint of the enlightened reform movement. However, for many, it simply represents a gesture from the court rather than one of protest. Some analysts have suggested that in this canvas painting, Goya anticipated social realism of the nineteenth and twentieth centuries. Nevertheless, the sketch produced in 1786 that apparently corresponds to the painting and which is entitled *El albañil borracho* (The Drunken Bricklayer) returns to a straightforward humorous theme, as indicated by the title.

Los pobres en la fuente (The Poor at the Fountain) was the third cartoon to be apparently drawn up along the lines of ideological and social protest. It dates from the same period. Like The Snowstorm and *The Injured Bricklayer*, the picture focusses on Winter. Whereas *The Injured Bricklayer* reflected Charles III's provisions for accidents at work, the *Poor at the Fountain* can be seen as a portrayal of the king's policy on helping widows and orphans.

Niños con perros de presa (Children with Hunting dogs), dating from 1786-87 seems out of place in a series about the seasons of the year although it is probable that it belonged to the piece dealing with the conversation of the king, also from the Pardo palace. *Cazador al lado de una fuente* (A Hunter Next to a Fountain) and *Pastor tocando la dulzaina* (A Shepherd Playing the Flute), painted at the same time, have been iconographically linked to *El otoño* (The Autumn) but these two lintel pictures apparently accompanied *La nevada* (The Snowstorm). *Gatos riñendo* (The Cat Fight) also dates from 1786-87. It lacks the characteristic technique of Goya and is in bad condition. The series is conclud-

Francisco de Goya. *The Threshing floor or The Summer.*
Canvas. 276 χ 641cm. Ref. n° 794.

Francisco de Goya. *The Injured Bricklayer.*
Canvas. 288 χ 110 cm. Ref. n° 796.

ed by another work from the same date - *Marica en la rama de un árbol* (A Magpie on a Tree Branch). This is the only cartoon by Goya that has been preserved to this day without restoration work or alterations although some analysts have questioned whether Goya was indeed the artist concerned.

La ermita de San Isidro el día de la fiesta (The Hermitage of San Isidro on the Day of the Festival), a composition from 1788, formed a part of another series of designs for tapestries commissioned in order to decorate the princesses' bedroom at the Pardo palace. Of these designs, five sketches and a cartoon remain. Whereas the religious aspect of the festival is portrayed in the picture of the hermitage, the secular side predominates in the sketch entitled *La pradera de San Isidro* (San Isidro Meadow). Goya sets an array of figures against a splendid panoramic view of Madrid. They represent all social classes and all sections of society. The brilliance of the artist's free-flowing brush-strokes blends in perfectly with the hustle and bustle. Various compositive influences have been suggested ranging from Spanish baroque to contemporary Italian and French artists staying in Spain.

La gallina ciega (Blind Man's Buff) from 1788-89 is the only surviving cartoon from this series. It has been regarded as breaking away from the traditional countryside festivities and moving towards *Déjeuner sur l'herbe* by Manet. However, *Blind Man's Buff* has also been interpreted as a symbol of blind love. The sketch for this painting, made in 1788, is also on display in the Prado. *Las mozas de cántaro* (Girls Carrying Jugs) from 1791-92 forms part of a series of twelve tapestry cartoons intended for the king's study at the Escorial palace. Goya made serious objections to this project and this was the last series of cartoons with which he was entrusted. Without diminishing the importance of a hidden allegorical theme, in this case female chastity, the picture presents a natural credible image moving away from previous rococo work and the style of Bayeu. *Los zancos* (Stilts), produced in the same period, alludes to the vanity of worldly triumphs and the vicissitudes of fortune. *La boda* (The Wedding), also from 1791-92, expresses a similar theme. In common with contemporary literature, the picture condemns forced marriages. This composition confirmed that in subsequent cartoons Goya was to abandon the decorative function in

favour of forms of expression that were more appropriate to his personal concerns.

El pelele (The Simpleton) from 1791-92 clearly meets the king's demands by providing humorous countryside themes in this series. The picture may have an allegorical and satirical meaning in terms of the manipulation of man by fortune or women. *Muchachos trepando a un árbol* (Boys Climbing a Tree) and *Las gigantillas* (short women with large heads) date from 1791-92. Perhaps they symbolize the transience of ambitions. However, this does not reduce the possibility that the second refers to the political and social instability unleashed in the wake of the French revolution.

Religious painting

Goya and Velasquez were both court painters and their work is mainly devoted to secular or lay themes, unlike Spanish art in general. However, Goya did include some religious elements in his pictures. *El Cristo crucificado* (Christ Crucified), produced in 1780 when Goya applied for a place at the San Fernando Royal Academy, shows an ideal figure with clear borrowings from Mengs. As a result of the circumstances in which it was painted together with the logical influential factors, it is a painting of a conventional academic nature. *La Sagrada Familia* (The Holy Family) from around 1780-89 is another work that is not very characteristic of Goya's style. Neither does it flow smoothly enough. *La Inmaculada Concepción* (The Immaculate Conception) from 1784 apparently came from the collection of Goya's friend, Jovellanos. Only in very recent times has it received much attention.

Unusual and dramatic religious emotion does feature much later in *El prendimiento de Cristo* (The Seizure of Christ) from 1798. This is a very loose schematic sketch of the famous canvas painting in Toledo cathedral. From the perspective of romanticism, emphasis has been placed on the extent to which the definitive painting was influenced by the lighting effects of Rembrandt, whose engravings are so reminiscent of Goya's.

Las santas Justa y Rufina (Saints Justa and Rufina), made in 1817, was a sketch for the great canvas painting produced for Seville cathedral through the action of the erudite Juan Agustín Ceán

Francisco de Goya. *Blind Man's Buff.*
Canvas. 269 χ 350 cm. Ref. n° 804.

Francisco de Goya. *Christ Crucified.*
Canvas. 255 χ 154 cm. Ref. n° 745.

Bermúdez, a fervent friend of Goya. The date of the sketch is indicative of new developments in the colouring and the brush-strokes, the results of Goya's last phase. In this preparatory study, these techniques are harshly and brusquely applied. As in the case of the definitive painting, however, the sketch provides evidence that the recommendations made by Ceán Bermúdez in an attempt to redirect Goya towards a convincing image of construction were delivered in vain.

The portraits

As a portrait painter, Goya has left an enormous artistic legacy. His work reached a climax in the last five years of the eighteenth century. *Cornelio Vandergoten,* a painting signed in 1782, achieves only limited success and does not match the heights already reached by the artist at this juncture. The portrait of María Teresa de Vallabriga is from 1783. She was the wife imposed on Prince Louis after he had been forced to accept a morganatic marriage. The picture shows evidence of patronage by the prince. This, together with the assistance of Floridablanca, facilitated Goya's professional and social advancement. *Carlos III, cazador* (Charles III, the Hunter) was painted in about 1787. The picture is a replica of the one in the Fernán Núñez collection, based on designs by Velasquez. The monarch did not pose for this portrait and his face must have been from another picture.

In 1789, on the occasion of the enthronement ceremony for the new king, Goya painted his portrait together with that of his consort, the first that he had made of the august royal couple. For some experts, Goya's portrait of *Carlos IV* (Charles IV) follows the guidelines laid down by Velasquez in terms of technique and colour and even in the composition although it portrays the court scene in ways which were unknown to Velasquez. Indeed, in the background, we can see a large ermine-lined cloak and a crown. These emblems of authority are also present in the portrait of *La reina Maria Luisa con tontillo* (Queen Maria Luisa with a Wide Skirt), a painting believed to be a copy by some historians. This portrait of the queen is reminiscent of the technique and artwork of Velasquez. There is the added feature of the wide skirt which is similar to the rounded wide skirt from the seventeenth century.

The portrait of Tadea Arias de Enríquez, painted in about 1790, follows European artistic conventions in presenting an aristocratic lady against the background of a garden, mixed here with an open landscape in a vaguely pre-Romantic style. The subtle clarity of the costume perfectly matches the elegance shown by the subject of the portrait.

The canvas painting entitled *Un garrochista* (A Horse Rider Brandishing a Stick), made in about 1791-92, constitutes a special case because hidden behind this typical image of rural Spain is a portrait of Godoy. Certainly, this is a sketch for an equestrian portrayal of the favourite, perhaps to commemorate Godoy being granted the title of Duke of Alcudia. The camouflage over the figure of the favourite following his downfall in 1808 is, according to some experts, the work of Goya himself.

El general Antonio Ricardos (General Antonio Ricardos) from 1793-94 is apparently a study for his full-figure portrait in front of a cannon. This particular picture clearly shows additional work by another artist in the way that the costume is painted and in the distinctive features. *El duque de Alba* (The Duke of Alba), a portrait from 1795, presents the consort of the famous María Pilar Teresa Cayetana with a music score from Haydn. As a great music enthusiast, she commissioned musical works from the composer. This portrait poses the awkward highly-debated question of whether Goya had a great deal of contact with English portrait painters of the time. Here, the figure of the aristocrat seems to follow the basic tenets of the English style. At least, the records show that this picture had just come from England.

In 1795, Goya produced a picture of Francisco Bayeu along the lines of a self-portrait by his brother-in-law who had recently died. Goya creates a superb reinterpretation, as much anti-academic as simplified, with free gleaming touches within a very limited range of colours. Around the same time, he painted the portrait of *María Antonia Gonzaga Caraccciolo, marquesa de Villafranca* (Maria Antonia Gonzaga Caraccciolo, the Marchioness of Villafranca). Goya also painted the portraits of other members of her family at about this time.

In his *Autorretrato* (Self-portrait) from approximately 1796-97, Goya presents himself with a sewing frame representing his artistic profession in accordance with conventional formulas that go back to the very beginning of this subgenre. On the other

Francisco de Goya. *Charles III, The Hunter.*
Canvas. 207 χ 126 cm. Ref. nº 737.

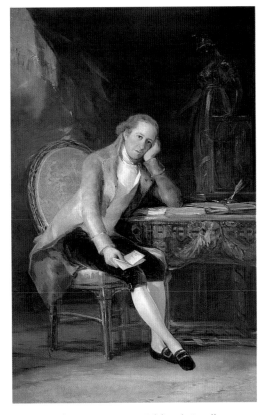

Francisco de Goya. *Gaspar Melchor de Jovellanos.*
Canvas. 204 χ 033 cm. Ref. nº 3236.

hand, Goya preferred to portray himself without this kind of status symbol. The resultant image, showing him with rebellious long hair and an obsessive look, has been regarded as an authentic representation of the so-called romantic Goya.

In 1798, Goya painted the portrait of his friend, the politician and Enlightenment theorist *Gaspar Melchor de Jovellanos*, who had recently been appointed Minister of Justice and Grace. With a magnificent technique including outstanding white and golden touches, Goya painted a typical portrait of a melancholic subject. The painting can fulfil the additional role of an allegorical composition. That is the reason why Goya included the statue of Minerva. Incidentally, this statue rests against the coat of arms or the Royal Asturian Institute of Gijón, the reformist institution with which Jovellanos tried to provide fresh impetus for his native region.

There is some doubt as to whether a portrait from around 1798 is indeed that of "Josefa Bayeu", Goya's wife. The splendid artwork in the part of the painting corresponding to the body and also on the veil and the sleeves shows how much the artist had developed by what was then the peak of his career. The influence of contemporary English painting is again said to be responsible for the composition of *El general José de Urrutia* (General Jose de Urrutia), completed in about 1798 as a commissioned picture for the dukes of Osuna, who had a liking for British art. The inscription is written on a military instruction, a ploy that Goya had already used before and one that other artists would take up until well into the nineteenth century.

To follow chronological sequence, proceed to the first floor.

Joaquín Company, a portrait from around 1800, is one of several paintings of this archbishop attributed to Goya. Perhaps it was merely a preparatory piece.

La condesa de Chinchón (The Countess of Chinchon), from 1800, is one of Goya's most famous portraits. It was undoubtedly the most important work by Goya in private ownership until its recent acquisition by the museum. The picture presents María Teresa de Bourbon y Vallabriga, daughter of the ill-fated prince Louis. She married Godoy in 1797. As her brother cardinal Louis had renounced his aristocratic title, she did not become known as countess until 1803. Through a splendid use of light and colour, Goya portrays her seated and alone in an indistinct

neutral interior space. She is wearing a crown made up of ears of corn, the sign of fertility, as Maria Teresa was then expecting the favourite's child. But the portrait projects melancholy rather than hope.

After 1800, Goya painted the portrait of her brother *El cardenal Luis María de Borbón y Vallabriga* (Cardinal Louis Maria de Bourbon y Vallabriga). He enjoyed a meteoric ecclesiastical career as the archbishop of Seville and of Toledo after his family's fortunes had been restored as a result of Maria Teresa's marriage to Godoy. As in the other two existing versions, the pattern of Velasquez's work is evident.

In 1804, Goya signed the portrait of *María Tomasa Palafox, Marquesa de Villafranca* (Maria Tomasa Palafox, Marchioness of Villafranca). She was an academic with a keen interest in the arts. In the picture, the Marchioness, in turn, is painting the portrait of her husband. The strange iconography is supported by rich shades of lavish colour. Against a neutral background, they combine admirably with the splendid aristocratic furnishings.

La marquesa de Santa Cruz (The Marchioness of Santa Cruz), a signed portrait from 1805, is an extremely well-known canvas painting. The outstanding features are the extraordinary artwork, which has been exceptionally well-reserved, and the strange iconography. This picture was recently acquired by the Prado. It has been interpreted as a personification of the Muse Euterpe but her emblems do not match the lyre carried by the marchioness. In any case, the composition refers to the artistic tastes of the refined aristocracy, whose representative figure is evidently linked to the figures of the somewhat earlier Majas.

From a collection of miniature paintings made for the same family, the Prado exhibits those of Manuela Goicoechea (1805) and Juana Galarza (1805-1806). These are beautiful and idealized paintings of middle-class women.

The free-flowing brush-strokes and the dark range of colours anticipate the restrictive intensity of his final portrait of *La duquesa de Abrantes* (The Duchess of Abrantes). Like her sister, the marchioness of Santa Cruz, she is portrayed as a Muse. The bold streak and mellow subject matter in Goya's late work do not diminish from the fact, pointed out by analysts, that this was to be his last portrait in a light colour range. In approximately 1824, Goya

Francisco de Goya. *The Countess of Chinchon.*
Canvas. 226 χ 144 cm. Ref. n° 2000/3.

painted the portrait of the playwright Manuel Silvela, seen here not as a typical intellectual but instead as an undistinguished member of the middle-class. The dark colours and the diluted completion are characteristic of this phase. By 1827, Goya was living in semi-exile in Bordeaux. There, in that year, he signed the portrait of the banker Juan Bautista Muguiro. In the picture, the thick brush-strokes and the quiet colours are particularly evocative of Goya's last style, characterized by great simplicity. By this time, Goya was completely immune from current trends, which had become immersed in Neo-classicism.

Besides the tapestry cartoons, the religious themes and the portraits, Goya enjoyed great success with genre painting and pictures from everyday life, where he was able to apply his keen powers of observation and his critical awareness. *Los cómicos ambulantes* (The Travelling Comedians) dates from 1793-1794. It is a small oil painting interpreted by some as a reference to the scandalous threesome comprising Godoy, Maria Luisa and Charles IV. In any case, the picture has been seen as an anti-authoritarian gesture. The painting of *La duquesa de Alba y 'La beata'* (The Duchess of Alba and the Pious Woman) presents a delightful scene of domestic privacy. Signed in 1795, the picture shows that Goya was familiar with the famous Cayetana.

The extremely well-known Majas cannot be categorized according to a genre as they lack the pretext of a story-line. These paintings were probably commissioned by Godoy, who later owned them as a part of his collection. Goya got into serious trouble with the Inquisition as a result of the pictures. Some experts still uphold the theory that the series was commissioned by the Duchess of Alba. In this case, she would have been the subject of the portraits. *La maja desnuda* (The Nude Maja), from around 1797-1800, breaks with the mythological or allegorical excuses which had been used up until then in order to justify the female nude. In this sense, it is a revolutionary work of art in iconographic terms and it anticipates artistic styles that came much later. It is certainly true that the Maja's features do not match those of the Duchess of Alba. On the other hand, it has been consistently argued that Goya altered the duchess's features in the painting so that she would not be recognised. It may be supposed that *Las majas* represent a distant idealised portrayal by Goya of his friend and patron, the duchess.

La maja vestida (The Clothed Maja) dates from about 1800-1805. The subject of the painting does not appear to be a low-class 'maja', judging by her apparel. Neither does she seem to be the aristocratic 'pseudo-maja' however. In view of the fact that these paintings were registered in the Hall of Female Nudes created by Godoy, it can be supposed that Goya found inspiration for both pictures in that very same place. At least, he would have been encouraged to use his technique of comparison and contrast. The fountain could have come from a work by Titian.

EUROPEAN PAINTING IN THE EIGHTEENTH CENTURY
Rooms 79, 78, 77, 76, 84, 83, 82, 81 and 80

The advent of the Bourbon dynasty explains why eighteenth-century French painting is so significantly represented, both qualitatively and quantitatively, in the royal collection and consequently also in the Prado Museum.

Susana acusada de adulterio (Susan Accused of Adultery) is a bombastic work of condemnation by **Antoine Coypel** (1661-1722). The picture was painted in about 1695-96. It reveals borrowings both from Flemish baroque and also from the decorative Roman style. Like other paintings from this period with Biblical themes, it was later used as a design for the Gobelin tapestry. **Charles de la Fosse** (1636-1716) produced Acis and Galatea in which he re-creates the Rubens tradition technically, chromatically and compositively.

Hyacinte Rigaud (1659-1743) painted his famous portraits of Philip V and his august grandfather in 1700. These pictures are now in the Louvre. One year later, in 1701, he painted a portrait of *Louis XIV*, armed and standing out against the background of a battlefield. In this dramatic portrayal, what shines out is the artist's French palatial reinterpretation of courtly elegance in the Van Dyck style. The portrait of Maria Ana Victoria de Borbón was painted in 1724 by Nicolás de Lagillièrre. He was another of the great exponents of genre supported by Versailles. His mature profuse artwork presents the princess, then the fiancée of Louis XV, in a very official style, so inappropriate to the Spanish royalty.

Jean-Baptiste Oudri (1686-1755) produced a superb matching pair of portraits in around 1716.

Francisco de Goya. *The Nude Maja.*
Canvas. 98 χ 191 cm. Ref. nº 742.

Francisco de Goya. *The Clothed Maja.*
Canvas. 95 χ 190 cm. Ref. nº 741.

They featured José de Rozas y Menéndez, *Primer Conde de Castelblanco* (The First Count of Castelblanco) and his wife Lady Mary Josephine Drummond. Oudry was the most notable pupil of Largillièrre. In approximately 1738, **Louis de Silvestre** *el Joven* (Louis de Silvestre The Younger) (1675-1760) painted the portrait of *María Amalia de Sajonia* (Maria Amalia of Saxony) as the queen of Naples through marriage to Charles VII (later Charles III of Spain). She is dressed in the Polish style against a magnificent monarchic background.

The French painters who were operating in Spain for the new dynasty are prominently represented in the museum. As a portrait painter, a role in which he would soon be replaced by some of his compatriots, the versatile **Michel-Ange Houasse** (1680-1730) presented his image of Louis I, still a prince. The picture was signed in 1717. In the painting, the king is wearing apparel pertaining to the French Order of the Holy Spirit. This enables the artist to deploy a splendid grey-silver palette. In about 1720, as part of a vast series on royal locations, he painted *Vista del monasterio de San Lorenzo de El Escorial* (View of the Monastery of San Lorenzo de El Escorial). This direct study anticipates modern landscape painting in an extraordinary way. Two canvas paintings by Hovasse on a mythological theme form a matching pair. *Bacanal* (Bacchanalia) from 1719 and *Ofrenda a Baco* (Offering to Bacchus) painted a year later demonstrate the artist's command of this genre by means of a very wide-ranging synthesis combining influences as diverse as Titian, Poussin, Watteau and Coypel, the latter in turn being a conveyor of Rubens' work.

Jean Ranc (1674-1735) was a portrait painter and a pupil of Rigaud. However, he was already somewhat out of fashion and tended to use meticulous detail. The museum has on display an interesting royal series by this artist headed by *La familia de Felipe V* (The Family of Philip V), a sketch from about 1723 for a large canvas painting since lost. In this picture, some of the characters adopt similar postures to the ones seen in separate portraits by the same artist as if these single portraits were offshoots from the majestic whole in the same period. Ranc also painted *Felipe V a caballo* (Philip V on Horseback). This is an allegorical portrait with the personification of victory leading the monarch to success in the middle of the battlefield. This painting is based on another picture by Ranc, which is now lost, showing the regent of France, the Duke of Orleans.

In 1723, Ranc painted the portraits of *Felipe V* (Philip V) and his second wife Isabel de Farnesio. This is a princely pair of official portraits that gave rise to numerous versions. Leaving aside the spectacular nature of Rigaud's painting and taking up a more restrained approach in which the virtuosity of detail is paramount, Ranc conventionally presents the king as a warrior against a natural background and the queen in a cloak in the interior of a palace. In approximately 1724, Ranc set about painting the official portraits of *Fernando VI, niño y Carlos III, niño* (Ferdinand VI as a child and Charles III as a Child) as princes of Spain but not without giving them a certain wit and childish candour. Taking the interpretation to its logical conclusion, it has been suggested that Ferdinand's melancholic character is already visible in the painting. Turning to madness, this would later prove fatal. Charles is portrayed with a book, flowers and an exotic bird – illustrating his future passion for science.

The portrait of *Don Felipe, duque de Parma* (Philip, Duke of Parma) was painted in about 1737-42 by **Louis-Michel Van Loo** (1707-1771). It is exhibited in the museum. This picture was probably a preparatory study for the enormous and symbolic canvas painting *La familia de Felipe V* (The Family of Philip V), signed by Van Loo in 1743. The artist would continue in the service of the Spanish crown during the reign of Ferdinand VI and would contribute to the setting up of the San Fernando Academy.

Antoine Watteau (1684-1721) painted in an ambiguous, impenetrable and intricate style. He set the standard for rococo art and proved the driving force behind this movement. *Capitualaciones de boda y baile campestre* (A Marriage Ceremony and a Country Dance) dates from around 1712-13. In the picture, Watteau uses very delicate artwork to evoke his own personal aesthetics of Flemish and Dutch origin. The theme of the painting clearly leads back in this direction. *Fiesta en un parque* (A Party in a Park) is very closely connected to the above-mentioned picture without forming a matching pair. Painted around the same time, it is a piece of extremely high quality in which the subtlety of the brush-strokes, the very refined toning and the accurate portrayal of an uncertain atmosphere perfectly match the frivolousness of

Hyacinthe Rigaud. *Louis XIV.*
Canvas. 238 χ 149 cm. Ref. nº 2343.

Michel-Ange Houasse. *Bacchanal.*
Canvas. 125 χ 180 cm. Ref. nº 2267.

the imprecise subject matter, not without a vague touch of melancholy. Rococo gallantry is seen here at its most sophisticated.

Françóis Boucher (1703-1770) painted *Pan y siringa* (Pan and Syringe) in about 1760-65. It deals with a theme from the Metamorphoses by Ovidio, the basis for several other versions. All the other versions were rectangular whereas this one is oval. The artwork is free-flowing with a nimble rhythm and a wealth of colour. The picture is related to a series of designs for the Gobelin tapestries. Jean Pillement painted two *Paisajes* (Landscapes) in 1773. They form a matching pair and by means of versatile colouring, lyrical tension and a nostalgic undercurrent, the two pictures express the artist's characteristic late rococo sensitivity, already directed towards a pre-Romantic spirit. Pillement also painted *Naufragio* (Shipwreck). The picture dates from about 1790-1800. According to the inscription on the reverse side, it was painted during his stay in the small French town of Pezenas. This is a typical demonstration of alarmist end-of-the-century sentimentality spurred on by a sense of the sublime. Although rather reluctantly, some Spanish artists such as Goya himself could not fail to succumb to this vague Pre-Romantic gloominess.

Claude-Joseph **Vernet** (1714-1789) painted *Marina: vista de Sorrento* (Seascape: A View of Sorrento) in about 1745-50. It may refer to a dramatic narrative. This is an imaginative composition in the rococo spirit with borrowings from the seventeenth-century Dutch school and also featuring Roman classical scenery. The picture could be one of the two seascapes acquired by Louis XVI in Paris for Charles IV, still a prince. *Paisaje Quebrado* (Broken Landscape) dates from the same time in the Italian period. With a typically wild landscape, this melodramatic painting contains a construction over a precipice reminiscent of the palace of Caprarola in 1781. Vernet was commissioned by Charles IV to produce a series of six canvas paintings for the country cottage belonging to the prince at The Escorial. These included three pictures exhibited here in the museum – *Paisaje con una cascada* (Landscape with a Waterfall), *Paisaje romano a la puesta del sol* (Roman Landscape at Sunset) and *La cometa* (The Comet). This latter picture has an extremely vertical format which provided a great challenge as far as the composition was concerned. The second of the three pictures brings to mind similar pieces by the artist mentioned next.

Hubert Robert (1733-1808) was a painter of monuments obsessed by the grandeur of architecture up against the smallness of man. In about 1780-90, he completed *El coliseo de Roma* (The Coliseum of Rome). It is a characteristic example of Pre-Romantic sensitivity expressed with a mature technique and varied contrasts of light.

The Italian School from the eighteenth century is well-represented at the Prado Museum. This display culminates in Tiepolo as a painter in the service of the king of Spain. Gaspar Van Wittell, **Vanvitelli**, was a Dutchman by birth. Born in 1652 or 1653, he died in 1736. He specialized in landscapes and in scenes of death from nature. In 1697, he painted *Venecia, vista desde la isla de San Giorgio* (Venice seen from the Island of San Giorgio), reflecting his professional development as the creator of the new concept of a sweeping view of the city scene with a rational and studied portrayal of architecture as well as people. A matching pair is formed by *Alrededores de Nápoles* (The outskirts of Naples) and *La gruta de Posilipo* (Posilipo's Cavern). These works are possibly from his final phase. *Posilipo's cavern* was so successful that eleven versions of the picture have been kept. Each version was produced at regular intervals between 1702 and 1715.

Cristo servido por los ángeles (Christ Served by Angels) was in all likelihood the work of two artists painting in collaboration. **Alessandro Magnasco** (1667-1749) created the small but dramatic figures that stand out as much as the mellow absorbing landscape very probably painted by both Magnasco and Antonio Francesco Peruzzini (died 1724).

Giovanni Paolo Panini (1691-1765) painted the matching pair of canvas pictures entitled *Ruinas con una mujer dirigiendo la palabra a varias personas* (Ruins with a Woman Addressing Several People) and *Ruinas con San Pablo Predicando* (Ruins with Saint Paul Preaching). These are typical examples of his 'veduta' concept of classical architecture, more brilliant than exact. *El cardenal Borja* (Cardinal Borgia), painted later than 1721, is considered to be the best portrait by the versatile **Andrea Procaccini** (1671-1734). It illustrates the artist's Spanish period. An architect and civil servant as well as a painter, he became interested in art through the Roman group of Carlo Maratti.

San Juan Bautista (Saint John the Baptist) dates from around 1730. It is very characteristic of

Watteau. *A Marriage Ceremony and a Country Dance.*
Canvas. 47 χ 55 cm. Ref. n° 2353.

Orace Vernet. *Seascape : a View of Sorrento.*
Canvas. 59 χ 109 cm. Ref. n° 2350.

Francesco Solimena (1657-1747) and his Neapolitan settings. A work of great quality and vibrant chiaroscuro, it makes up a series along with another two pictures from the royal palace in Madrid. *La educación de Aquiles* (Achilles' Education) by Sebastiano Conca (1680-1746) depicts the ephemeral set-up in the papal city in 1727 in order to celebrate the birth of Prince Louis Antonio, son of Philip V. Panini used the scene as a sketch for a picture of his, now in London. At the invitation of the architect Filippo Juvara, Conca contributed to the decoration of the room devoted to the king's enterprises at the palace of La Granja. He did so with the canvas painting *Alejandro Magno en el templo de Jerusalén* (Alexander the Great at the Temple in Jerusalem). A 1736 sketch for the picture is exhibited at the Prado. By resorting to the well-known story of Alexander, the gallery programme intended to extol the virtues of Philip V.

Giuseppe Bonito (1707-1789) was commissioned by the future Charles III to paint the picture entitled *La embajada turca en Nápoles, año de 1741* (The Turkish Embassy in Naples in the Year 1741). Bonito was famous for his skill as a portrait painter. In this picture, the wealth of colour expresses the eighteenth-century fascination for exotic themes. The plan to decorate the conversation room at the palace of Aranjuez was initiated in 1748. A matching pair made up of two large and dramatic canvas paintings formed a part of this plan. The pictures in question were *La copa en el saco de Benjamín* (The wineglass in Benjamin's sack)and *José en el palacio del faraón* (Joseph in the Pharaoh's Palace), the latter by Jacopo Amigoni or Amiconi (1682-1752), a typical travelling artist from the eighteenth century. The little-known Francesco Battaglioli (c. 1725-c. 1796) painted *Vista del palacio de Aranjuez* (A View of the Palace of Aranjuez) and *Fernando VI y Bárbara de Braganza en los Jardines de Aranjuez* (Ferdinand VI and Barbara of Braganza in the Gardens of Aranjuez). In these two pieces, the painter's delightful artistic style recreates two scenes from a party organized in 1756 to celebrate the King's Saint's day.

A Neapolitan educated in Rome, the great fresco painter Corrado Guiaquinto (1703-1766) decorated the royal palace in Madrid and was one of the driving forces behind the new San Fernando Academy. He had a great influence on Spanish art. Guiaquinto painted *La justicia y la paz* (Justice and Peace), dating from 1753-54. The picture displays his characteristic rich contrasts of colour in soft colour ranges. *El nacimiento del sol y el triunfo de Baco* (The Birth of the Sun and the Triumph of Bacchus) was a sketch made in 1761 for the so-called *Salón de columnas* (Hall of Columns) at the royal palace. Guiaquinto also painted *España rinde homenaje a la Religión y a la Iglesia* (Spain Pays Homage to Religion and the Church), a piece from 1759. Both of these pictures are full of allegories with abstruse meanings. The two paintings also reveal Guiaquinto's exceptional talent for complex and intricate compositions.

Antonio Joli (c. 1700-1777) was another travelling artist. As a *"vedutista"* (a pupil of Veduta), his work links up with that of Gaspar Van Wittel, Vanvitelli. Joli painted two curious documentary pictures based on an historical event in 1759 – *Embarco de Carlos III del puerto de Nápoles vista desde el mar* (A View from the Sea as Charles III Sets Sail from Naples). Pompeo Girolamo Batoni (1708-1787) specialized in painting portraits of those travelling through Italy. In this case, he presents a portrait of Charles Cecil Roberts. The picture evokes the typical image of someone on a 'Grand Tour'. The setting for the portrait is the outskirts of Rome and the subject appears among archaeological remains in front of an architectural background. The San Fernando Academy holds a replica of the painting, signed in 1778. From the same date and of a similar type, *Un viajero en Italia* (A Traveller in Italy) shows the subject sitting down next to a classical bust in the interior of a room.

Giambattista Tiepolo (1696-1770) was a late exponent of the Venetian School. He died in Madrid, the city where he had arrived in order to decorate the royal palace. He is mainly represented in the Prado Museum by a series of pictures from his last phase or Spanish period. The enormous canvas painting now entitled *La Reina Zenobia ante el Emperador Aureliano* (Queen Zenobia Facing Emperor Aureliano) was created at some time between 1717 and 1735 although there is a great deal of debate about the precise date. This balanced composition has very pleasant colouring. The piece was known as *La continencia de Escipión* (The temperance of Scypion) when it was acquired by the State in 1975.

Tiepolo arrived in Spain in 1762. Shortly before, perhaps in 1761, he painted *El Olimpo o el triunfo de*

Tiepolo. *The Olympus.*
Canvas. 86 χ 62 cm. Ref. nº 365.

Venus (Olympus or the Triumph of Venus). This is the only remaining sketch from a series intended for the Empress of Russia. In this sketch, he anticipates the structure and, in line with his customary way of working, he even includes some designs for one of his Madrid vaults. Once he had applied the finishing touches to the palace decoration programme, he set about the only completely individual or personal series of his long career, namely the seven canvas paintings for the church of San Pascual Bailón in Aranjuez. He worked on this series between 1767 and 1769. However, in 1770, the freshly-hung paintings were replaced by others from Mengs, Bayeu and Maella, as the twilight art of Tiepolo with its delicate contrasts of light and intensely mellow quality was incompatible with the academic rigidity resulting from the advent of classicism. The museum holds several paintings from this series. Owing to the above-mentioned narrowing down of aesthetic values, the pictures suffered serious damage.

Vision de San Pascual Bailón (The Vision of San Pascual Bailon) is the picture on the main reredos. It is known in its entirety due to a sketch and an engraving. Two fragments showing the subject of the painting and an angel are exhibited on the same panel. Saint Pascual is kneeling while the angel is bearing the monstrance. Tiepolo also painted *San Francisco de Asís recibiendo los estigmas* (Saint Francis of Assisi Receiving the Stigmata). This signed canvas shows the extent to which Tiepolo knew how to utilize the dramatic potential of colour in harmony with the climax of the narrative, in line with Venetian tradition. Whereas this painting displays religious unction, *La Inmaculada Concepción* (The Immaculate Conception) gives an impression of elegant secularity, far removed from Spanish baroque encoding of this contradictory Marian theme. Moreover, it goes against the collective spirit. This signed painting follows the compositive outline of the picture made by Vicenza.

Ángel con corona de azucenas (An Angel with a Lily Crown) is one of the two fragments to have emerged from *San José con el Niño Jesús* (Saint Joseph with Jesus the Child). It makes a negative impact within the series due to its inferior quality. The picture contains a substantial contribution by Tiepolo's son Giandomenico who collaborated in this series to a certain extent. Although it includes the design for the messenger from heaven who appeared to Saint Pascual Bailon, *Abraham y los tres ángeles* (Abraham and the Three Angels) was omitted from the commissioned work for Aranjuez. Nevertheless, it is a work of art from the painter's Spanish period in which the same exquisite touch is evident.

After coming to Spain with his father and then having returned to Venice, Giovanni Domenico or **Giandomenico Tiepolo** (1727-1804) made a series of paintings on *La pasión de Cristo* (The Passion of Christ) for the monastery of San Felipe Neri. The work was carried out in his native city between 1771 and 1772. The emotive use of colours once again emphasizes what some have interpreted as claustrophobic dramatism.

German art from the eighteenth-century is only represented by the great Bohemian artist **Anton Rafael Mengs** (1728-1779) who was very famous in his time. His first stay in Spain from 1761 to 1769 coincided with a major realignment in monarchical tastes towards the classicist ideas that Mengs had assimilated through contact with the theorist Winckelmann. In the Prado, we can get a good idea of Mengs' work, mainly in his role as a portrait painter although some of his pictures on religious themes are also exhibited.

The two *Cabezas de apóstol* (Heads of an Apostle) date from around 1764. They are complete studies for *La ascensión* (The Ascension) in Dresden cathedral, a painting made in Rome and inspired by "Raphael the Divine." Also in the papal city in approximately 1770, Mengs produced a third version on wood of *La adoración de los pastores* (The Adoration of the Sheperds). This was closely related to the version by Correggio in Dresden and therefore constituted a tribute to his other great Renaissance influence.

Mengs created his royal portraits with inexorable meticulous accuracy, confident design and a wealth of colour. From a present-day aesthetic perspective, we should recognise the brilliance, precision and elegance with which he portrays the subjects in his court portraits. The signed portrait of *Fernando IV, rey de Nápoles* (Ferdinand IV, King of Naples), painted in about 1760, presents a formal or official figure. The subject of various replicas, this picture constantly surprises observers with its enormous architectural background.

The portrait of **Carlos III** (Charles III) shows the king in armour and from the knees upwards in an

Anthon Raphael Mengs. *Charles III.*
Canvas. 154 χ 110 cm. Ref. nº 2200.

ostentatious display. This portrait forms a matching pair with that of *Maria Amalia de Sajonia* (Maria Amalia of Saxony) who is pictured seated in an interior room. Mengs may have painted these portraits on his arrival in Spain in 1761, when the queen had already died. In contrast to the relatively domestic atmosphere in his wife's portrait, the picture of the King is another official portrait, also the subject of a number of versions. It has been suggested that the portrait of the king reflects concepts present in those by Velasquez and Van Loo. Another matching pair of pictures is formed by the portraits of *Carlos IV* (Charles IV) and *María Luisa de Parma* (Maria Luisa of Parma) in their role as the Prince and Princess of Asturias. The prince is portrayed as a hunter against a background of a game preserve while his wife appears in court costume. She is looking out at the landscape from a garden. The portraits were painted in about 1765, the year of their wedding. In the first of these portraits, traces of Velasquez have once again been identified.

During Meng's stay in Florence in 1770, he completed another series of commissioned royal portraits, this time featuring the great dukes of Tuscany *Leopoldo de Austria and María Luisa de Borbón* (Leopold of Austria and Maria Luisa of Bourbon). This matching pair of high-quality canvas paintings attains an extraordinary degree of virtuosity in the apparel worn by the daughter of Charles III. Pictured together, *Los archiduques Fernando y Maria Ana de Austria* (The Archdukes Ferdinand and Maria Ana of Austria) are the children of the subjects in the previous portrait. Both paintings were completed in the same year. The archduke and archduchess are portrayed with an assumed childlike attractiveness that entirely gives way to the intense and refined shades of the tapestry. This Florentine series from 1770 was completed by the portrait of another young member of a royal family – *El archiduque Francisco de Austria* (Archduke Francis of Austria), the future emperor. Once more, the magnificence of the materials outshines the supposed childlike innocence of the protagonist.

Meng's magnificent **Autorretrato** (Self-portrait), painted on a panel in approximately 1761-1765 is one of the many that Mengs undertook in order to please his legion of admirers. The sketched artwork was perhaps unfinished.

The strained relations between Spain and England account for the relatively small number of eighteenth-century British paintings exhibited in the Prado. The display is limited to individual portraits, the result of recent acquisitions. *Retrato de un eclesiástico* (A Portrait of a Clergyman) was painted by **Sir Joshua Reynolds** (1723-1792). It is a youthful work from about 1756-60 and bears no resemblance to his subsequent "great style". **Thomas Gainsborough** (1727-1788) painted the portrait of Mr. Robert Butchert of Walthamstown in about 1765. Here again, the picture is not that of a mature artist. However, Gainsborough had developed a much more mature style by the time he painted the portrait of the renowned Jewish-Portuguese doctor Isaac Enrique Sequeira in about 1775. The free-flowing artwork reflects the feigned natural elegance of the subject.

Probably painted on the ocasión of her engagement in approximately 1789, the portrait of Miss Marthe Carr by **Thomas Lawrence** (1769-1830) is one of his early canvas paintings in which his firm touch and the vibrant uninhibited freedom of his style are already visible. Lawrence's studio participated to some extent in painting the portrait of *John Fane, X conde de Westmoreland* (John Fane, Tenth Count of Westmoreland). Produced in about 1806, this high-quality work of art is less direct and spontaneous. The ostentatious figure is wearing the cloak of a lord with the insignia of the Order of 'Jarretera'. *El retrato de Master Ward* (The Portrait of Master Ward) was painted by **George Romney** (1734-1803) in about 1790. In the portrait, Romney gives a higher priority to the demands of fashion than to psychological depth or an exact representation of his characters. The picture exemplifies his skill in portraying children and youngsters.

In *El retrato de Mrs. MacLean of Kinlochaline* (The Portrait of Mrs. MacLean of Kinlochaline), painted in about 1800, **Henry Raeburn** (1756-1823) informally portrays this Scottish lady with very fluent and energetic brush-strokes within a very limited range of colours. Swiss by birth but particularly successful in London, the cosmopolitan and prolific **Angelica Kauffman** (1741-1807) painted the portrait of Anna von Escher Van Muralt in about 1800. It is an appropriate example of her elegant compositions and includes a classical Roman landscape in the background.

Anthon Raphael Mengs. *Self-portrait.*
Panel. 62 χ 50 cm. Ref. n° 2197.

THE CASÓN DEL
BUEN RETIRO
NINETEENTH-CENTURY ART

THE CASÓN DEL BUEN RETIRO:
NINETEENTH-CENTURY ART

The Casón del Buen Retiro served as a venue for festivals or parties in the palace complex. It was built according to a design by Alonso Carbonell and completed in 1638. The lavish fresco on the dome of the great central hall was painted in about 1697 by Luca Giordano or Lucas Jordán and remains to this day. It was accompanied by an allegory of the Order of the Golden Toisón. The Casón del Buen Retiro would now be unrecognisable in comparison with the original building, following the many modifications that have been made. The façade shows a number of different styles. In 1894, the nineteenth-century collections were taken out of the Prado in order to initiate the *Museo de Arte Moderno* (The Museum of Modern Art). Since 1971, these collections have been housed in the Casón del Buen Retiro.

Among the collections of sculptures, very unequal in terms of importance, some exhibits reflect the art of the most prestigious international exponents of Neoclassicism. **Antonio Canova** (1757-1822) is represented by an excellent model of Hebe and a good workshop copy of *Venus y Marte* (Venus and Mars). A version of Hermes by Bertel Thorwaldsen (1770-1844) is also exhibited. Modelled in 1840 and cast four years later, the *San Jerónimo Penitente* (Penitent Saint Jerome) by José Piquer (1806-1871) involved an aesthetic renewal with baroque associations.

A number of works chart the course of official sculpture until well into the following century. They include Sagunto, an eclectic piece by **Agustín Querol** (1860-1909), *Eclosión* (Blossoming), a modernist creation by Miguel Blay (1866-1936) and *Hermanitos de leche* (Little Foster Brothers), a very unfashionable piece by Aniceto Marinas (1866-1953). These compositions were given prestigious awards at the national exhibitions of 1906, 1908 and 1926 respectively.

Spanish art from the beginning of the nineteenth century fluctuated between the prolonged pursuit of eighteenth-century court designs and foreign Neoclassicism which lacked the right artistic climate. The meticulous **Vicente López** (1772-1850) belonged to the first school. In 1802, he produced an allegorical painting very much in the baroque style in order to immortalize *La visita de la familia de Carlos IV a la Universidad de Valencia* (The Visit by the Family of Charles IV to the University of Valen-

cia). Among the artist's many and generally elaborate portraits, the most outstanding are the official and conventional picture of Fernando VII (Ferdinand VII) from 1814, the very lavish portrait of María Cristina de Borbón in 1830 to commemorate her wedding with the said monarch and, above all, the extraordinary picture of Francisco Goya from 1826. The latter was presumably unfinished. Sufficient indication of its quality is provided by the fact that it has become the standard image of the Aragonese painter on account of its spontaneity, conviction and psychological perception, even overriding Goya's self-portrait.

Bernardo López Piquer (1800-1874) was a son and pupil of Vicente López. His portrait of Queen María Isabel de Braganza, signed in 1829, alludes to the creation of the Prado museum.

Among strictly Neo-classical Spanish painters, one of the most outstanding was **José de Madrazo** (1781-1859). His *Muerte de Viriato* (The Death of Viriato) was painted in about 1808 and inspired by both David and Flaxman. **Juan Antonio de Ribera** (1779-1860) was another leading Neo-classical artist. Here, he is represented by a pair of canvas paintings from different dates – *Cincinato abandona el arado para dictar leyes a Roma* (Cincinato Abandons the Plough to Impose Laws on Rome) and *Wamba renunciando a la corona* (Wamba Relinquishing the Crown). The two pictures were painted in about 1806 and 1819 respectively. They also show the influence of David. In 1815, **José Aparicio** (1773-1838) painted the portrait of *La reina de Etruria con sus hijos* (The Queen of Etruria with her Children). In this picture, Aparicio dislays his French Neo-classical style which is nevertheless very rigid, hardly avoiding frontal views.

Eugenio Lucas Velázquez (1817-1870) was an exponent of the Madrid romantic movement. He is represented by several scenes characteristic of his bold streak, similar to that of Goya. They include *Sermón a las máscaras* (A Sermon to the Masks), signed in 1855 and forming a matching pair with *La revolución y la ronda* (The Revolution and the Patrol). Both pictures display mellow artwork with some very bold touches. The artist is also represented by pictures with a bullfighting theme such as *Mujeres en el balcón* (Women on the Balcony)) from 1862 and painted in dark grey and brown colours and also *Las presidentas* (The Women Presidents).

José de Madrazo. *The Death of Viriato.*
Canvas. 307 χ 460 cm. Ref. nº 4469.

Federico de Madrazo. *The Countess of Vilches.*
Canvas. 123 χ 87 cm. Ref. nº 2878.

Leonardo Alenza (1807-1845) was a 'costumbrista' artist, a painter of typical everyday scenes from local life. He also belonged to the Madrid romantic movement and was likewise a good portrait painter. He used a very free-flowing technique in creating *Borracho* (Drunk) and *La azotaina* (The Beating) which are typical reinterpretations of *Caprichos de Goya* (Goya's whims). In Alenza's *Autorretrato* (Self-portrait), there is evidence of the disease that would soon end his life.

José Gutiérrez de la Vega (1791-1865) from Seville painted in the style of Murillo and expressed a personal sense of romanticism with morbid sensual suggestions. Whereas in the sweetly-created *Santa Catalina* (Saint Catherine), he presented a nude bust in *Maja Sevillana* (A Maja or Characteristic Girl from Seville) from the 1840's, he reverted without an allegorical pretext to the eroticism of the Venetian 'poems' from the sixteenth century.

Antonio María Esquivel (1806-1857) also from Seville, was an exponent of the merged Andalusian and Madrid Schools. In 1841, he developed a previous sketch in order to produce a great canvas painting reminiscent of Murillo – *La caída de Luzbel* (The Fall of Lucifer). In 1846, the artist signed *Los poetas contemporáneos* (The Contemporary Poets), a cheerful collective portrait revealing a complex composition and a skilful technique. These aspects are, however, eclipsed by the picture's inestimable worth as an iconographic document.

Within the Andalusian romantic-costumbrista movement, we can highlight *El presente* (The Present) and *El baile* (The Dance), paintings signed in 1866 by Valeriano Domínguez Bécquer (1834-1870) as part of an official series of commissioned pictures designed to reflect Spanish traditions. Another noteworthy pointing is *Procesión del Corpus en Sevilla* (The Corpus Christi Procession in Seville), signed in 1857 by Manuel Cabral y Aguado-Bejarano (1827-1891). Bathed in brilliant light, the picture shows the departure of the procession under the presidency of the dukes of Montpensier.

Jenaro Pérez Villamil (1807-1854) created the Spanish romantic landscape in the style of the Scot David Roberts. Villamil painted a self-portrait together with highwaymen in his marvellous *Vista del castillo de Gaucín* (View of the Castle of Gaucín).

A lone figure in the romantic-realistic phase, Federico de Madrazo (1815-1844), son of the Neo-classicist José, was resigned to giving up important business in favour of portrait painting, a genre in which he was unrivalled during the middle of the century. His portrait of *El niño Federico Flórez* (The Boy Federico Flórez) from 1842 was created, exceptionally, against a background landscape. In 1848, he painted the majestic ostentatious portrait of Isabel II which formed a matching pair with a now lost picture of the king's consort.

Spanish romantic portrait painting reached a peak with that of *La Condesa de Vilches* (The Countess of Vilches), signed in 1853. In contrast to his customary palette of dark grey and brown colours, Madrazo applies a wealth of colour with the effect of further emphasizing the unconventional posture of the character, an aspect perhaps taken from Ingres. Signed in 1854, the portrait of General Evaristo San Miguel is considered to be his best military portrait with full decoration.

The portrait of Carolina Coronado was painted in 1855. With a black mantilla and closed fan, this romantic literary lady projects a sincere informal image.

Raimundo de Madrazo (1841-1920) was the son of Federico. In 1887, he signed a vibrant portrait of *Maria Cristina de Habsburgo* (Maria Cristina of Hapsburg). As the inscription indicates, it is a study of her natural appearance.

Various works of art by the great but ill-fated Eduardo Rosales (1836-1873) are on display at the Prado Museum. They provide evidence of the wide-ranging subject matter used by the artist in reviving old Spanish painting. From that time onwards, nineteenth-century painting bridged the gap with this previous Spanish art, thus concluding an interval characterised by foreign influence. Signed in 1864, the *Testamento de Isabel la Católica* (The Last will and Testament of Isabel the Catholic) a picture with a complex composition, indeed constitutes a return to traditional Spanish painting and in particular to Velasquez. The painting's impressive quality overrides its role as a historical picture, the great official genre promoted during the second half of the century by national exhibitions only to subsequently fall into marked disrepute. Later, the appropriate critical reappraisal tried to reverse this decline.

In 1869, Rosales signed the *Presentación de don Juan de Austria a Carlos V* (Juan of Austria Being Introduced to Charles V). The picture reveals a lim-

Rosales. *The Last Will and Testament of Isabel the Catholic.*
Canvas. 290 χ 400 cm. Ref. n° 4625.

Francisco Pradilla. *Doña Juana the Mad.*
Canvas. 340 χ 500 cm. Ref. n° 4584.

ited palette and mellow modelling. It made a great impression due to its small format, so unusual in these retrospective themes. Like its sketch, *La Muerte de Lucrecia* (The Death of Lucretia), a picture signed in 1871, involves a truly revolutionary technical transformation giving rise to very fluent artwork, with lively drawing, a restrictive range and a great emphasis on volume. In the same year, the artist painted the portrait of *La condesa de Santovenia* (The Countess of Santovenia), Conchita Serrano, the daughter of the famous general. There is a complex variety of pink shades in the picture. It not only demonstrates his ability in this other genre but it also constitutes one of his masterpieces.

The Catalonian **Mariano Fortuny** (1838-1874) was also a leading figure in nineteenth century Spanish painting. Like Rosales, his life was cut short at an early age. Fortuny developed a style characterised by preciosity with great international success. He made a decisive contribution to the fashion for *cuadritos de "casacones"* (small squares like those on coats) in a mock eighteenth-century setting. Between 1864 and 1867, he produced the great historical canvas painting *Maria Cristina e Isabel II pasando revista a las tropas en 1837* (Maria Cristina and Isabel II Reviewing the Troops in 1837). This contemporary chronicle was hung as an adornment in the palace of Castile in Paris where the said queen had settled following her downfall.

With very limited resources, Fortuny completed *Fantasía sobre Fausto* (A Dream about Faust) in 1866. In this painting, a vision of the Goethe legend forms in front of the pianist Juan Bautista Pujol while he performs a piece by Gounod. Signed in Rome in 1869, the painting entitled *Un marroquí* (A Moroccan) illustrates the artist's great interest in Arabian themes. *Viejo desnudo al sol* (An Old Man Sunbathing Nude) from 1873 anticipates the dark grey and brown colours of Sorolla. The following year was to be his last but Fortuny still produced these paintings – *Los hijos del pintor en un salón japonés* (The Painter's children in a Japanese Room), *Desnudo en la playa de Pórtici* (Nudity on Pórtici Beach) and *Paisaje de Pórtici* (A Pórtici Landscape). They show his achievements in terms of light and the divisive artwork which had provided a new orientation for his short-lived career by this time.

Historical painting arrived late in Spain and indeed persisted there when it had lost all of its purpose in the rest of Europe. Rarely has this genre been so well developed than in the work of Rosales. In 1858, **Eduardo Cano de la Peña** (1823-1897), the great sketch artist, signed *El entierro de don Álvaro de Luna* (The Burial of Alvaro de Luna). However, the picture lacks compositive unity. In 1864, **José Casado del Alisal** (1832-1886) signed *Rendición de Bailén* (The Surrender of Bailen). This well-produced work constitutes a tribute to Velasquez's *Las lanzas* (The lances). The theme derives from both tradition and history. **Francisco Pradilla** (1848-1921) signed the painting entitled **Doña Juana la Loca** (Juana the Mad) in 1877. This is a very well-known canvas painting with studied tension arising from the setting.

The *Conversión del duque de Gandía* (The conversion of the Duke of Gandia) is a very melodramatic painting signed in 1884 by **José Moreno Carbonero** (1860-1942). *Los amantes de Teruel* (The Lovers from Teruel) was the work of **Antonio Muñoz Degrain** (1843-1924). Also signed in 1884, the artist evokes the tightly-packed atmosphere with an accomplished technique. The genre culminates in the work of **Antonio Gisbert** (1834-1901) represented by *Fusilamiento de Torrijos y sus compañeros* (The Execution by Firing Squad of Torrijos and his Companions). This is an exceptional, vivid and effective portrayal of an incidence of repression in 1831.

A forerunner of the naturalist movement, **Martín Rico** (1833-1908) was a rebellious pupil of Villaamil. He was close to the Barbizon group. In *Orillas del Azañón (Aragón)* (The Banks of the Azañón, Aragon) from 1858, he demonstrates his realist concept of the landscape, although still with romantic touches. **Carlos de Haes** (1826-1898) was of Belgian descent. The Museum holds many of his studies of objects painted in their natural states. Later, he used these studies to produce the definitive pictures in the studio. In 1876, the artist signed the canvas painting entitled **Los Picos de Europa (La canal de Mancorbo)** (The Picos de Europa Mountains) (The Mancorbo Channel). The picture demonstrates solid drawing together with accurate chromatic and lighting effects, all arising from the way he developed his sketches.

Whereas the panel *Sendero (Aránzazu)* (Path. Aránzazu) presents very free-flowing touches with rich harmonies of colour and clearly-defined volume, the canvas painting entitled *Paisaje de montaña* (Mountain Landscape), probably a picture of the Sierra de Guadarrama mountains, reveals a more

Sorolla. *Children on the Beach.*
Canvas. 118 χ 185 cm. Ref. nº 4648.

Carlos de Haes.
The Picos de Europa Mountains.
Canvas. 168 χ 123 cm. Ref. nº 4390.

restrained colour scheme with glimpses of his northern European legacy.

After Haes had paved the way for 'plenairism', **Aureliano de Beruete** (1845-1912) took it to its utmost consequences. Two versions of the same theme – *Orillas del Manzanares* (The Banks of the Manzanares) – one dating from 1878 and another from 1907 illustrate his artistic leap from a style reminiscent of the Barbizon group and influenced by Haes to a much more vibrant technique together with his impressionist style. *El Guadarrama* and *Paisaje de invierno. Plantío de Infantes* (A Winter Landscape. The Prince's Royal Garden) were both painted in 1911. They reflect the last bold artwork by Beruete, the exponent of light. A *Paisaje* (Landscape Painting) signed in 1860 by Ramón **Marti y Alsina** (1826-1894) reveals the application of pleasant materials in order to exemplify the role of the genre creator in the Catalonian context.

The three great exponents of Valencian art from the end of the nineteenth century and the beginning of the twentieth are represented reasonably well in the museum. The painting entitled *Portada del palacio de Dos Aguas en Valencia* (The Front of the Dos Aguas Palace in Valencia) is a very free-flowing piece with a rich texture signed by **Francisco Domingo Marqués** (1842-1920). Conversely, his *Autorretrato* (Self-Portrait) from 1884 corresponds to photographic realism from the end of the century.

Pinazo and Sorolla epitomize Valencian art in terms of the use of light, the debatable 'luminismo' from the east coast of Spain, a regional alternative to impressionism. This movement had already been anticipated by *Barca en la playa* (A Boat on the Beach), painted in 1880 by **Ignacio Pinazo** (1849-1916). Later, in 1898, he made *La lección de memoria* (The Memory Lesson) in which he displays dark grey and brown shades in an authentic Spanish style.

Joaquín Sorolla (1863-1923) was very famous in his time. We can highlight three pictures corresponding to different genres and periods. Signed in 1894, *Aún dicen que el pescado es caro* (They Still Say that Fish is Expensive) represents a delayed response to the fashion for social themes. However, the atmosphere is reminiscent of eighteenth-century realism. Sorolla also painted the splendid portrait of

Aureliano de Beruete, signed in 1902. The range is very restricted as in a tribute to Velasquez. *Niños en la playa* (Children on the Beach) from 1910 displays superb lighting effects in line with the artist's most individual and advanced works.

The style of the "Franciscan" or pure **Darío de Regoyos** (1857-1913) can be categorized as occupying a position between impressionism and pointillism. He painted the picture entitled *La playa de San Sebastián* (San Sebastian Beach) and the landscape painting *La viña* (The Vineyard) in which he demonstrates his free-ranging brush-strokes and his lack of a fixed colour scheme. Within Catalonian modernism, **Santiago Rusiñol** (1861-1931) achieved success as a landscape painter. *Jardín de Aranjuez* (Garden of Aranjuez) from 1908 is characteristic of his style and contains a magnificent wealth of colours.

The Casón holds a very limited selection of foreign painting from the nineteenth century. The few pictures it houses are, however, highly regarded. The romantic Scot **David Roberts** (1796-1864) was Villaamil's master. Two very beautiful panels by Roberts are on display – *La Torre del Oro* (The Golden Tower) from 1833 offering a nebulous, almost dreamlike vision and *El castillo de Alcalá de Guadaira* (The Castle of Alcala de Guadaira) including magnificent views against the light. The portrait of *La marquesa de Manzanedo* (The Marchioness of Manzanedo) was signed in 1872 by the highly prestigious and influential Jean-Louis-Ernest Meissonier (1815-1891). The painting provides evidence of his stupendous mastery of detail.

Paul Baudry (1828-1886) enjoyed a great deal of respect during his lifetime. In 1862, he signed *La perla y la ola* (The Pearl and the Wave). This painting of a female nude constitutes the epitome of technical professionalism applied decoratively in the service of high society. The picture belonged to emperor Napoleon III. In 1868, **Lawrence Alma Tadema** (1836-1912), a British artist of Dutch descent, signed a painting entitled *Escena pompeyana* (A scene from Pompeii) or *La siesta* (The Afternoon Sleep). This picture reflects the artist's highly individual and decadent reinterpretation of classical aesthetic values.

Aureliano de Beruete. *The Guadarrama Mountains.*
Canvas. 56 χ 102.5 cm. Ref. n° 4254.

Santiago Rusiñol. *The Aranjuez Gardens.*
Canvas. 134.5 χ 140.5 cm. Ref. n° 4630.

INDEX OF ILLUSTRATIONS

Bayeu, Francisco **141**

Bataglioni, Francesco **13**

Bermejo, Bartolomé **19**

Beruete, Aureliano de **191**

Bosch, Hieronymus **25, 27**

Boticelli, Sandro **31**

Brueghel de Velours **101**

Bruegel, Peter **29**

Camarón Boronat, José **143**

Carreño de Miranda, Juan **139**

Cartari, Giulio **57**

Claudio Coello **141**

Correggio **37**

Dughet **75**

Dürer, Albrecht **29**

Fra Angelico **31**

Greco, El **47, 49, 51**

Goya, Francisco de **147, 149, 151, 153, 155, 159, 161, 163, 165, 167, 169, 171**

Guercino, **75**

Haes, Carlos de **189**

Herrera, Francisco de **137**

Houasse, Michel-Ange **173**

Jordaens, Jacob **99**

Juanes, Juan de o Masip, Vicente Juan **21**

Leoni **53**

Lorena, Claudio de **73**

Madrazo, Federico de **185**

Madrazo, José de **185**

Martínez del Mazo **137**

Mengs, Anthon Raphael **179, 181**

Murillo, Bartolomé Esteban **133**

Padilla, Francisco **187**

Paret y Alcázar, Luis **143, 145**

Patinir, Joachim **25**

Pereda, Antonio de **135**

Poussin, Nicolás **71**

Raphael **33, 35**

Rembrandt **77**

Ribalta, Juan **105**

Ribera, José de **107**

Rigaud, Hyacinthe **173**

Rosales **187**

Rubens, Peter Paul **81, 83, 85, 87, 89, 91, 93, 95**

Rusiñol, Santiago **191**

Sánchez Coello **3**

Sánchez Cotán, **105**

Sorolla **189**

Stomer **79**

Teniers, David **103**

Tiepolo **177**

Tintoretto **45, 47**

Titian **7, 39, 41, 43**

Van der Weyden, Roger **23**

Van Dyck, Anton **95, 97**

Van Eyck, Jan **21**

Van Ostade, Adriaen **79**

Velasquez, Diego de **111, 113, 115, 117, 119, 121, 123, 125, 127, 129, 131**

Vernet **175**

Veronés, Pablo **43, 45**

Vos, Paul de **101**

Watteau **175**

Zurbarán, Francisco de **109**